Mia

THE LIFE OF
MIA FARROW

Mia

THE LIFE OF MIA FARROW

EDWARD Z. EPSTEIN
AND
JOE MORELLA

Delacorte Press

Published by
Delacorte Press
Bantam Doubleday Dell Publishing Group, Inc.
666 Fifth Avenue
New York, New York 10103

Library of Congress Cataloging in Publication Data

Epstein, Edward Z.
    Mia : the life of Mia Farrow / by Edward Z. Epstein and Joe Morella.
        p.   cm.
    ISBN 0-385-30446-3
    1. Farrow, Mia, 1945–   . 2. Motion picture actors and actresses—
United States—Biography. I. Morella, Joe. II. Title.
    PN2287.F35E6   1991
    791.43′028′092—dc20
    [B]   90-21808
                                                                     CIP

Manufactured in the United States of America

Published simultaneously in Canada

July 1991

10 9 8 7 6 5 4 3 2 1

RRH

Mia

**THE LIFE OF
MIA FARROW**

A Personal Encounter

MIA FARROW and Woody Allen are standing alone, apart from the other guests.

They are at a private gathering, critic Judith Crist's annual "Survival Party" in the Crists' spacious Riverside Drive apartment in Manhattan. It's late January, just before the New York Film Critics Awards, and many of the New York movie world's leading opinion-making critics and public relations people are in attendance.

Although there are other film stars at the party, and although it's a sophisticated crowd, Mia and Woody are clearly attracting the most attention.

Woody has attended several of these parties over the years —Mrs. Crist is a longtime, loyal Woody admirer. Diane Keaton was Woody's companion at a couple of previous "Survival" soirees. But now Mia Farrow stands by him. If this were a scene in one of his films, the dour expression on his face would represent perfectly his character's discomfort at being here, at being at any social gathering.

1

Mia is sweet and polite when approached, but the couple is definitely not inviting cocktail party conversation.

People try not to stare, but who can help it? This couple is famous. Hot. Mia hates being stared at. But dealing with this well-behaved group has to be child's play for her. After all, for years she's been pursued relentlessly by hostile paparazzi, nosy press—and merely curious civilians—in all corners of the globe. She's contended with plenty of unwanted attention in the course of her very colorful, still unconventional life. One assumes that by now very little can faze her.

Observing Mia, one is impressed. She wears the mantle of larger-than-life celebrity gracefully. She's a survivor. Certainly no longer the wide-eyed teenager, the "scrawny kid," as so many accounts described her through the years.

She's still a beauty. Always was. Even if she hadn't become a major star, she would have found plenty of work in "the business." The high cheekbones and huge, luminous blue-gray eyes and perfect complexion are instant indications to any casting director that hers is a photogenic face. Over forty, she looks ten years younger and her soft voice is unique.

But behind the very delicate and vulnerable Madonna-like facade resides an amazingly resilient, adventurous, fearless, curious, risk-taking spirit.

Mia and Woody briefly move through the Crist crowd. Mia has spotted a couple of acquaintances. She leads the way. An uncomfortable-looking Woody follows. Mia wears no diamond jewelry or flashy clothes. She doesn't have to. She stands out without it. She has presence. Always did.

Her life has been as colorful (if not more so) than the voluptuous movie queens that she appears to be the antithesis of. Liz, Lana, Cher *et al.* have made their journeys through life often drenched in glamour and glitter. Mia has traveled many of the same roads, only in plain clothes and without makeup.

And unlike many other stars of her caliber, she seems to have had the ability to appreciate it all. And to emerge from the maelstrom strong and whole.

When her film career foundered badly several years back, she simply turned on the in-person electricity, climbed onto a Broadway stage, and became a star there. And now, like the legendary phoenix, her film career has risen—with Woody Allen's help—from the ashes.

In the very beginning hers was a Star-Is-Born story personified. Mia made it fast and she made it big. Back in the swinging sixties only Elizabeth Taylor and Richard Burton surpassed the frenzied media attention heaped onto barely-out-of-her-teens Mia Farrow. It was a baptism by fire once the budding television star linked up with the legendary Frank Sinatra, a man of fifty. The courtship alone put Mia on the covers of *Life, Look,* and virtually every other major magazine throughout the world. Then the marriage. The nasty rumors of physical abuse. The separation. Her journey to India. The divorce. ("She was shattered," relates close friend Garson Kanin today.) Others in Mia's position would have drowned in the publicity whirlpool. The attention didn't abate and was often contemptuous and hostile.

Mia, the quintessential flower child of the era, survived.

With conductor-and-composer Andre Previn, "a powerhouse on the podium" whose audience was supposed to be far more "highbrow" than Sinatra's, came more unflattering and intimidating headlines. Out-of-wedlock children. Previn's acrimonious and painful divorce from Dory Previn. Previn's marriage to Mia. His purported infidelities. Hers. Their divorce.

And then came Woody. The world's most talented, famous, and neurotic bachelor (with two ex-wives). The comedian who, out of the spotlight, often appeared as carefree and fun-loving as an undertaker. A man who ostensibly detested attracting attention but who wore white sneakers, jeans, and a tam hat to black-tie film premieres—and then complained about being photographed.

Almost a decade ago, the Brooklyn-born Allen Stewart Konigsberg began a personal and professional relationship with Maria de Lourdes Villiers Farrow Sinatra Previn that has apparently worked on many levels, for both of them, to the present day. Theirs does not appear to be an operatic-style *grand passion* but a very practical, comfortable, and friendly relationship between two sophisticated adults who have found and sustained something deeply meaningful.

How they have maintained their successful relationship is especially intriguing in light of the incredible pressures—and temptations—constantly in play for two people in their situations.

People at the Crist party know that although the couple's life-style together is supposedly very private, the gates open when there is a movie or cause to publicize. Everyone also knows (and possibly envies the fact that) they maintain separate apartments—Mia's, a huge dwelling on the West Side of Manhattan's Central Park; Woody's, a penthouse on Fifth Avenue. Mia continues to retain her individuality zealously while at the same time espousing a communal philosophy of life. She is one of the few people who have succeeded in having both feet firmly planted in two worlds.

The world of the Establishment has never been Mia's cup of tea, though her roots burrow deep into its foundations. Obviously the Catholic concept of family and commitment—Mia is one of seven brothers and sisters, all reared religiously—is ingrained in her nature: She has nine children (five adopted). But although Mia, in 1987, gave birth to Woody's first child—a son, Satchel, who looks *just* like him—as far as anyone knows, they've exchanged no formal marriage vows.

The years have proven Mia Farrow to be a strong-willed creature of contrasts and contradictions. Avant-garde. Traditional. Fragile. Strong. Ambitious. Spiritual. Superstitious. Practical. Supersensitive. Steely-tough. . . .

"She may look very fragile, but she's quite strong," says her mother.

A shy-looking Mia and Woody say their good nights to Judith and Bill Crist and are off into the cold New York night. To observers she remains as aloof and mysterious as ever. A fascinating anomaly. A waiflike gambler at life whose biggest risks, emotionally and professionally, have paid fabulous dividends.

To try to understand a woman like Mia Farrow, one must reach back to her past.

The old maxim says the apple doesn't fall far from the tree. In Mia Farrow's case this is particularly apt.

Chapter One

ONE NIGHT in 1929 in Dublin teen-aged Maureen O'Sullivan, a high-spirited Irish beauty with a great sense of fun and adventure, attended the closing party for the glittering Dublin International Horse Show.

Frank Borzage, an eminent Hollywood director, was seated at the table next to hers. Everyone at the party was talking about Borzage. He'd won one of the first Academy Awards, for his direction of the silent film classic *Seventh Heaven*. The film had been an enormous success all over the world, and Borzage was in Ireland scouting locations for a new film.

The room was filled with attractive young people, many trying to catch Borzage's eye. Then, as now, almost everyone wanted to be in the movies.

He noticed Maureen O'Sullivan. She was with a handsome young escort and they were drinking champagne and seemed to be having a glorious time. When her escort wanted to leave the party, Maureen had a strong feeling she should stay. She suggested one more dance.

When they returned to the table after their dance, Borzage's business card was waiting for Maureen. Was she interested in appearing in films? Please come to his office tomorrow at 11:00 A.M.

In the morning the previous evening seemed dreamlike to the young girl. But when she spotted the business card, she asked her mother, "Can I go?" After all, many of Maureen's close friends were eager to be in Borzage's new film. It was *Song O' My Heart* and would star the great Irish tenor, John McCormack. Some of the girls in Maureen's set had already been interviewed. But none had been chosen for anything more important than extra work.

Maureen wasn't expecting anything to happen—she didn't consider herself a beauty. The meeting with Borzage didn't impress her. She felt he looked at her like a dentist when he asked her to smile.

Borzage, however, was impressed. He made a screen test.

The next step: He would have to get permission from Maureen's father to proceed if he wanted to cast her in the film.

O'Sullivan was a military man. He'd been a major in the Connaught Rangers and had been wounded in World War I. Maureen had been born before the war in Boyle, County Roscommon, on May 17, 1911. The family eventually moved to Dublin, and Maureen received her education at a convent school, Roehampton, which was located near London. (One of her classmates was another actress-to-be, Vivian Hartley, later Vivien Leigh.) The O'Sullivans were people of means, and Maureen and her siblings always had nannies (as would Maureen's children).

Maureen's father was not the kind of person to perceive of the acting profession as anything but notorious, especially in these "Roaring Twenties" when actresses, in particular, seemed to be in the vanguard of shockingly liberated attitudes and behavior. And Maureen would have to travel to Hollywood, the very heart of the den of iniquity.

The major's answer to Borzage's request: *no.*

The wily Borzage said he understood—and stated that if he were in the major's shoes and Maureen was his daughter, he'd most likely feel the same way! Borzage added, as an afterthought, that he wouldn't tell Maureen the major's reply had been negative. Instead, he said, he'd tell the girl that her screen test had been disappointing—then she'd never have any reason to blame her father.

But that evening, according to Maureen, when the major overheard his son and two daughters praying for their sister Maureen's success, hoping that she would have a good test and go to Hollywood, he had a change of heart.

And so began what would shortly become a successful career—though not as successful as it might have been, since Maureen O'Sullivan wasn't then, and never became, a relentless self-promoter. She would later note that it was those people who "pushed themselves" who would be remembered best.

Maureen, although a well-bred young woman, was a fun lover and a romantic at heart. Her penchant for kicking over the traces would certainly be emulated by her daughter, Mia, decades later. But Maureen's enjoyment of good times did not preclude the more conventional priorities ingrained in Catholic colleens of her generation: husband and family. She was very family-oriented.

But as 1929 drew to a close and a new world of experiences loomed before her, Maureen O'Sullivan put thoughts of husband and children aside. She was going to Hollywood. First, however, certain scenes were to be shot on location in Ireland.

Her starting salary for the Borzage picture was decidedly mundane, around fifteen dollars a week, and at first she had no dialogue scenes in the picture.

One day Borzage asked her if she could learn lines quickly. She didn't know what he was talking about, but she knew enough not to say no. She learned the speech he gave her, and one line, spoken to the actor portraying her brother in the picture, held great personal significance for her at that point in time: "I'm going a long way away and I don't know when I'll be back." There was a catch in her throat and tears welled up in her eyes as the scene was filmed.

Borzage was greatly impressed. He felt she had enormous, indeed extraordinary, ability as an actress.

But Maureen recalled years later that when they redid the scene on a Hollywood soundstage, she could never duplicate the tearful poignance that had so spontaneously occurred in front of the cameras in Ireland.

Maureen O'Sullivan was eager and willing to try her wings. She has recalled that it wasn't that she was unhappy at home. She hated leaving her father, but she couldn't wait to get out into the world. "Boy, did I fly! So many parents forget how it feels to be young."

Borzage was making films for the Fox Film Corporation, which was headed by blue-eyed Irishman Winfield Sheehan. The studio put Maureen under contract.

She has remembered vividly how she was all alone in this country at eighteen, with no relatives, nobody. She felt very lonely in this strange new world, and the way she felt would have a lot to do with her eventual decision to have a very large family.

Maureen's illusions about Hollywood were no different than anyone else's. Her contact with the town had consisted strictly of seeing its movies. The Hollywood of the early thirties was, as far as the public was concerned, drenched in glitter, glamour, and sex appeal. How one looked was the paramount consideration. The drop-dead European allure was currently top box office, epitomized by femme fatale Greta Garbo and her successful new rival, Marlene Dietrich. Exotic Latin beauties like Dolores del Rio were also "in," and the epitome of American sophistication on screen was the svelte and stylish brunette fashion plate Kay Francis.

Into this mix of lacquered hair, thick makeup, and false eyelashes, Maureen O'Sullivan's quintessential, fresh-faced colleen looks were like a breath of fresh air. Not that Maureen viewed it that way. She felt her looks inferior to those of the fashionable, gorgeously seductive femmes fatales. But Fox viewed O'Sullivan both as a possible successor to Janet Gaynor, their fresh-faced number-one box office star; and as a threat to her as well, if Gaynor proved to be too demanding in upcoming contract negotiations.

Fox put O'Sullivan to work, fast. But the films were forgettable. The titles conjure up what was going on in the marketplace in these years when Hollywood turned out hundreds of pictures per year: *So This Is London, Just Imagine, The Princess and the Plumber, A Connecticut Yankee,* and *Skyline.*

Just as Mia Farrow would be thrust into the grueling world of day-and-night television production three decades later, O'Sullivan and other actors on her level in the 1930s worked very long and hard hours in these days before the Screen Actors Guild. Sometimes the cameras rolled seven days a week, night and day. She might be working on two or three pictures at a time. Often actors collapsed from the strain—Maureen was no exception.

One day, emotionally and physically exhausted, she became hysterical on the set. She was unable to stop crying and couldn't go on. But she wasn't a quitter. Even at her wit's end, she knew she didn't want to go home to Ireland, not before she had become a success.

An understanding crew set up a cot for her right on the set so that she could sleep it off and get some desperately needed rest. Decades later she'd vividly recall this incident and how difficult it had been to fall asleep with all the activity of movie making continuing on around her.

The powers-that-be didn't shed any tears over her dilemma (or any other actor's). Maureen would recall the bosses from this "golden era of Hollywood" as "absolutely heartless."

What made it worthwhile, and fun, were the good films and the good directors, like Tay Garnett and George Stevens.

And it was during this period that Maureen met John Farrow. She was in Manhattan, taking in the nightlife, which in those days included a trip uptown to Harlem's fabulous Cotton Club. Her date that evening was the young musical genius and genuine character, Oscar Levant (they became great friends).

Handsome, dashing John Farrow, a writer, was at the club that evening with the glamorous Hollywood star he was dating, Dolores del Rio. But he spotted Maureen, and for most of the evening couldn't take his eyes off her.

Maureen didn't think Farrow very gracious; in fact she found him impossible. "He was awful," she recalled. On the dance floor he kept pushing up against her, saying how sorry he was.

"The next thing I knew we were all outside," recalled Maureen, "he was looking for his car—'Oh, I beg your pardon.' He was really getting rather fresh, which I enjoyed. Fun. He got in his car and he went away."

Farrow, too, was under contract to Fox, a fact Maureen learned later and by accident. Back in Hollywood, having lunch one day in the studio commissary, she saw him at the writers' table. His intense blue eyes continually focused on her. It was a replay of what had happened at the Cotton Club.

Maureen was in the skimpy costume she was wearing for her current picture and in later years she joked, "No wonder he was looking!"

She decided to outstare him. "I stared and I stared till he had to go on eating his lunch!"

Maureen shortly encountered Farrow again while trying to locate a director's office. "John never believed this," she wryly observed, recalling the meeting. She entered Farrow's office by mistake.

"There John sat," she recalled, "twiddling a pencil, his legs on the desk."

They had friends in common. One of Maureen's friends was the actress Janet Gaynor, and Farrow's good friend was Gaynor's husband, Lydell Peck.

After some chitchat Farrow got to the point: "Would you do me the great honor of having dinner with me?"

"When?"

"Two weeks from tonight."

Maureen later laughingly recalled her reaction vividly: "Lord, he's booked for two weeks? I don't have a date for two weeks!"

In two weeks she would turn nineteen (Mia's age when she met Frank Sinatra).

• • •

John Farrow has been described by his adult daughter Mia as a very tough but also gentle man. Very strict. Opinionated. A paradox. Priest and lover. Strong. Weak. Powerful. Incompetent. In other words, highly complex and complicated. A man whose interests and ambitions were incredibly diverse—and often at odds. Here was a man who wanted to be the pope, a poet, and also Casanova. Mia found him to be many people at once, good and bad. She said in retrospect that she admired him.

John N. B. Villiers-Farrow was born in Sydney, Australia, on February 10, 1904. His father, Colonel Joseph Rashmere Villiers-Farrow, was, like Maureen O'Sullivan's father, a distinguished soldier. He'd fought bravely in Indian and South African campaigns.

The boy was educated, intermittently, at Wellington College in Australia and at Winchester College in England. He would remain a lifelong Anglophile (and saw to it, decades later, that daughter, Mia, attended English schools).

A handsome lad, tall, blond and blue-eyed, weighing in at 165 pounds, John Farrow had an adventurous spirit and was eager to experience all the world had to offer. He was fearless —he ran away from home when he was eleven. At fourteen he enlisted in the Royal Navy. The rigid discipline, however, irked him, and he resigned from the Royal Naval Academy after only a year of training. His next endeavor: the merchant marine service. He was a private, first class, with the U.S. Marines in 1920 and '21. He spent six months in the U.S. Coast Guard in 1924.

By the age of twenty-five he had been to most of the world's ports. He'd traveled around Cape Horn on square-rigger grain ships. He had become a first mate (and for decades afterward held officer's papers for both sailing and steamships). He even participated in scientific expeditions.

John Farrow had another talent: He discovered he could write, and some of his short stories were published while he was still in the navy.

In 1927 Farrow was traveling from Tahiti to New York. He loved Tahiti and had actually compiled French- and English-Tahitian dictionaries. He was also interested in history. But en route to New York he stopped in Hollywood. He had written a play and wanted to sell it. Apparently he liked Tinseltown, because he remained there and eked out a living writing, first, for magazines.

Then, according to some accounts, it was a Boston-born movie producer, Charles R. Rogers, who gave him his first assignment to write for the screen. Other accounts bring Rogers into the story later. In any event it is fact that Farrow's good looks and knowledgeable, authoritative manner—courtesy of his naval training and many years at sea—were assets, and Farrow made fast progress. Within a year he'd worked on eight pictures, writing titles for some, screenplays and adaptations for others. Some were top pictures of the day, such as *Ladies of the Mob,* which starred Clara Bow and was directed by William Wellman; *Three Week-Ends,* another Clara Bow starrer; and *Wolf Song,* directed by Victor Fleming. In 1929 Farrow wrote the titles for a classic film, *The Four Feathers,* a Merian C. Cooper production. (In a few years Cooper's *King Kong* would become another classic.)

But Farrow's path to success encountered an obstacle. The young man's personal life suffered a heavy, though fortunately unpublicized blow.

He was taking a course at the Catholic University at Loyola in San Francisco. His version of the story was that on campus he was ardently pursued by an attractive girl who was the daughter of a wealthy San Francisco man. The family was Jewish.

Reports are that when the young woman became pregnant, Farrow would not immediately agree to marry her. Her father's influential lawyers had Farrow arrested. Maureen O'Sullivan has recounted the ordeal: "The lawyers got John taken to prison in San Francisco in chains and thrown in the hold for three days."

Of course Farrow and the girl were subsequently married. And divorced.

When, not too many years later, Farrow was one of the leading Catholic scholars in the United States, he was terrified that this information would become public. Consequently he assiduously avoided personal publicity, no easy task in view of the fact that his religious books were best-sellers, and he was a successful Hollywood director.

But that was all to come. When Maureen O'Sullivan first met John Farrow, they were both on the threshold of what promised to be very colorful and exciting lives.

• • •

Maureen's career, while at Fox, had not really taken off, although she'd appeared in two pictures opposite the studio's top male star, Will Rogers. But she didn't like America's most famous and beloved humorist. She also felt Rogers didn't like her. She was just relieved that he kept his distance.

As expected, the studio had indeed used Maureen as a pawn in contract negotiations with Janet Gaynor. After they came to terms with Gaynor, Fox dropped Maureen's option. For a brief period she free-lanced. She got the glamour treatment for a 1932 United Artists release, *The Silver Lining.* Her makeup and costuming were ludicrous: heavily made-up eyes and low-cut necklines. In later years she laughed at it, thinking she looked like "a female Dracula."

However, she wasn't unhappy with the salary: $300 a week, a huge salary in Depression-era America. In Hollywood terms of the day, though, it was nothing. Loretta Young, an actress even younger than Maureen, was earning over $1,000 a week. William Powell and Kay Francis were at the top, each pulling down $6,500 a week (at a time when there were breadlines all over America). The queen of the Hollywood pack was sleek, golden-haired Constance Bennett, whose $30,000 per week stood, for many years, as the all-time high for any actor or actress's salary.

Maureen was happy to be working and she has told a story that sheds light on Mia Farrow's future attitudes about material things. When Maureen first came to California, she could've bought property on Ventura Boulevard, which was offered to her for $100 an acre, but she turned it down. She said to herself, here was a deal that would make her so rich she would never really know who her friends were. She admitted, however, that some people thought she was crazy.

Maureen made pictures for Warner Bros. and Universal. The Warner's experience was glorious—a role in *One Way Passage,* a highly romantic story and one of Maureen's all-time favorite films. Tay Garnett was the director and he became lifelong friends with Maureen and John Farrow. (He became godfather to their second daughter, Prudence.)

But at Universal the young Maureen found she had to contend with Carl Laemmle, Jr., the pushy son of the studio's founder. Junior Laemmle, the head of production, kept a sharp eye out for new, beautiful young actresses on the lot. Laemmle asked his cousin, Paul Kohner (later a top agent), to introduce him to Maureen. Then he invited her out to dinner. She found him to be an abrasive young guy, a real turnoff, a nasty Hollywood character. She refused to have dinner or anything else to do with him personally. (Like Mia, many years later, there were certain Hollywood games Maureen refused to play.) Needless to say, a Universal contract was not in Maureen's future.

But her Irish leprechauns were looking out for her, because in 1932 she landed a contract at MGM, the leading studio of the day—the home of the brightest stars and most talented behind-the-scenes people in the industry.

Maureen, twenty-one, was in the big time.

She'd taken up residence at the colorful Garden of Allah Hotel. Farrow lived nearby at the Ronda Apartments. He was often seen at the Garden of Allah's swimming pool. Sheilah Graham, a sometime tennis partner of Farrow's, recalled that Farrow had a snake tatooed on the upper part of the inside of his left thigh. He posed for long periods at the end of the Garden's diving board wearing short swimming trunks, and the snake appeared to be emerging from his reproductive organs.

$$\bullet \quad \bullet \quad \bullet$$

Maureen had to be aware from the onset that the competition on the Metro lot for the leading female roles in Leo the Lion's pictures was almost laughably formidable: Joan Crawford was at the very peak of her career, as was Norma Shearer (who was married to the head of production, Irving Thalberg). Myrna Loy was on the way up. Rosalind Russell was under contract. Platinum-blond bombshell Jean Harlow was the studio's undisputed sex symbol, and of course Garbo reigned supreme.

It is a tribute to Maureen O'Sullivan's individuality and uniqueness that she survived and flourished in this hothouse environment of drop-dead glamour and sexual allure, though the studio did launch an effort to make her conventionally "sexy." But she has freely, almost proudly, admitted that she was never a very ambitious person, and ambition was as essential in Hollywood as oxygen is to a plant.

Maureen of course got to know the stars on the lot, and admired many of them. Joan Crawford was an exception. Maureen remembers her as a phony and didn't mind saying so, because "she *was* a phony."

The picture Metro initially cast Maureen O'Sullivan in was

one of the studio's all-time winners—a film that put Maureen on the career map: *Tarzan the Ape Man.* The director, W. S. "Woody" Van Dyke, worked fast but not at the expense of quality. He was also very attractive, and Maureen liked him very much. Van Dyke was very pleased at her ability to be creative and spontaneous without requiring endless retakes (a trait to be passed on, apparently, to her daughter Mia). He would use her again.

This picture would in effect haunt the mature Maureen, as the film lived on and played to succeeding generations. For years she didn't like being referred to as Jane, because people always made stupid jokes, such as "me Tarzan, you Jane." But Maureen grew to realize she was part of movie folklore and graciously accepted the attention.

It's interesting that she detested Cheetah, the chimp, and referred to him as "that bastard." It seems the primate bit her whenever he could. (Maureen said the apes were all homosexuals, eager to wrap their paws around Johnny Weissmuller's thighs. The apes, according to Maureen, were jealous of her, and she loathed them.)

Maureen's personal life was typical for the day. For publicity purposes the studio linked her name with as many eligible young bachelors as possible. She was dating handsome Irish star James Dunn, and in 1932 was reportedly engaged to him. After their breakup, it was said that she was going home to Ireland.

But 1933 was the year she was engaged to "Johnny Farrow, a ladies' man who knows how to pick them," observed columnist Sidney Skolsky.

It's fascinating how many personality traits of the young Maureen O'Sullivan were echoed decades later in the personality of her daughter Mia. Maureen, as Mia would be, was typed in the public mind as the sweet, virtuous girl on the screen. At the age of twenty-one, the outspoken Maureen was stating publicly that she was tired of it. She was "a little tired of being so good."

She was also described as "good-natured but obstinate," and while totally cooperative, "when she decides that she wants to have her own way, she has her own way." A description that applies one hundred percent to Mia. Furthermore, noted reports of the day about Maureen O'Sullivan, "she can sulk. She has a temper and can say things and throw things."

Like Mia, Maureen was also lauded as a total professional who took direction easily and was always eager to learn.

But perhaps the most startling similarity between mother and daughter concerns this bit of information about Maureen O'Sullivan that appeared in 1933: Maureen was thinking of adopting a Japanese baby. An unheard-of move for a young movie actress even to consider, let alone talk about. (Mia Farrow would eventually adopt three Korean and two Vietnamese children, one of them a handicapped child.)

• • •

The engagement of Maureen O'Sullivan to John Farrow lasted for three years, a *very* long time by Hollywood standards. Everyone wondered why. The answer was connected to the secret John Farrow was concealing: his first marriage.

Farrow, like Maureen, was Catholic. He was divorced. At one point Maureen and Farrow had reportedly journeyed to Ireland so that they could be married in the presence of her parents. Some reports even suggested they were already married and wanted to reconcile the O'Sullivans to that fact. The most probable reason for the trip was to introduce John to the family and obtain their permission. Hollywood gossips said that in Eire a rude circumstance confronted the young lovers when the Roman Catholic church still denied their request to marry.

But Farrow and O'Sullivan were resourceful and determined, with a philosophy that lighting candles made more sense than cursing the darkness. It took years, influence, and the kind of commitment—and patience—Hollywood people were not famous for. But there would be positive results.

Maureen O'Sullivan's private life was of growing interest to a nosy press. Ambition or no, her career was gaining considerable momentum.

John Farrow was newsworthy too. There was a minor contretemps with the Immigration Service at the beginning of 1934. It seems that Farrow was involved in a deportation proceeding, but he was cleared by the court, which said he had been the victim of a mistake. He was Australian. Friends believed he had gone to Mexico to reenter the country in compliance with an immigration formality. (Maureen had been quizzed on her immigration status the previous December.)

O'Sullivan was featured in two highly successful pictures in 1934: *The Thin Man,* directed by Woody Van Dyke; and *The Barretts of Wimpole Street.* She was wonderful in both films, although she didn't initially like herself in *The Thin Man.* (She did like William Powell, and they used to sneak off during filming and go to his house for a swim in the pool between shots. She said he was a beau of hers for a while.)

She also starred that year with top leading man Robert Montgomery in *Hideout,* another success. Maureen O'Sullivan was becoming a hot property.

She clicked in two more prestigious and successful films the following year. *David Copperfield* and *Anna Karenina* were both top-of-the-line Metro productions, produced by David O. Selznick and directed, respectively, by George Cukor and Clarence Brown.

Maureen was superb in *Copperfield.* It's peculiar that she wasn't a contender for the role of Scarlett O'Hara a couple of years later. *Gone With the Wind* was a Selznick venture too. George Cukor was the initial director, and Maureen's *Copperfield* performance was, in many ways, the ultimate screen test for that coveted role.

She was wonderful, too, in the Garbo picture *Anna Karenina,* and off-camera the actresses shared a pleasant camaraderie. Garbo chided her when Maureen avoided being too friendly, but Maureen had heard Garbo didn't like people trying to get too close. To Garbo's delight, Maureen often brought her fresh-baked Irish bread (made by Maureen's cook).

John Farrow meanwhile published a novel, *Laughter Ends.* He had by now directed his first films and was writing screenplays and working on another book, a biography of a famous priest. In 1935 he was also working on the screenplay for Maureen's latest Tarzan adventure, *Tarzan Escapes.* The picture dragged on and on in production, and Maureen became ill during a prolonged sequence in a studio-built "swamp." She chided Farrow about this long, difficult-to-film sequence, which she wished he hadn't written (and which was cut out of the final film).

On the social scene Maureen O'Sullivan and "Johnny" Farrow were one of the town's most attractive couples. By now she was sporting a beautiful square-cut diamond engagement ring, but it seemed they'd never be able to wed. And then came the news.

Maureen's father, in Dublin, was finally able officially to announce his daughter's engagement to John Farrow on August 12, 1936 (three years after Hollywood columnist Sidney Skolsky had reported it). Major O'Sullivan stated the ceremony would take place in Dublin "on a date yet to be decided." The vital and new information, however, was saved for last. Major

O'Sullivan announced that a special dispensation for the marriage had been granted by the Vatican.

The couple finally wed, not in Dublin but in Santa Monica, California, in Santa Monica Church on September 12, 1936. Mrs. Norman Foster (Sally Blane, Loretta Young's sister) was matron of honor. Michael Tandy, British consul, was best man.

There was a wedding breakfast and reception at Loretta Young's home, then the newleyweds were off on a brief honeymoon.

Chapter Two

THE FARROWS built a guest house on the grounds of their new Beverly Hills home on Beverly Drive, for the occasions when Maureen's parents visited. Maureen and "Johnny" quickly earned a reputation around town as wonderful hosts and delightful guests.

Garson Kanin, one of the fast-rising young writing-directing talents on the Hollywood scene, was under contract to RKO at the same time as Farrow. Kanin describes Farrow as "good-looking, with enormous charm, and I thought him an excellent director too. We met frequently on the lot and he was very charming and witty."

But there was an added facet to John Farrow—his scholarly bent and his intense interest in Catholicism and religion. Garson Kanin recalls him as "a rare sort. A *devout* Catholic, it was an important part of his persona. He took his Catholicism *very* seriously, very fervently."

Farrow's biography, *Damien the Leper,* was about the Roman Catholic priest who gave his life to the care of lepers in a colony in Molokai, Hawaii. Published in 1937, it became a huge success, one of the most commercial religious books of its day. So great was its impact that Farrow was named a Knight of the Holy Sepulcher by Pope Pius XI.

From this point on, John Farrow occupied a unique niche in Hollywood. He was certainly the only papal knight writing and directing movies, and just how Louis B. Mayer, Jack Warner, Sam Goldwyn, and the other Jewish movie moguls perceived this distinction boggles the mind (Zanuck wasn't Jewish, but everyone thought he was).

However, in the opinion of Garson Kanin today, all the current emphasis on the "Jewish-ness" of the old Hollywood is totally erroneous. "I think when one says Hollywood was Jewish-oriented, that's a misconception," states Kanin. "An example: W. C. Fields was once having dinner at Chasen's. He was raising hell about all the troubles he was having at Universal. He was saying, 'Those goddamn Jews, they're driving me crazy!' and someone said to him, 'Bill, there aren't any Jews at Universal. They're all Catholics,' and he said, 'That's right, they're the worst kind of Jews.'"

Kanin points out that D. W. Griffith was a dominant force in early Hollywood, and there was nothing Jewish about him.

"I never saw or felt that I was in friendly territory," states Kanin. "Statistically I think if you went all through the names of the executives, the players, et cetera, you'd find the same proportion of Jews as in any business. But I didn't ever feel that it was so dominated."

Some contend that it was. If, as some sources state, Hollywood didn't quite know what to make of John Farrow, apparently Farrow himself was confronted and torn by his own inner conflicts. Mia Farrow revealingly stated, years later, that the thing her father respected least was directing films—he never believed in it as an art form.

The year *Damien* was published, Farrow had already begun work on his next literary project, a massive undertaking that would take years to complete: a history of the papacy. Farrow was held in such high regard by the Catholic hierarchy that for this new book project, eventually titled *Pageant of the Popes,* Farrow's research in Rome was done with the aid of Vatican authorities.

And then there was Farrow the Hollywood director. His studio, RKO, was famous for producing the Fred Astaire–Ginger Rogers musicals and Katharine Hepburn's pictures. But Farrow's films, for the remainder of the thirties, were not exactly trend-setting blockbusters. His most successful pictures were *Sorority House, The Saint Strikes Back,* and a remake of *A Bill of Divorcement.*

In 1937 Maureen (whose 1936 pictures included the horror classic *Devil Doll* and the Marx brothers classic, *A Day at the Races*) was sent to England, along with heartthrob Robert Taylor, to star in *A Yank at Oxford.* The picture was made at MGM's London studios, and one of Maureen's old schoolmates from Roehampton was featured in the cast: Vivien Leigh.

The women never became close friends. Maureen later said Vivien's personality had changed; she didn't find her as likable. (Ironically Vivien Leigh would be instrumental in launching the young Mia Farrow's television career.)

Maureen's career at MGM seemed to have peaked by the late thirties. She was popular and a star, but not a first-rank star. Maureen herself has blamed this on her lack of ambition, coupled with her own insecurities and feelings of inferiority. Plus the fact that she was often not available for projects because she was busy working on a new Tarzan film, all of which had very long and arduous shooting schedules. (Two pictures that Maureen had been anxious to do, *Wuthering Heights* and *Our Town,* were filmed by other studios.)

For whatever reason, the Metro hierarchy never launched a campaign to build Maureen into a major star, nor did they purchase properties expressly for her talents or commission original properties to showcase her. Perhaps she was too versatile and professional for the powers-that-be to recognize her full potential. Certainly, three decades hence, at the time Mia Farrow was being launched into full-fledged stardom, the marketplace was far more friendly to all types of actresses. By then diversity was an asset, not a liability; it was welcomed, not ignored.

In any event *A Yank at Oxford* turned out well and was slated for release early in 1938. Maureen made six more films in 1938, including yet another Tarzan picture, to be released in 1939.

One of John Farrow's 1939 films was a melodrama, *Five Came Back,* starring Chester Morris, Wendy Barrie, and a promising twenty-seven-year-old actress, Lucille Ball, in the role of a prostitute. The picture was a surprise success (and Farrow remade it in the late 1950s as *Back from Eternity* with Anita Ekberg in the Lucille Ball role).

America's film industry was at a peak, creatively and commercially, and in 1939 it would produce a series of films that proved to be timeless, including *Gone With the Wind; The Wizard of Oz; Goodbye, Mr. Chips;* and *Wuthering Heights.* There were many others, and that year Maureen starred with Laurence Olivier and Greer Garson in *Pride and Prejudice* (released in 1940).

For the Farrows, however, 1939 was memorable for another reason: In May, Maureen gave birth to their first child, a son—Michael Damien Villiers Farrow.

• • •

When World War II began in October 1939, many British and British Commonwealth subjects felt the call to arms. It seemed the United States would never enter the European fray, so many men across the country journeyed to Canada to enlist. John Farrow joined the Royal Canadian Navy. He was second in command on an antisubmarine vessel, the officer in charge of depth bombs, fire hoses, and directing "abandon ship" in case of emergency. Farrow saw active combat. He discovered firsthand what it was like to be under attack. He observed how men, including himself, behaved under extraordinary circumstances.

But it wasn't an enemy shell that proved disastrous. While on duty in the Caribbean, Farrow was stricken with typhus. It was June 1941.

The prognosis was frightening. Doctors told Maureen her husband had no more than a year to live. Farrow was in and out of a dozen hospitals, subjected to every known treatment. He was finally sent back to Canada and then home—an invalid.

The doctors held out little hope. Farrow looked awful. He'd lost most of his hair and eyebrows and an enormous amount of weight. His skeletal appearance was disheartening, especially to him. He felt he looked like a freak. His mental condition was dismal as well. Maureen, desperate, took him to Palm Springs, praying he'd recover there.

Farrow recalled afterward how the futility of his situation was as terrifying as the reality of it. He said he almost went insane from worry. One can imagine how Maureen, with a new baby, must have felt during this traumatic period.

Farrow's outlook changed, miraculously, when Paramount Pictures sought him out to direct a film the entire movie industry considered extremely important to the war effort on the home front. *Wake Island* was based on the true story of a marine garrison's heroic last stand. The Japanese attack on Pearl Harbor on December 7 had plunged the United States into the world conflagration, and Hollywood was considered crucial to the government's propaganda campaign to keep public opinion properly focused.

John Farrow was considered an expert on men in war—the industry needed him. He later said the idea that *someone* still had some use for him immediately gave him a different outlook on life. It was like a shot of adrenaline. Technically he was on sick leave from the Royal Navy. Directing *Wake Island* was considered a service to the war effort, and he was ordered to do so.

Farrow was grateful that Lt. Col. Francis E. Pierce, of the U.S. Marine Corps, was technical adviser on the picture. Colonel Pierce, too, had won a fierce battle with deadly typhus, and Farrow was encouraged by his example.

Farrow's health remained shaky during production. He took frequent blood tests and received injections for a recently diagnosed liver condition. Farrow's bouts with typhus would recur, but each time, fortunately, with less severity. Eventually Farrow was rid of it, and his doctors referred to him as the miracle man.

The temporarily incapacitating illness, in retrospect, had at least provided one positive result in Farrow's life. In the dreary, disheartening weeks he had had to spend in a tiny Dutch hospital in Curaçao when he had been diagnosed with typhus, he was able to do some more work on his book about the papacy; that was what he devoted himself to during the long, painful convalescence at home.

Wake Island would prove to be a big critical as well as commercial hit and a turning point in Farrow's career. It was his first "A" picture for a major studio. He even won the coveted New York Film Critics Award as best director and an Academy Award nomination as best director. It seemed that the thirty-eight-year-old Farrow had finally broken into the Hollywood golden circle.

His book *Pageant of the Popes* also proved to be a hit, with reviewers as well as with the public. According to one critic, the book moved with "a steady pressure of nervous vitality." Another noted that while it was reverent, *Pageant* pulled no punches.

With all this success came the heavy-hanging specter of the old dilemma: how to cooperate and publicize all these endeavors without running the risk of exposing his "secret" private life—the marriage before Maureen and all the unsavory details.

The solution Farrow settled on was to do a very limited number of select interviews. And, one assumes, he held his breath and prayed nothing negative would result.

The forces were with him.

However, by refusing to go all out and cooperate with Hollywood's powerful publicity machine, he paid a price. According to his wife, years later, he never became famous enough so that top producers would jump any hurdle to hire him, as they would a Mervyn Le Roy, for example.

In later years it was Maureen who lamented the fact that others less talented than John would *not* be forgotten because they had played the self-promotion game. But her husband had dared not, and, considering his uptight era, perhaps the decision was the only one he could have made.

Farrow quietly accumulated a very impressive number of honors for his books and scholarly endeavors (in 1942 *Damien* was in its fifteenth printing and had been translated into eleven languages). Whereas publicizing movies was one thing, in the area of his books he drew the line on publicity because of the religious nature of the material. He literally forbade movie press agents from publicizing his awards. The publicity people were astonished by his reticence. To them Farrow seemed almost a blue blood. He had been named Knight of St. John of Jerusalem by King George V; Officer of the Crown of Rumania; he'd been decorated by France and Spain for scientific research into their national histories; and he was a Fellow of the Royal Geographical Society.

But despite their entreaties, and perhaps despite even some encouragement to cooperate with them from his wife, Farrow stood firm. No publicity. There would be rare exceptions, when Farrow would reluctantly go along, but for the most part the edict stood.

One of the exceptions had of course concerned *Wake Island*. He agreed to meet with reporters not only because the film celebrated the Marine Corps and the Allied cause—what American film of the day didn't?—but he had conquered typhus, and Farrow thought it important to let others who might have to face a similar medical ordeal know that recovery was possible.

To Farrow's embarrassment, the press made much of the fact that Farrow had contacted typhus while on a rescue mission aiding a freighter torpedoed by the Nazis. But Farrow bent over backward not to cast himself in the role of hero. Quite the opposite. When his vessel had been under attack, he recalled, a superior officer had called him a cold fish of a chap because he had seemed to remain so cool and collected. Perhaps, explained Farrow, he (Farrow) had merely been a good actor, for he had been acting in reverse. Hysteria under attack breeds more hysteria. It wasn't the danger that made men cowards, said Farrow, it was the thinking that bred fear.

Those on the set of *Wake Island* observed that John Farrow

usually issued orders quietly; his attitude, most of the time, was one of absorbed concentration. People didn't argue with him.

It's fascinating that Bette Davis observed decades later, after having been directed by Farrow, having known Maureen O'Sullivan, and having met and spent time with the whole family, that it was daughter Mia who had Mama Maureen's guts—and Papa John's toughness.

• • •

After *Wake Island,* Farrow's next assignment was another war epic, to be filmed in Canada with the full cooperation of the government: *The Commandos Strike at Dawn.* It starred Paul Muni. Then Farrow directed Loretta Young and Alan Ladd in *China,* another war tale.

Amid all this activity the Farrows had made a crucial decision concerning their personal lives. Maureen would retire from the screen and devote herself full-time to her family. They planned on having more children (one a year for ten years, Maureen said). She didn't want the children to be strangers to one another.

On another occasion she wryly noted that she didn't think John wanted quite so many. She could see a pained look on his face every time she told him she was pregnant. But, she related, he acted very Catholic about it, and so she selfishly went ahead and had children.

Farrow would be making plenty of money to support the family in style and to satisfy his interests in art and literature.

Maureen, at thirty-one, was still young and beautiful (the noted portrait painter Sir John Lavery had, not too long before, chosen her as one of the four most beautiful women—the other three were Loretta Young, Lady Diana Cooper and her sister, Vicomtesse Castleross). She could easily have gone on making films. At first it was assumed that the actress would do just that. It was a familiar scenario others had followed. The actress would have a change of heart, and before long she'd be back on the soundstages saying how wonderful it was to be back. After all, Loretta Young, also devoutly Catholic, said she was going to retire and raise a family. She'd married advertising executive Tom Lewis only a couple of years earlier, and Lewis expected her to retire. Things didn't exactly work out that way.

Maureen O'Sullivan, however, said she'd retire—and she did. The Farrows' second child, Joseph Patrick (Pat) Villiers Farrow, was born in November 1943. And on February 9, 1945, Maria de Lourdes Villiers Farrow entered the world.

Chapter Three

MAUREEN O'SULLIVAN once recalled that many years ago in Ireland, her mother—Mia's grandmother—was told by a fortune-teller that Maureen's eldest daughter's name would become a household word.

Mia, noted Maureen years later, was a girl who got what she wanted. She was born wise—and stubborn. The girl's birth was announced in Louella Parsons's column. In reporting it, Parsons incorrectly gave the infant's name as Marie, not Maria. Farrow telephoned her to point out the error, and Louella apologized, claiming it had been a typo. But everyone knew the columnist was notorious for making such mistakes. Parsons, who had been born Jewish, was now a devout Catholic, having converted the previous year. She was to be Mia's godmother.

And the new infant's godfather was a friend of the family, famed director George Cukor. With Parsons and Cukor as godparents, and O'Sullivan and Farrow as her parents, the baby was, in Hollywood terms, of royal blood.

Apparently Maria de Lourdes Villiers Farrow had a very active imagination virtually from infancy. (She later claimed she remembered being born!) She recalled, as an adult, that before she could even talk, she lived in her own magic kingdom and had a private name for herself: Mildred.

She adored her older brother, Michael, who returned the affection. Six years older than Mia, Michael was old enough to take a proprietary interest in her, but young enough to have fun with her. He called her Mouse because, as she grew, she changed from a fat infant to a scrawny child. The nickname stuck.

Over the next six years four more siblings would join the family: John Charles (John-Johnny), born a year after Mia; Prudence Anne (Pru-Prudy) in 1948; Stephanie Margarita (Steffi) in 1949; and Theresa Magdalena (Tisa), in 1951. (Maureen was forty the year Tisa was born.)

Over the next few years Maureen's responsibilities included running the house and sometimes chauffeuring the children to school in the station wagon. She was the president of the St. John's Hospital Guild in Los Angeles for two years and worked for the social service auxiliary of her church.

Maureen was back on a soundstage in 1947. She returned to films, under her husband's direction, in *The Big Clock,* in which she played the lovely, chic wife of Ray Milland. Ironically Maureen, who had made thirty-four movies, had to take a screen test! The studio told her they wanted to be sure she looked right for the role. What they meant was they wanted to see if she looked too old (she was thirty-six). Maureen, the consummate pro, didn't mind. She said she understood why they wanted the test and she thought they were right. Needless to say, she was cast and was excellent in the finished film. Her technique, and her looks, hadn't dimmed at all. The movie was a good suspense thriller, with Charles Laughton chewing up the scenery in a major role, and even nonfilm buffs will find it interesting to note that *The Big Clock* was the basis for one of Kevin Costner's big hits in the eighties, *No Way Out.*

John Farrow's career in the mid-to-late forties included some notable successes. In addition to *The Big Clock* there was *Two Years Before the Mast* and *The Night Has a Thousand Eyes. Alias Nick Beal,* another Ray Milland starrer, had a story right up Farrow's alley: Milland played the devil in a contemporary setting.

Farrow also directed his share of turkeys during these years, *The Hitler Gang* and *Copper Canyon* among them. There were many others.

Home life at the Farrows' wasn't like home life for the average American family. There were nannies for the children, and the children lived in a nursery separate from the main house. John Farrow liked to come home to a quiet house—his wife knew he "didn't like everything messed up"—and the children had their own wing, complete with a kitchen that opened up into Maureen's bedroom.

It's revealing that when Mia Farrow became a mother, none of her children had full-time nannies. Or lived in a "separate wing." Mia would have help come in, but preferred doing things herself.

Mia's introduction to the Catholic religion began early. She was a highly sensitive and impressionable child. When she saw a nun for the first time, she became hysterical. She was four years old. The rituals of Catholicism, with its formidable trappings and theatricality, apparently both attracted and terrified the child. (Later, when she was about ten, Mia said she wanted to become a nun. What appealed to her most was that if she became a nun, she thought then she'd be able to levitate "and stuff," and have visions along with the best of them.)

Mia's alter ego, Mildred, died when Mia turned six. The

"death" occurred aboard a luxury liner. The Farrow family was en route to Ireland and Mama Maureen took advantage of the opportunity: She told Mia that they were going to "drown Mildred." They theoretically put Mildred overboard and drowned her. To Maureen's relief they never saw Mildred again. Apparently Mia had been ready to let her go.

But Mia's imagination continued to flourish mightily. She recalled, as an adult, that she hadn't received a lot of attention as a child, which was probably a benefit, she thought, because when one is overlooked, one is left to one's daydreams. There wasn't the pressure that an only child, or two children, would have had. As a result, claimed Mia, she was a terrific daydreamer, and she read a great deal and felt free to do what she liked.

On another occasion the picture she described of her childhood wasn't quite so rosy. She stated as an adult that she wasn't afraid to be alone but that she was afraid of being lonely. She said she knew what loneliness was all about—and it had nothing to do with being with people. She had been lonely when she was growing up. She also said she was an insomniac by the age of eight.

In retrospect Mia Farrow has revealed that she hadn't really known her parents very well, but they certainly had represented a great deal to her. She recalled Maureen as a terrific mother, full of fairy tales, with a soft voice and a soothing manner, but not very involved in the more physical aspects of parenting, such as feeding and dressing the kids. But time shared with Mama was of top quality, Mia said. Her mother was a mystical figure to her, and Mia to some degree romanticized her, and her father too.

Maureen suffered a personal loss on Christmas Eve 1950: Her father died. The major left a sizable estate—close to

£70,000, almost $200,000 in American money. (Eventually Maureen reportedly received about a quarter of the estate.)

The Farrows lived on a lavish scale and didn't want for any of the physical comforts. The children, like all Hollywood kids of that era, were well insulated from the realities of the outside world. After Tisa's birth Maureen had gone back to work. The Farrows may have needed the money, and besides, although Maureen loved motherhood, she was also an actress who loved to work. In 1952 she was Ronald Reagan's leading lady in an opus titled *Bonzo Goes to College,* a sequel to the successful *Bedtime for Bonzo.* Maureen doesn't recall working with Reagan on the picture, but she does remember Bonzo, the monkey. Maureen and Reagan later worked together in a television drama, and she has recalled him as "pleasant." When Reagan became president and Maureen wrote him disapproving letters, he didn't answer. She had done the same with presidents Eisenhower and Kennedy, who sent her "lovely replies." She described Reagan as a man who obviously didn't like to be disagreed with.

Maureen costarred in *All I Desire,* with Barbara Stanwyck and Rock Hudson. She didn't like Stanwyck and was proud she had the guts to say so. Most people in Hollywood did like the veteran star, or said they did. But Barbara apparently didn't like Maureen, or the fact that the very feminine Maureen was as popular with the cast and crew as she was.

Although Maureen O'Sullivan's career seemed to be back on track, at this point she had to abandon her career once again. Another dreaded physical disease had invaded the Farrow household. In 1954 nine-year-old Mia contracted polio. The entire family had to be evacuated. Mia's clothes and toys were burned. Even her beloved Magic Box, which contained all sorts of little treasures and belongings that were magical to her, had to be destroyed.

Mia was taken to the polio ward at Cedars of Lebanon Hospital in Los Angeles. Maureen recalled what a really ghastly and very difficult experience that was for little Mia. The family would come see her every day, but they weren't allowed to get very close. Around her were children in iron lungs, and the girl in the bed next to hers died, which upset Mia terribly. Maureen remembered that before Mia went to the hospital, she had wrapped up all her toys and given them to her brothers and sisters, which Maureen thought was really very sweet. But what Mia didn't know was that because she was contagious, all those toys had to be burned.

It was a very difficult time. Polio was a crippling—sometimes fatal—disease. The family's prayers were answered. The child recovered, and there were almost no aftereffects—only a slight weakness in the left shoulder. (Certainly the trauma of polio had something to do with Mia, later in life, adopting a handicapped child.)

While Mia was recovering from polio, her eldest brother, Michael, was in a serious accident. One night in early 1955, very late, asleep in the Beverly Hills mansion, Maureen heard the screech of tires in front of the house. She instinctively felt something had happened and dashed outside, wearing only her nightgown. Michael had been hit by a car. The story was that Michael had been returning home from a movie, shortly after midnight, when the accident occurred.

The fifteen-year-old was taken to an emergency hospital, then to Cedars of Lebanon. He had head injuries and a fractured right leg. Maureen, dressed in her mink coat and nightgown, accompanied him to both hospitals. Michael recovered from the accident, but it was a trying time for the Farrow family.

Garson Kanin had been a visitor to the Farrow home during Mia's childhood years. "When I encountered her, she must have been around ten," recalls Kanin. "She was adorable. Looked exactly the way she looks now, except in miniature.

"She was an *extraordinary* child, in the sense of always being years beyond her age. I never can think of Mia as 'a little girl.' I don't remember a little girl. I remember a *small* creature —but she always was a young lady. She was always perfectly soignée, always neat as a pin, and she behaved with enormous dignity."-

According to Kanin, her brothers and sisters were quite different—not like Mia at all. "My recollection of her brothers is that they were kind of tough—little roughnecks, like all boys. But Mia was a little *lady*."

The Farrow kids were a close-knit clan. They loved each other. There was the usual fighting and competitiveness that characterizes any large family. Mia has recalled that at times they ran pretty wild and could be "pretty savage."

But Mia recalled that good manners always surfaced when, in the evenings, the children were dressed in their best when company was over. However, when put back in the nursery, one presumes they returned to an atmosphere of mild bedlam.

The Farrows all attended church together on Sundays. They went to the Church of the Good Shepherd in Beverly Hills (because of all the stars who belonged, a wag nicknamed it "Our Lady of the Cadillacs"). The Farrows were an extraordinarily attractive family. "They were *all* beautiful," recalled Rosalind Russell. "You didn't know which one to look at first."

The rich and famous of the film world were regular visitors to the Farrow home. Mia has recalled one particular female visitor, a beautiful brunette. What impressed the young Mia was that the lady spoke to her as an equal, not as a baby. She wasn't interested in Mia's dolls or her clothes; she wanted to know what Mia wanted to do in life, what she wanted to be. The lady was Ava Gardner. (Daddy had directed her in a picture for MGM, a Western filmed on location in Utah, and there were reports that Ava had disliked Farrow because he'd been sadistic in his treatment of the horses. There were also accounts describing how he'd fly to Los Angeles on Saturdays, "fly back the next morning with an armful of call girls to carouse and fornicate all through the Sabbath, then turn up on the set on Mondays with a hangover, cursing at everyone.")

In Hollywood the Farrow kids sometimes visited their dad on the set. When Mia was ten, she and her brothers and sisters visited the Warner Bros. lot where John Farrow was directing *The Sea Chase,* a picture starring John Wayne and Lana Turner. The Farrow brood had their names monogrammed in large script on their little matching shirts; that way there was no chance they'd be taken for "outsiders." The children posed for pictures with the actors, and ten-year-old Mia looks soberfaced indeed, posed alongside the radiant Lana (then thirtyfive).

Lana, in her memoirs, didn't recall the visit of the Farrow kids. But she clearly remembered John Farrow. She wrote that before the picture, she knew Farrow only by reputation—as a womanizer. On location in Hawaii she found that her hotel room was directly next to Farrow's, connected by a sliding door. Lana suspected that the director had something extracurricular in mind. She complained to the production manager, who was "reluctant to talk to Farrow about it." An intermediary acting on Lana's behalf warned the front office that Lana would return home "if something wasn't done." Lana was subsequently told that "Farrow . . . had not taken my attitude lightly. He couldn't understand what in the world was on my mind. He hadn't dreamed, et cetera, et cetera, he had just thought it would be a good idea to be close so that we could discuss the script." Lana wryly noted that from that point on, directing the picture, Farrow was very abrupt with her and "gave me almost no direction at all." He snarled at her if she missed a line. "And he was not very pleasant with the other actors either."

A friend had this to say about the Farrow marriage: "They stayed married to each other. They kept having babies. They went to church. John, in addition to producing important films, wrote serious books. . . . It was all very odd in film circles."

Others have described John Farrow as a hard-living, roguish Irishman whose fortunes were less than predictable. Farrow's career flourished in the fifties. The pictures he was associated with varied widely in quality, but one classic emerged from the lot: *Hondo,* with John Wayne. The men became fast friends.

Another film that might have been Farrow's crowning achievement (and also earned him a fortune) ended up being directed by another man. Things had begun promisingly. Farrow was signed by flamboyant producer Mike Todd to write and direct Todd's first picture, *Around the World in Eighty Days.* But it soon became apparent that an irresistible force had met an immovable object. Farrow completed preproduction and began the film. He directed the Spanish sequence. But he quit after disagreements with Todd, retaining credit as screenwriter. This was vitally important, because Farrow subsequently won an Oscar—his only one—for the script.

Although today John Farrow's name doesn't mean much celebrity-wise, he was, in the 1950s, famous enough to be considered subject material for the popular network television show *This Is Your Life.* Each week host Ralph Edwards would surprise an unsuspecting celebrity and proceed to haul out people from the person's past to pay homage to him or her. Usually the celebrities were well past their prime, like Buster Keaton or Stan Laurel. Or they were in total retirement, like

Bebe Daniels. *This Is Your Life* put the spotlight back on yesterday's headliners, and supposedly the attention often revived a sagging career.

John Farrow was slated to be a subject, even though his career was still big. Perhaps his colorful life was the lure, plus the seven children, Maureen O'Sullivan, and the books he'd written and awards he'd won.

Somehow Farrow learned the show had its eye on him. He hit the roof and told his wife in no uncertain terms that if ever she cooperated and he ended up on the show (often the husband or wife of the subject participated in elaborate subterfuge to preserve the element of surprise), their marriage was *over.*

Maureen got the message. It wasn't easy, but somehow she talked *This Is Your Life* out of using John Farrow as a subject.

• • •

The Farrow children attended parochial school in Los Angeles. After her bout with polio, Mia returned to school. But the youngster continued to hate the regimentation. From the age of six until around eleven she invented a marvelously creative method of getting out of class. She kept a tooth in her pocket. If she'd had enough of a particular class, she simply said she had an awful toothache and produced the tooth from her mouth. It worked like a charm.

Her many foibles and eccentricities did not go unnoticed by her parents. According to Mia's adult recollections, before she turned twelve, she underwent a period of sustained analysis. She recalled it as a "jiffy course," in which someone attempted to "stick me together."

When Mia was twelve, the entire Farrow family—parents and all seven children—went to Spain, where John Farrow was to direct an epic adventure film, *John Paul Jones.*

While all the traveling around that the Farrows did was perceived as exciting and fashionable, it wasn't necessarily the best way to raise a family. Mia's girlhood has been described as tough, uncertain, and gypsylike.

The children were enrolled at the American School in Madrid. One day Mia shook up a seltzer bottle, aimed it at the ceiling, and let go. She was thrown out of school. Maureen then sent the clan to a Spanish school. Mia recalled she didn't learn much there either—but she discovered she loved to paint (she said it was good for the soul).

One of the stars of *John Paul Jones* was the legendary Bette Davis (then almost fifty years old). Bette took an immediate liking to twelve-year-old Mia (in later years Mia would refer to Davis as her "great ally"). Davis subsequently recalled what a "lonely little girl" Mia was. Mia struck up a friendship with Davis's daughter, B.D. (Beedee), and Mia made a deep impression on Bette, who observed that Mia had been born "with an old soul. She lived all alone in her own world."

Bette was also obviously impressed that Mia was just like the young Bette Davis had been as far as a life's goal was concerned. Davis later recalled that Mia had known, without a doubt, that she was going to be an actress, although, according to Davis, young Mia was "quite mousy-looking then." But she had brains, recalled Bette, and "in a most gentle way" she was solid steel.

Mia and her brothers and sisters all had small parts in *John Paul Jones.*

Her father was not pleased with Mia's expressed interest in acting. He did not want her, ever, to become an actress. "I never saw a happy actress," he told her with the knowledge of a lifetime. It was then decided that Mia be sent off to a convent school in England. As far as John Farrow was concerned, the farther away she was from Hollywood and its pitfalls, the better.

While Mia was at school, a traumatic event—a terrible tragedy—struck the Farrow family.

Thirteen-year-old Mia received the devastating news while at school in London: Her brother Michael, only nineteen, had been killed in a plane crash back in California. He had been the person closest to her. Her idol. Her confidant. Only the week before she had received a letter from him, in which he wrote, "Dear Mouse, I hope you are growing."

The death was a calamity for all. "It quite simply destroyed the family," Mia acknowledged years later, saying that after that tragedy the rest of the kids sort of fell into their own plots of soil and grew.

John Farrow, still in Spain filming *John Paul Jones,* said he and his wife hadn't even known Michael was taking flying lessons. They had been expecting him to rejoin the family overseas for Christmas. In tears Farrow flew to Los Angeles, taking the over-the-pole route. Maureen was following by plane the next day. She was too upset to talk with anyone or make any comment. She was with the other children.

The accident had been a collision of two small planes over the San Fernando Valley. In addition to Michael, two others had been killed—young Farrow's twenty-one-year-old flying instructor, David Johnson; and, flying alone in the other plane, thirty-nine-year-old Donald Preneville.

The planes had collided at about six hundred feet. It had been a bright, sunny day. The aircrafts fell two hundred yards apart at opposite sides of a gravel pit near the airport.

A witness was quoted: "It was terrible. They just seemed to seek each other out."

One can only imagine the heartbreak the parents suffered. Mia did not go to the funeral: She couldn't bear to acknowledge the finality of what had happened. Perhaps also her parents didn't want to submit her to the additional trauma of attending the funeral.

Over two hundred mourners attended the Requiem Mass at the Church of the Good Shepherd. John Farrow was a member of the Marine Corps Reserve, and a Marine Corps Honor Guard performed at graveside.

The tragedy certainly crystallized for young Mia the realization of just how shaky a world it was, how short and tiny life could be. Her life's philosophy was forged from this tragedy: One must live in the *now* and take advantage of every opportunity.

She went to church every morning—and later said religion was very seductive. She didn't know exactly what she wanted but she did know she wanted to be something bigger than herself, since she had learned the hardest way possible that a life's journey could be six weeks or six months—or nineteen years. At the age of fourteen, still thinking about becoming a nun but wanting to be an actress, too, Mia realized that all she really wanted to do was to act out her fantasies. She could *play* a nun, she didn't have to be one.

For the time being, however, she had to finish school. Over the years she was suspended from school many times for misbehavior. Mia, it seems, was always on the lookout for magic and excitement. Where there was none, she tried to create some. Or at least shake up the status quo. One day, for example, to offset the deadly dullness of study hall, she smuggled in an alarm clock and set it off. The clock rang loudly for over a quarter of an hour before the nuns were able to shut it off. They were not amused.

Mia later said that the nuns didn't know what to do with her. She was always apologizing for something. They were always telling her she had to be responsible. One summer she accompanied some nuns and postulants on a trip to Egypt. In Luxor she got lost for a whole day and night. They were going out of their minds trying to find her. She had become completely engrossed in wandering among the ruins, couldn't speak the language, and couldn't find her way back. Eventually they found each other.

But then, back in England, Mia went too far when she conducted secret guided tours behind the sacred door and into the cloisters where the sisters resided. Mia charged her classmates for these excursions (doughnuts and change) and she pointed out specific items on the "tour"—for example the crown of thorns on the Mother Superior's bed.

One day, as she was pointing to the crown of thorns, they heard nuns approaching. Panic-stricken, Mia pulled her "customers" behind some curtains. They all stood, breathlessly, shaking with fright, their feet pointed sideways so as not to protrude beyond the curtain and reveal their presence.

The ensuing moment of silence was deceiving. The curtains were suddenly pushed aside, and a glowering Mother Superior eyed the intruders. Mia's punishment: solitary confinement.

Of course, there were also good times at school in England. On one occasion Mia portrayed Amahl in *Amahl and the Night Visitors.* She sang in church and acted in Christmas pageants. She recalled how the school building was old and freezing cold, but there were warm memories because she had made some wonderful friends.

Chapter Four

To be an actress—how many young girls harbor that divine ambition? How very few succeed? And fewer still succeed the way Mia did.

She recalled that the first part she ever played was a tree—and she was "a very good tree."

Acting was a release for her, an escape. It was magical but also structured, as far as she was concerned; she could experience something with a beginning, a middle, and an end. There would be other desires: explorer, astronaut. Very impractical for Mia, obviously; she realized most places had been discovered, and one had to become a test pilot before one became an astronaut.

But an *actress.* That was achievable—perhaps even on the highest level. As Bette Davis observed, "Mia will always decide where she is going."

Where she went, after London, was back to California. Almost sixteen, she was enrolled at Marymount, a Catholic prep school for girls in Los Angeles.

She has recalled that the nuns in California really turned her off. How her parents must have blanched at remarks on her report cards. Mia was asking disturbing questions about religion! But Mia would not be dissuaded. She had questions, she wanted answers. And she observed that the nuns appeared more interested in fund-raising than in answering her questions.

By this time the opposite sex, of course, was beginning to arouse Mia's adolescent curiosity. The boys, however, were hardly running after her.

She has recalled a dance for teens at the Beverly Hills Hotel. She and a girlfriend were wallflowers. Then a boy walked toward them. Mia was thrilled—until the boy invited her girlfriend to dance. Mia, mortified, was the sole remaining female on the sidelines. She later recalled she turned around and held her face so that she wouldn't cry and managed to walk, not run, to the checkroom and ask for her coat. They weren't permitted to give it to her—the students were all supposed to check out at the same time. So Mia clambered underneath the counter, took her coat, and ran out of the building and all the way home (it was about a half mile). She ran into the garage and sat on an empty gasoline drum, crying, until 11:30. Then she went around the house and let herself in. Maureen asked her if she'd had a good time and she answered yes and went to bed.

Mia realized that her socks and flat chest were hardly assets at the dance. So the next day she remedied the situation: She bought nylons and falsies.

In drama class at Marymount, she discovered she could *make* people react to her, notice her; she could manipulate people, and all through the "marvelous game of pretending, where I didn't have to be me."

While at Marymount she competed against young students

from seventy other schools throughout the state (it was a National Forensic League competition) and won a gold medal for her readings from *I Am a Camera* and *Our Town*.

John Farrow, however, was apparently still opposed to his talented young daughter's aspirations of becoming an actress. One didn't challenge the formidable Farrow at home. He felt Mia hadn't had enough formal education. One can, to an extent, sympathize with Farrow's way of thinking. How many top stars had he known who were not only unhappy but pathetically uneducated and not remotely equipped to deal with the business or social side of show business.

Mia was sent back to England to attend Cygnet House, a first-rate finishing school located outside of London. It was very British and upper-crust, a school where one learned about wines and wallpaper, among other essentials. Seventeen-year-old Mia loathed it and most of the girls in it. She felt she didn't fit in and became belligerent. She knew she couldn't remain there. She longed to see the world, India in particular. She wanted to study Indian religions and meet their holy men. She vowed that she would one day.

Mia was as tough-minded as her father. Her future was unclear. According to one source, Maureen wrote to Mia and pleaded with her to come home to Beverly Hills and complete her final year of high school. Mia returned to the States, but it appears that attending Cygnet House was considered the completion of Mia's formal education.

In the mid-to-late 1950s John Farrow had a special production contract with RKO. He could write, produce, and direct his own films. However, the mercurial Howard Hughes sold RKO to the General Tire and Rubber Company, which stopped producing films and relied on renting out the studio's facilities. Farrow turned to directing for television.

In 1961 Maureen had been approached to do a play, *A*

Roomful of Roses, in Chicago. The offer intrigued her; she had the time; the children were all away. She loved to act (she had told Mia to become an actress only if she truly loved to act). To her surprise her husband told her to go ahead and do it. He thought it would be the right thing to do, that perhaps she would have to go back to work at some point because, after all, who knew what the future held?

If Maureen was alarmed by her husband's attitude—and what wife wouldn't have been—did he have some premonition about something?—she didn't show it. She followed his advice. The play was a hit.

One day she was slated to make a promotional appearance for the play on columnist Herb Kupcinet's popular Chicago-based TV show. She entered the wrong studio by mistake and found herself on camera with a panel of experts discussing the Cold War and devising a long-range strategy for contending with it.

Mia Farrow's mother handled herself exactly the way the adult Mia would have under the same circumstances. Maureen volunteered a strong opinion and said she didn't know why the United States needed a long-range policy because there really shouldn't be a Cold War, should there?

At home playwright Sumner Arthur Long was watching the program. Long's new play, *Cradle Will Rock,* was about a woman around Maureen's age with adult children who discovers, to her family's shock, that she's pregnant.

Long was taken with Maureen's remark about the Cold War because that was exactly the kind of remark the character in his play would have made—"dumb, but sensible."

Maureen was sent a copy of the play. It was a comedy. Did she want to do it? Yes. It played successfully on the summer-theater circuit on the East Coast in 1962.

Legendary producer-director George Abbott saw it and

thought the play could make the transition to Broadway, with a few changes. Long got the message and worked on a new version for months. But suddenly Maureen wasn't sure that she either should—or could—do it. Broadway wasn't summer stock. She wasn't a fearless young girl anymore—she was fifty years old, the mother of seven children. Doubts assailed her. She discussed it with her husband. He urged her to do it.

Again she followed his advice.

The play was retitled *Never Too Late,* and the wheels were in motion for a fall 1962 opening.

On October 24 the play was scheduled to open in New Haven, Connecticut. Several hours before opening-night curtain Maureen received a telephone call from a reporter, who told her her son Patrick had been arrested in California on a narcotics charge. Did she have any comment? (According to a published Associated Press report, police said they found narcotics and a hypodermic needle in Patrick's room.)

Maureen was nonplussed. She told the reporter her son had been in the hospital with hepatitis and had just been released. She said she hoped and prayed it was something the doctor had given him. She explained that he was a wonderful boy, that he was in the merchant marine and had just returned, and emphasized that she had never seen "any signs of this thing in Pat. Oh, it can't be true."

She certainly hadn't been forewarned about the problem. No one had called her from the Coast to tell her about it. (It later turned out that no one had wanted to upset her on opening night.)

Opening night!

How was she to get through the play? She hoped she wouldn't spoil it—but it was a comedy, and how, she agonized, could she be funny now? How, she repeatedly asked herself, was she going to get through it?

Maureen's fellow actors were aware of how distraught she was before stepping onstage. She was weeping just before she went on (and wept after the show). But the cast knew she wouldn't let them down, that she wouldn't let herself down. "She's a very strong person," observed an onlooker. "She acted as if she's been doing this all her life."

Bette Davis had once observed about Maureen O'Sullivan that the lady had *guts*. Maureen obviously did. She not only got through it, she also got wonderful reviews. "Miss O'Sullivan did a lovely job," wrote New Haven *Journal-Courier* critic Florence Johnson, who liked the play as well. Other critics were equally, if not more, enthusiastic and flattering.

The play had something to say that Maureen related to and considered important. She observed how an actress could easily have played the part for farce—a kind of "leering, one-joke thing about middle-aged pregnancy." But Maureen saw it as much more than that. Her character is overjoyed at the unexpected baby because it enables her to get her husband back. The husband has forgotten he loves his wife. The late-in-life baby enables husband and wife to find each other again. For Maureen the play was comedy only on the surface; underneath it was serious and poignant and had an important message for women.

When the curtain came down that night in New Haven, it was back to reality. Patrick Farrow's problem would not be quickly resolved, but as always life for the Farrows went on. They were survivors, traumas notwithstanding.

• • •

Never Too Late opened on Broadway and was a resounding hit. Maureen O'Sullivan, at fifty-one, experienced a new high; she became a Broadway star for the first time.

She didn't shun publicity the way her husband did. In fact

she was a natural at it, always providing provocative, quotable opinions and ideas. She had both a sense of humor and the gift of gab—and the press loved her. As 1962 came to a close, her star was in orbit.

Her family was very proud.

Mia, who had made her decision to become an actress, joined her mother in New York. The timing was certainly right for agents, casting people, producers, and directors to meet the beautiful, blond teenage daughter of a star who had just been reborn.

Maureen had already spoken to columnists about her talented daughter, telling them to pay attention to her. She saw to it that her friends, like theatrical lawyer Arnold Weissberger, who knew everyone important in show business, invited young Mia to his New York parties. Teenagers wouldn't ordinarily fit in with Weissberger's ultrasophisticated guests, but Mia was no ordinary teenager.

Mia got to know Kirk Douglas (later reports said she had a flirtation with him). He was appearing on Broadway at the Cort Theatre in *One Flew Over the Cuckoo's Nest,* across the street from *Never Too Late,* which was at the Playhouse Theater. Douglas recalled that Mia "spent many nights watching *Cuckoo's Nest* while she waited for her mother. Several times after the theater I took them both out to dinner. I didn't know which way to turn, they both were so beautiful."

Douglas was impressed not only by Mia's beauty but by her intelligence. "It wouldn't surprise me if Mia has the highest IQ of any actress I know."

Their paths would cross again.

The doors of opportunity opened for Mia. Nothing happened overnight, but in retrospect she didn't suffer a long wait. (In later years she noted that she didn't have the kind of faith in herself that would have supported a long wait; if things hadn't worked out in a reasonable time, she would have tried something else.)

Mia took as naturally to the New York theater scene as the proverbial duck to water. She sounded intelligent and mature when she spoke and was self-sufficient and resourceful. She also happened to appear ethereal and vulnerable and, according to those on the scene, radiated star presence from every pore.

Not long after her arrival in New York she encountered Salvador Dali, then in his late fifties. The controversial, eccentric, legendary painter was noted not only for his surrealistic art but for his personality and talent for self-promotion. His sometimes bizarre appearance and demeanor reflected his genius for showmanship and concealed a razor-sharp intelligence that had propelled him to the very pinnacle of success in the world of art—and beyond.

Mia and Dali met in an elevator at the St. Regis Hotel. She'd been invited to a party, which she suspected would be very dull and hadn't wanted to go. She went anyhow. When she entered the elevator at the St. Regis, she didn't want to get out. She rode up and down trying to collect her wits before making an entrance at the party.

Dali, holding his famous cane, was sitting in a chair facing the elevator and kept seeing Mia every time the elevator went by and the doors opened. She thought he was waiting for someone, but it turned out he'd been invited to the same party and, like Mia, didn't want to go.

He finally stepped into the elevator and rode up and down with her a few times. Then he turned to her and said, "Good morning!"

It was evening, but as far as Mia was concerned, she thought he was right.

They became good friends (Dali and his wife even invited

Mia to visit them in Spain). Mia said she shared the artist's philosophy of life: *Live* everything, each moment, as if you're truly alive.

She later explained that Dali both confirmed and helped her express her own feeling about life. And she said he helped her to gather up enough energy to actually live that way instead of trying to change herself into something more conventional.

They both briefly went to the party at the St. Regis that evening. According to Mia they marched over to the food table, seized a bunch of canapés—and left.

They saw more of each other. Dali was not exactly the kind of mentor every mother would want for her daughter. Mia's reflections about him have been somewhat soft-focus. Dali has been described by some as "really a crazy man." He was always looking to set people up—be they celebrities, socialites, or simply good-looking nobodies—to participate in some sexual situation that titillated his erotic fantasies. He'd fashioned clay copies of male and female genitalia, and more than one beautiful male or female visitor to one of his inner sanctums has reported on the artist's attempts to coax them into participating in a kinky tableau. Sometimes Dali would tempt them with a third or fourth partner and utilize his clay models to indicate how, for example, two men might enjoy coitus with one woman.

Little Mia Farrow was somehow able to float above the glaring pitfalls inherent in this potentially hazardous friendship. She kept her innocence intact while apparently retaining Dali's interest and affection. No mean feat for a convent-educated seventeen-year-old.

On one occasion Mia, with Dali, unexpectedly found herself witnessing a Greenwich Village orgy. She has recalled she wore a long white dress, and she and Dali simply stood there and watched. She recalled how deeply involved the participants were. Impressionable Mia had a strange feeling that they were performing a ballet—and said years later that she honestly still didn't know what the participants were doing.

Columnist Earl Wilson, for one, was dubious about Mia's radiant innocence. He observed that teenaged Mia Farrow was more worldly than many three times her age.

• • •

A totally unexpected blow struck the Farrow family soon after Maureen's triumphant Broadway debut. In January 1963 John Farrow died of a heart attack.

He was found dead in their Beverly Hills home by his son Pat. There was a telephone book by Farrow's side, leading to speculation that perhaps he had tried to call for help. He was fifty-six years old.

The last couple of years hadn't been easy. Farrow had continued to work. Despite ill health, he directed for television, helming several episodes of the NBC Western series *Empire.* The demands of television shooting were very rigorous. Speed was the keynote. Never mind doing it right, just do it. It was exhausting work.

Maureen learned of the tragedy in New York. It was once again a terrible time for all. Maureen was overwhelmed by decisions she had to make about her own life and the children and schools and money and where to live. At first she wanted to settle everything at once. She wanted to tie up loose ends and "make everything orderly."

But it wasn't that easy. A galvanizing force was suddenly gone from their lives. The person who had made the decisions and called the shots and taken care of the things that had to be taken care of was gone.

Maureen had been married for twenty-seven years and experienced most everything life had to offer. But now she faced one experience that was totally alien to her: She had never been a widow.

She took a week's leave from the show and returned to California to arrange for the funeral with a High Mass. Mia could not bear to go to this funeral either.

When she finally visited the cemetary where her father and brother were buried, a peculiar thing happened. When she got close to the burial plot, the lawn sprinklers suddenly sprang on. She started to run, trying to avoid getting wet and trying to find her father's and brother's graves. When she located them, she stood there for about five seconds, getting drenched by the sprinklers—and then she ran away.

Maureen returned from the Coast with all her children: Tisa, now twelve; Steffi, fourteen; Prudence, fifteen; John, seventeen; and Pat, nineteen.

But it appeared that it was eighteen-year-old Mia who now became the one all would consider the strong one, the one who could be relied on for advice, support, and direction. And according to those who've known her for years, Mia continued in this role through the ensuing decades. She was often the strong parental voice and support for her siblings and even her mother. After John Farrow's death Maureen O'Sullivan was uncertain about many things. It was her moment of struggle— to decide which way her life should go. She considered moving back to California, to a small town. She could manage financially without working and be home with the children. But that might be a bleak solution, a dreary life for all concerned. She wanted to continue leading the kids into the worlds of literature, music, and art that their father had shared with them.

O'Sullivan decided to stay with the play and her career. And to provide the Farrow children with greater opportunities.

Chapter Five

ONE DAY Mia took the subway downtown to the Gramercy Arts Theater. Supposedly no advance phone calls had been made on her behalf. Even though her mother was starring on Broadway and her father had been a major Hollywood director, Mia Farrow was one of the crowd, auditioning just like any of the other girls in the group. They were casting for a replacement in an Off-Broadway production of *The Importance of Being Earnest.* Carrie Nye (later Mrs. Dick Cavett) was leaving the role of Cecily.

Mia Farrow got the part. It was only afterward, according to Mia, that the producers learned who she was.

One of the actors in the cast of this revival was Jack Merivale, Vivien Leigh's loyal, longtime, and intimate friend. Merivale was extremely impressed with Mia Farrow. That evening at dinner with Vivien and Garson Kanin and his wife, Ruth Gordon, Merivale raved about the young actress. Kanin of course had known Mia and the whole family, and Garson and Ruth's close friend George Cukor was her godfather.

The Kanins and Vivien Leigh went to see Mia Farrow in the show (for which Mia had received excellent notices, but no one had yet read them—there was a newspaper strike).

After the performance Mia was, in Kanin's words, "rendered speechless" on meeting Vivien Leigh, the lady who'd played the role of the legendary Scarlett O'Hara (and who'd been Maureen's schoolmate).

Vivien not only praised Mia's performance, she was so taken with her that, according to both Garson Kanin and Mia Farrow, the actress was directly responsible for bringing Mia to the attention of 20th Century-Fox. (Vivien had "called up everybody," according to Mia.)

The timing was right. The studio had an ambitious TV project on the drawing boards, and casting director Harvey Mann thought Mia was perfect for one of the leads. A contract was offered.

Mia had no interest in doing television. Even if she were interested, the contract called for a commitment of *years,* and she later claimed that she didn't know if she had enough professional discipline to undertake such a venture.

She refused to sign.

In true Hollywood tradition, that made the powers-in-charge want her all the more. What, they wanted to know, was all the fuss about? Most contracts were multiyear agreements. Her mother's old MGM contract tied up a player for seven years, and the industry hadn't changed that much regarding newcomers. But times were changing. With promises of movie work and working out their differences, Mia was finally persuaded to sign.

Around this time brother Patrick had another run-in with the authorities. He was fined several hundred dollars and placed on three years' probation for illegal possession of dangerous drugs. Reports said that he was already on five years' probation following a conviction for narcotics possession the previous spring. The court was told he was under the care of a psychiatrist.

Patrick and millions of other young people were on the threshold of a turbulent time in American history. The words of President John F. Kennedy back in 1960 had been eerily prophetic: "We stand today on the edge of a new frontier —the frontier of the 1960s, a frontier of unknown opportunities and perils, a frontier of unfulfilled hopes and threats."

It was to be a decade of assassinations and "Ban the Bra," of "Student Power" and "The Silent Majority." "Hippy Power." "Flower Power." "God Is Dead."

And drugs.

It was to be a decade of youth rebellion, of renunciation of material things, and of a search for inner peace. The Farrow family would run the gamut, since it would also be a time of multimillion-dollar star salaries, outrageous behavior, and a totally uninhibited life-style for the idols of the new generation.

Mia Farrow would walk the tightrope between both worlds.

• • •

Mia did appear in a motion picture (her contract specified she would appear in at least five films) before she did TV. She replaced sexy blond Swedish actress Britt Ekland (whose jealous new husband, Peter Sellers, had forced her to give up the role) in an adventure film, *Guns at Batasi.* It was filmed in England.

Mia could hardly complain about typecasting. Although everyone thought she was the virginal, radiant innocent personified, here she was, in her first film, required to be a seductress. She tackled it enthusiastically and even posed in sheer lingerie for magazine layouts to promote the film. But, as was the case with a contemporary of her mother's, Loretta Young, when the attempt was made to make Mia conventionally sexy, Mia Farrow somehow looked less like a love goddess and more like an intense young girl in church.

In any event the picture was experience for her in front of the camera. Commercially the movie proved to be a bomb. Meanwhile *Peyton Place* was the series Mia was slated for. Its success was not a long-shot. The blockbuster novel had been one of the biggest best sellers of the 1950s, and an important one. It foretold, in its revelations of small-town life and sexual reality, of the "moral revolution" soon to sweep over the country. The 1957 film version of *Peyton Place* had been 20th Century-Fox's biggest grosser to date.

The TV series was breaking new ground in terms of its programming: *two* nights a week, a first for television.

Mia thought it would last only a couple of weeks.

Meanwhile her mother was about to enter the medium. She had stayed with *Never Too Late* for almost a year and a half. The motion picture rights to the play had sold to Warner Bros., but Jack Warner was notorious for casting strictly Hollywood box office names in the studio's film versions of Broadway hits. Playing the lead in the picture hadn't been in Maureen's contract.

What she did next was unexpected, and for her, a first. In early 1964 she joined the NBC *Today* show, as cohost with Hugh Downs. Producer Al Morgan gambled that Maureen's likability and gift of gab and her familiarity with the show-business scene would pay off in drawing new viewers to the show.

But Maureen wasn't thrilled with or suited to the very fast-paced world of live television journalism. The experience turned out to be a total disaster for her. Among other problems, there was negative chemistry between Maureen and cohost Hugh Downs, who later observed that Maureen "couldn't develop a definite notion of how broadcasting worked . . . a lovely lady but a lame broadcaster."

Maureen, for a number of reasons, was definitely out of her element. Judith Crist was appearing on the *Today* show at this time and found O'Sullivan to be not the brightest woman in the world: "I wasn't surprised at the tales of her being dominated by John Farrow."

One report claims that during her stint on *Today* O'Sullivan "was unknowingly abusing prescription drugs." She later explained, "My husband had just died. It was a very bad moment in my life. I had to support the children. The doctor had given me tranquilizers."

In August 1964, not long after Mia had begun filming *Peyton Place,* Maureen left the *Today* show in a blast of unflattering publicity. She'd lasted barely more than six months. (Barbara Walters was her replacement.)

Fears concerning her uncertain future loomed large and threatening. Surprisingly Maureen's *Never Too Late* Broadway costar, Paul Ford—hardly a Hollywood draw—had been signed to re-create his role of the husband in the film and was involved in the casting of the picture. Maureen asked him if she would get to play Edith in the movie.

Ford wasn't sure. He informed her that the studio thought she wasn't the type! In Hollywood the more things change, the more they stay the same. Maureen screen-tested for the role. Why not? She'd had to screen-test for a role in her own husband's movie back in 1947, not too long after her peak years in films.

She tested on a Friday. After the test her agent advised her to return to New York. They'd let her know.

The same instinct that had told her, so many years earlier,

not to leave the party at which she was discovered by Frank Borzage was still with her. She remained in Hollywood. She soon learned that Jack Warner didn't think she looked right in the test. Would she do a second one? Yes.

She got the part.

•   •   •

Mia began *Peyton Place*. She felt she had been cast as the ugly duckling. She viewed actress Barbara Parkins as the attractive, sexy one (so did the story line), and the brunette actress seemed to Mia very beautiful, everything a real star should be.

Mia's work on the set, acting in front of the cameras, was only part of the job. The gates of the power world of big-time studio publicity swung open, and she entered the arena like a doe-eyed gladiator. And like a gladiator, she suffered wounds.

Her opinions and thoughts tumbled out like water over a precipice. She revealed a lot of herself at the time. She stated that she became an actress because she couldn't stand being anonymous. She said she didn't want to be just one of the Farrows, third from the top and fifth from the bottom, although she said she found it fun to be part of a big family— because in a way it relieved her of the responsibility of being herself.

The future mother of nine, back in 1964, said she didn't want many children herself; a child needed more love and affection than he or she could get in a large family.

Mia claimed she loved getting up in the morning and going to the studio (she rode her bike to work and roller-skated on the lot), and considered herself very lucky, and her life exciting.

She was an individualist from the outset. In a short while she moved from her small apartment, in which, she said, too many people had left bad vibrations, into a small duplex in Beverly Hills, complete with fireplace. It became what she referred to as her sanctuary.

She bought herself a white four-door Jaguar. She bought a guitar and sang folk songs at the Troubadour, the trendy new nightclub in West Hollywood. She claimed she wasn't in touch with her own generation, because most of her friends were older, like Dali. But she had at least one *very* young friend as well.

Kimberly Beck was a ten-year-old actress on *Peyton Place,* and when her godfather, Jack Haley, Jr., came to visit his pal Mia and goddaughter Kimberly on the set, he often observed the camaraderie between the two. Kimberly adored Mia, because Mia had the ability, and the patience, to behave as though she were Kimberly's ten-year-old friend.

Mia's overall life-style certainly reflected the direction her generation was moving in. Mia loved California. She loved the sea and horseback riding. She bought a horse and named it Salvador. She kept him on a small ranch in Malibu and rode on her days off. She didn't use a saddle or gloves, and often her hands were cut from the leather reins. She loved the dense Malibu hills—because no one could find her there.

She said she thought of her life as a beautiful garden where she walked barefoot behind a high wall. Sometimes she went outside, but if people intruded, she went back behind the wall.

People did intrude. Only a couple of months after *Peyton Place* debuted, in the fall of 1964, Mia went back to New York to spend Christmas with the family. When she went ice-skating with her sister at the Central Park rink, it didn't take long for people to recognize her. It was almost like a scene from *Day of the Locust:* Within minutes she was mobbed—and terrified. It wasn't a pleasant experience.

She became fearful of crowds and panicked whenever she

had to go shopping in department stores. She used this as an explanation regarding the "strange clothes" she wore. Actually her sense of style was way ahead of the pack. She preferred the kind of colorful, comfortable, shapeless little smock-type dresses that would in time become the "uniform" of an entire generation.

Mia was happening. *Peyton Place* was a hit in its first season, making stars of Mia Farrow and Ryan O'Neal. It was O'Neal who brought Mia to meet makeup and hairdressing wizard George Masters. Masters had cut O'Neal's hair, and he wanted Masters to do something with Mia's. Masters later recounted how Mia was at her hair constantly, cutting it off, snipping or whacking a piece here and there. "She hated her hair," he said, and said it was a mess when he took over—anything would have been an improvement.

He began trying to get it in shape, cutting and streaking it, giving it some style. He gave her eye-makeup lessons at the same time and said she got as annoyed with her eyes as she was with her hair. According to Masters, Mia never knew what to do with either her hair or her eyes, and she didn't seem to be able to learn, much as she really wanted to and tried. He gave her twenty eye-makeup lessons and said she never did learn how to do it herself.

But Masters found her to be a sweet girl, one of the nicer of the younger stars, always pleasant and down to earth.

Peyton Place was stirring considerable controversy, winning both praise and condemnation. But everyone was talking about it—and watching it, and there were discussions about expanding the format to *three* nights a week.

Lana Wood, younger sister of Natalie Wood, also played a leading character on the show, a girl from the wrong side of the tracks who chased after the character played by Ryan O'Neal. Lana observed that it was a case of life imitating television, except that the chase was reversed. She said Ryan was as handsome as they come, with a wicked sense of humor and a desire to bed as many of the *Peyton Place* actresses as he could.

Lana described Mia as painfully thin, a girl who ate spinach and cottage cheese every day for lunch. And Lana, too, said that Barbara Parkins was expected by all to be the young femme fatale of the show. According to Lana, Parkins could be either friendly or haughty, depending on how the mood struck her, and moods struck her often.

Dorothy Malone, Ed Nelson, and Tim O'Connor were regulars, too, and most of the group enjoyed playing practical jokes. Ruth Warrick played the matriarch on the series and was quite a perfectionist, which made her a target for the jokesters, including Mia.

One week, according to Lana Wood, Warrick had been insisting on retakes, as usual, and things got out of hand. There was a long scene coming up with Ruth in which Mia, Lana, and most of the other regulars also appeared. Unknown to Ms. Warrick, the kids took bets on how many takes the actress would insist on. When Ruth Warrick completed the scene in one take, she then made the mistake of turning to Mia for reassurance. Mia's money was on take three and she therefore appeared doubtful and suggested another take. This continued on until about take five, when the owner of the money on take five—Lana—cheered Ruth when she was done. (Eventually Warrick learned what was going on. She wasn't amused. In fact, according to Lana Wood, she walked off the set, threatened to call the Screen Actors Guild and report them all, and demanded an apology. She got one. They all felt terrible, but, said Lana, not because they had been betting on her but because they'd been found out.)

The character Mia portrayed, Allison MacKenzie, was representative, apparently, of millions of young girls of the day, girls Mia's age trapped in the mores and conventions of a society they had not created and had no voice in, but searching desperately for meaning and love in their lives.

Mia said she portrayed Allison MacKenzie well because she knew her: "I know every inch of her. I *was* Allison Mac-Kenzie."

Series director Walter Doniger (the other director was Ted Post) described Mia as being able to make instant contact with her inner self to reflect the conflicts in a girl's growing to maturity.

The shooting schedule was very arduous and demanding; it certainly didn't leave Mia leisure time to loll on the beach and reflect on life in the privacy of her "sanctuary." Despite some of her later statements—at one point she was quoted as saying that *Peyton Place* was a *terrible* series—it was anything but a routine experience for her. It was highly important in her development. Garson Kanin said that *Peyton Place* was Mia's academy and that, working daily under great pressure, she learned to speak, to listen, to relate, and to create.

The series gave her confidence; she was no longer fearful nor anxious about having put herself in jeopardy.

Mia's family didn't think much of *Peyton Place,* however. Watching with some of her children at home one evening, back in New York, Maureen ventured, "Who's going to tell her?" It turned out not to be necessary; according to Maureen, Mia knew the score without anyone telling her.

There was no reason to believe that anything would change. A contract was a contract. Mia, like many other actors, might complain, but all were required to do their jobs. Mia was lucky to be in a hit.

However, something unusual happened. Something that set Mia Farrow apart from every other young actress of her generation.

She met Frank Sinatra.

Chapter Six

THEY MET on the Fox lot. It was October 1964. Mia had some time off and was fooling around the set of *Von Ryan's Express,* Sinatra's current film. Her version of the meeting: Actor Edward Mulhare was there, and Sinatra was climbing out of one of the freight cars used in the picture. Mia was embarrassed and wanted to get out of their way. She realized she must have appeared a strange figure, half girl, half tomboy. The men said nothing.

To Sinatra, however, she was absolutely radiant. He recalled later that she wore something white and sheer, and he thought she looked like an angel (in fact she was wearing an ankle-length nightgown she'd appropriated from studio wardrobe).

Mia's account of the story continues: She had a friend on the set, who would let her ride the motorcycles and little cars that were part of the props and paraphernalia for *Von Ryan's Express,* which was a war movie.

When she saw Frank again, Mia found her voice: "Hello, Mr. Sinatra."

One day, in Mia's version, one of Sinatra's friends saw her swinging on the bars with her lace pantaloons showing, and he said, "Hey, kid, how old are you?"

"That's hardly a question to ask a lady."

Frank asked her to sit with them a moment. She was so nervous, she dropped her purse and everything spilled out. Frank invited her to a screening of one of his pictures (she had never seen a Sinatra picture!) and she went. She liked him instantly—to her he rang true. He was what he was. They saw each other from time to time—not steadily.

That was how it began, according to Mia.

There are other versions. Actor-producer Brad Dexter was a close friend and business associate of Sinatra's at the time (he'd literally saved Sinatra's life—the singer had almost drowned swimming in the ocean on location for a film in Hawaii). Dexter, who had a role in *Von Ryan's Express,* recalled that Mia had invited herself on the set every day for a week, observing and admiring Frank. Then Sinatra, Dexter, and cinematographer William Daniels were about to fly to Palm Springs for the weekend. As they were on their way off the soundstage and passed the young actress, Sinatra off-handedly told her he'd see her later, explaining that he and his pals were off to the desert for the weekend. According to Dexter, Mia took Frank by surprise when she asked to go along. Sinatra explained the private jet only accommodated three, but if she wasn't kidding, he'd have the plane return for her. According to this account, that's just what happened, and Mia and Frank had their first weekend in Palm Springs, and the romance was launched.

There can be no doubt there was a strong sexual attraction —there is voluminous evidence that Frank Sinatra is a very sexually oriented man. No matter if a lady was famous or unknown, a princess or a showgirl, a call girl, a secretary or a star, once intent, time, and place were established, Sinatra got right to the point: "Let's go to bed." It seems reasonable to believe that his modus operandi with Mia was consistent with his past behavior (which didn't alter at all in the future). Obviously he was smitten with Mia from the start.

The screening Sinatra had taken her to was of *None But the Brave,* which he'd directed as well. Mia is supposed to have told him that she thought he was a better director than her father.

Mia had met Sinatra the man (she thought him super-looking), a flesh-and-blood person she could relate to. Had she been dazzled by Sinatra? "Well, who wouldn't be dazzled by Frank Sinatra, especially in those days?" reflects Garson Kanin today. "He was attractive, he was powerful, he was glamorous, he was funny—he was a remarkable fella." And Kanin, friend of both parties, does not dismiss the suggestion that Sinatra was dazzled by Mia. In his opinion they dazzled each other.

But there was another Frank Sinatra that one eventually had to contend with: the Legend. Famed bandleader/trumpet player Tommy Dorsey was there when Sinatra first emerged as a superstar, back in the forties, with Dorsey's band, and Dorsey summed up for many what the Voice could often be like behind the scenes: "He's the most fascinating man in the world, but don't stick your hand in the cage."

The Monster was another appellation used to describe the former boy singer from Hoboken, New Jersey. Over the years everyone clustered around and kowtowed to him as though he were a king, observed shrewd longtime Sinatra watcher Hedda Hopper, adding, "I am sure he believed he was." *That* Frank Sinatra was an awesome, arrogant, larger-than-life, often volatile, sometimes violent, hostile and downright mean creature about whom millions of words had been written. Around whom storms of controversy had raged. When Mia came into Frank Sinatra's life, his past already consisted of adventures, amorous and professional, that novelists would be laughed at for inventing. There were even reported suicide attempts.

"If I'd done half of what I'm supposed to have done, I'd be in a bottle in the Smithsonian," he once quipped.

He'd done plenty. And more than ever, Sinatra was the stuff headlines were made of. And he was approaching his fiftieth birthday. Two of his three children were older than Mia, who would be twenty in four months.

Mia, however, was a girl who believed in diving right into things. She wasn't afraid of commitment. According to Mia, Frank was the same way.

It was a while before the public learned about their blossoming relationship. But the news spread like wildfire around the Fox lot and throughout behind-the-scenes Hollywood. Suddenly, virtually overnight, Mia Farrow became one of the "special" ones, a new personality whose aura in the industry took on a glow. *Peyton Place* had made Mia Farrow a hot property, but there had been many similar hot properties over the years who turned out to be flashes in the pan.

There was only *one* Frank Sinatra, however, and if he took an interest in someone, everyone's curiosity was piqued. *What* did he see in her? *Why* her? *Who* was Mia Farrow?

To Mia's eventual dismay the seeds were sown for her private life to become a source of intense, unrelenting scrutiny by the press and public. "When I first started going with him, there was havoc in my life," she recalled. But the choice had been hers.

Sinatra of course had been in the caldron many times before. He had, he claimed, developed a thick protective shell (an arguable claim). But Mia hadn't, and her life would literally never be the same.

Mia said, later on, she often wondered what he saw in her. It wasn't a mystery to those who knew her. She was in fact very beautiful, a golden-haired, porcelain-skinned, high-cheekboned, saucer-eyed aristocrat. She embodied a characteristic Sinatra was always highly impressed by: class. She was a fresh new face. Sweet. Smart. Young. She may have loathed the European convent and finishing schools she had attended, but they had done their job: Mia had a polish, a veneer that placed her far apart from the ordinary group of what Sinatra would have referred to as "broads."

Furthermore she also possessed a trait that Sinatra was strongly attracted to—independence. It was as ingrained in Mia as her skin. She wasn't one to be told what to do (usually she would then do the opposite).

They saw each other quietly, mostly in Palm Springs, where Sinatra was most comfortable. People didn't bother him there. He could come and go without causing a riot. The couple were often seen dining at Ruby's, one of Sinatra's favorite restaurants.

Women in the Sinatra social set who met and got to know Mia viewed her differently than men did. Edith Goetz, for example, later characterized her as very clever, self-knowing, and focused in her goals. Some others saw her as ambitious, shrewd, and manipulative.

Men responded to Mia differently. She brought out their protective instincts. Sinatra had been very moved by her wallflower tale; and her sparsely furnished duplex apartment had touched him, too, in its poignant reflection of her sensibilities.

Mia's best friend at the time, Liza Minnelli, said that Mia had fallen in love with Frank at first sight.

Sinatra's eldest daughter, Nancy, left no doubt about her father's feelings concerning Mia Farrow. She revealed that her dad had fallen in love—hard. Nancy conjectured that perhaps her famous father was afraid of becoming a middle-aged man. But Nancy junior later had to readjust her thinking regarding his affair with Mia.

Mia would reflect, years later, that her favorite times with Sinatra were when they were completely alone.

But Sinatra was rarely alone.

He had decided it was time for him to enter middle age. The Swinger had even changed tailors—an image as "diplomat" was a more becoming and suitable one, Sinatra felt. And he'd largely stopped running with his famous Rat Pack—flamboyant cronies such as Dean Martin, Sammy Davis, Jr., Peter Lawford, and Joey Bishop.

The group he currently palled around with were old-line Hollywood, a very "social" set. Big money and power were prerequisites. The worldly Goetzes, Bill and his wife "Edie," were part of the group. Edith Goetz, eldest daughter of Louis B. Mayer, was acknowledged to be top dog on the Beverly Hills social circuit. She and her husband were the Joneses everyone tried to keep up with, pretty much an impossible task. Their art collection, for example, would prove to be worth more than $50 million. Edie's jewelry was world-class. (Mia Farrow had no use or desire for diamonds—she thought them "hilarious." She would, however, acquire some in the near future.)

Old Sinatra crony and business associate Jack Entratter, then president of the Sands Hotel in Las Vegas, and his wife, Corinne, were in the inner circle. Others included actresses who were all contemporaries of Maureen O'Sullivan's, only most were older (and far richer) than Maureen: Rosalind Russell, Merle Oberon, and Claudette Colbert. Their husbands were all older than Frank.

Frank was perhaps jumping the gun on his fear of middle age. His looks were still intact, and so were his voice and energy level. But he'd grown sensitive to the constant references to his life-style and reputed gangster affiliations. ("If I hadn't made it in show business, I'd have been a mobster myself," he once boasted.) Now he wanted a group of friends with impeccable credentials.

Meanwhile, as Mia's popularity on *Peyton Place* soared, her bosses envisioned a very long-running and prosperous series, with Mia an integral part of their plans. They were flabbergasted that Frank Sinatra had taken a serious interest in their ingenue. He telephoned her on the set frequently (to check up on her) and was spending weekends with her in Palm Springs. In the old days the studio would have tried to interfere, to manipulate, but these were no longer the old days. And no one interfered with Frank Sinatra.

The Palm Springs weekends were certainly not run-of-the-mill gatherings. His friends observed Mia closely, and the women in particular found her fascinating.

Corinne Entratter observed Mia's aloofness and indifference to some of the guests one weekend and thought to herself that, without doubt, Frank was going to marry this one.

There were photographs of Ava Gardner all over the house, even in some of the bathrooms, the kitchen, and the living room. According to those on the scene, Mia was smart enough to say nothing about them.

One lady who took notice of Mia was Jacqueline Park, a former actress and the intimate companion of movie mogul Jack L. Warner. (Sinatra had a multimillion-dollar production deal with Warner Bros.) Ms. Park had also once had a brief affair with Sinatra. At Sinatra's Palm Springs home one weekend Ms. Park told Mia she'd known John Farrow. Mia's response surprised her: words to the effect that her father had been such a paragon of virtue he should have been the pope. Mia was unaware that Ms. Park had had quite a romance with

Farrow, and the worldly beauty recalled him fondly as anything but pure and holy!

When Jacqueline asked Mia if she was happy with Sinatra, Mia replied she knew they were going to be married, it was her destiny and she couldn't change it if she wanted to. In Ms. Park's opinion Mia was searching for a replacement for her adored father (an assessment that, decades later, Mia would in fact echo).

Wily British-born columnist Sheilah Graham, ironically a longtime friend of Maureen O'Sullivan's and John Farrow's, broke the story of the budding Sinatra-Farrow relationship, admitting later that she'd complicated young Mia's life by doing so. The bombshell quickly led to Mia's first taste of what might be termed bitch journalism, with many reporters and editors going for the jugular.

What obviously triggered this approach was Mia's attempt to deflect questions about Sinatra with the old "we're just good friends" and "one's personal life is one's own affair" routine. They weren't buying it.

So if Mia would talk only about her work, and in an interview had eighty percent positive things to say, and twenty percent negative, it was the negative comments (along with negative editorializing) that found their way into print. Example: "I read the book *Peyton Place*. . . . It's not a literary masterpiece, but I have to say something kind about it."

Sheilah Graham continued to report on the romance. At first there had been an effective "no comment" news blackout from all parties, and the story had effectively died down. Mia did not discuss the matter of being in love with Frank again, according to Sheilah Graham, "on orders of Sinatra, her studio, and the sponsors of her very successful *Peyton Place* TV series." But Graham was persistent. She subsequently informed her readers that Frank and Mia were still seeing each other.

Sinatra was furious at the columnist. Her story had opened a Pandora's box of negative comments. But Sinatra had not broken off the relationship with Mia, even after she'd publicly revealed her feelings about him, which proved how deeply he felt about her. When Lauren Bacall had made the mistake of going public about their romance only a few years earlier, Sinatra had ended the relationship abruptly. (In her memoirs Bacall bitterly referred to him as "a complete shit".)

Those who envied Mia Farrow (and they were legion) might not have been too anxious to change places with her if they had known all the facts—not only about Frank Sinatra's unpredictable and chameleonlike personality, but about life in a seemingly glamorous goldfish bowl. It was more like a minefield, and most of the time the linchpins couldn't be avoided. Irate women's groups, even the PTA, began petitioning the studio and the sponsors regarding Mia's behavior. The PTA claimed Mia was an idol of the youth of America and how dare she carry on in her private life in such an "obscene" way. But Mia was adamant that she'd never led her life with the intention of being an example to anyone. She was just trying to do her best. She couldn't show anyone the way, so it really didn't matter very much whether they approved or not. Her attitude was that it was nobody's damn business anyhow.

There would be many forms of harassment to contend with. One of the things Mia learned was never to eat any food people sent her. One cake she received in the mail was sent to the studio lab and tested. It was full of pure arsenic. The incident was kept under wraps.

Certainly in the mind of the TV viewing public, Mia and Allison were one. For all practical purposes it was the angelic young Allison in whom the much older and "jaded" Frank Sinatra was interested.

Mia was given the opportunity by Frank to function as his hostess on social occasions at the Palm Springs abode. But he learned she wasn't very adept at seating arrangements, and on one occasion Sinatra told her not to bother, he'd do it himself. The day after this episode Sinatra received a letter from Mia: She was sorry, she just wasn't enough of a sophisticate and she'd understand if she never heard from him again.

She heard from him the next day.

Mia was now temporarily living in the luxurious two-bedroom guest cottage, complete with swimming pool, belonging to Saul and Helen Berner. Located in the posh Los Angeles suburb of Brentwood, the cottage, which offered complete privacy, had been the home of many stars over the years.

The Berners watched over their property with eagle-eyed devotion, and they always knew when Frank was visiting, which was often. Sinatra drove a flashy sports car, and right behind it was a car containing his bodyguards. The Berners weren't thrilled by the bodyguards, and Mia, aware of this, usually ran out to Frank's car as soon as it pulled up. According to Mrs. Berner, Mia was an ideal tenant: She was always cognizant of keeping the house and grounds in tiptop shape, the way the Berners liked it. If one of Mia's guests accidentally dropped a piece of paper on the driveway, Mia picked it up.

Mia's young friend Kimberly Beck was sometimes Mia's houseguest at the cottage, and on occasion Mia would take the child swimming in Sinatra's pool (he, too, was renting a house in Beverly Hills).

The attention riveted on Mia was all getting to be a bit much for her. She began to lose weight (which she could not afford) and became ill. Outsiders were barred from the *Peyton*

Place set. She couldn't stand the whispering and the pointing fingers when she was trying to work.

The attention did not abate. Suddenly she was *famous*. She later claimed she hadn't brought it on herself, but there it was, hot and heavy, as though she had pursued it for fifty years. *Peyton Place* director Walter Doniger felt that Mia Farrow represented something new in the American culture. In his view she wanted to grow up; on the other hand she was afraid to. She was, according to Doniger, a girl in search of herself, and in his opinion as long as she kept projecting that conflict, she'd be a really big star. Mr. Doniger obviously had his finger on the pulse of what was happening with American youth of the mid-1960s.

Meanwhile Mia Farrow was socializing with a group that many ambitious directors, producers, actors, and actresses sought to know. There was Thanksgiving dinner at the Goetzes. And for Christmas Sinatra gave Mia a solid-gold cigarette case, lovingly inscribed and signed "Francis." (One report subsequently noted she'd filled it with marijuana cigarettes she'd rolled herself.)

Sinatra's formidable mother, Natalie ("Dolly"), was sought out for comment on the romance. At this stage the very outspoken and gutsy Mrs. Sinatra didn't realize the importance of Mia in Frank's life. She said her son was doing what he'd done many times before, helping a girl to become a star. He'd do it again. In Mrs. Sinatra's opinion Mia was a nice little girl. The matriarch reminded one and all that Mia was younger than Frank's kids. And she added that if she had any influence with Frank, she would use it to discourage any marriage.

• • •

It was the summer of 1965.

The great white yacht, *Southern Breeze,* floated majestically on the ripply surface of the Atlantic. It was anchored off Martha's Vineyard. Frank Sinatra had leased the 165-foot vessel from Houston shipbuilder W. C. Edwards. It had a crew of sixteen. The cost (depending on which source you consulted) was either $7,000 or $14,000 per week, and Sinatra had leased it for a month for a leisurely cruise along the New England coast.

The voyage had begun from decidedly unglamorous Flushing, New York. Guests were picked up en route. Aboard were Frank; Mia; Claudette Colbert and her husband, Dr. Joel Pressman; Rosalind Russell and her husband, Frederick Brisson; and financier Armand Deutsch (heir to the Sears Roebuck fortune).

If Sinatra had been some anonymous millionaire and Mia an anonymous young girl he'd fallen in.love with, the lovers could have luxuriated on the splendid, romantic, and peaceful cruise Sinatra certainly had in mind.

But invasion of—and loss of—privacy is part and parcel of the awesome price "legends" have to pay.

Perhaps Sinatra had naively reasoned that they could get away from it all by simply heading out to sea. (Not that he was particularly comfortable at sea; when asked how he liked the yacht, he replied, "It rocks.")

Mia could hardly have been thrilled by the limited activities available on board. She was always comfortable with older people, but on this cruise most everyone sat around and played backgammon.

It was a friend's opinion that Sinatra "had pulled Mia into this group and forced her on them, and neither she nor they liked each other."

This view is questionable. Claudette Colbert and Rosalind Russell were not exactly bankers' wives. They were highly successful, sophisticated, world-famous actresses, friends of the

Farrows for over thirty years. Roz Russell in fact subsequently told a business associate that she had liked Mia very much: "I didn't know how the hell to tell her that the world was going to come down on her like a fist on a grasshopper once the whole business was really out in the open and Frank's enemies had their say."

Both Claudette and Roz pooh-poohed the marriage rumors, with Claudette going so far as to say she didn't think Frank would marry such a young girl.

With the development of the telescopic lens, photographers could literally track a person almost anywhere. Once the word got out that the *Southern Breeze* and its famous passengers were off the shores of Massachusetts, the press began showing up like mosquitoes at a picnic. The hot rumor was that Frank and Mia (who had known each other now for ten months) were already married. It wasn't true.

When Sinatra spotted the unwanted intruders, who'd rented a launch and captured pictures of Sinatra and Mia standing together at the boat's railing, he angrily ordered the captain to sail to Hyannis Port, twenty-five miles away. That was where the Kennedy family compound was located. He hoped that privacy would be available there.

As Mia and the rest of the world knew, Sinatra had been one of the late president's staunchest supporters and one of his closest Hollywood friends. Their relationship, however, had been abruptly curtailed by JFK after the election was won. Sinatra was furious and mortified, but he'd remained on good terms with Kennedy family patriarch Joe Kennedy. (It had been Robert F. Kennedy, a man Mia and millions of other young people throughout the country idolized, who'd been responsible for his brother severing the Sinatra tie. He'd feared that JFK's image would have suffered irreparable damage if certain information ever leaked out. Sinatra and Peter Lawford, a Kennedy brother-in-law, had been instrumental in orchestrating President Kennedy's extracurricular love life. Revelations involving the president's relationships with Marilyn Monroe and Judith Campbell could've caused a scandal the likes of which modern-day Washington hadn't ever seen. With Sinatra's knowledge, Campbell had been having simultaneous affairs with both JFK and mobster Sam Giancana, a close Sinatra buddy.)

Mia Farrow was barely out of parochial school when all this had occurred. Now, as Sinatra's lady, she was about to meet some of the principals.

Sinatra went on shore and visited former Ambassador Kennedy, who'd suffered a debilitating stroke. Mia accompanied him. Sinatra knew his old buddy would perk up at the sight of a pretty young blonde. (Mia, wearing her hair pulled back and no makeup, looked like a schoolgirl.)

However, despite everyone's efforts on the yacht to believe otherwise, the cruise was turning into a disaster. At Hyannis Port the yacht couldn't sail in close to the compound because the water wasn't deep enough. The captain had to drop anchor several hundred yards out in the harbor.

The next day a jet-black speedboat from the compound sped out to the yacht. There was sudden pandemonium in the ranks of snooping photographers offshore: Aboard the speedboat was a very familiar-looking brunette in dark sunglasses, black sweater, and white slacks, a white bandanna tied around her head.

Jacqueline Kennedy! What a scoop! Shutters clicked away furiously as the figure disembarked from the speedboat and went on board the yacht. The shots subsequently appeared on many front pages, with snide captions and headlines identifying the woman as the late president's revered widow, who was stopping off to see Frank Sinatra and his new love.

There was lots of egg on many fourth-estate faces a couple of days later. Mrs. Kennedy had denied all—and she was telling the truth. Embarrassed Associated Press photographer J. Walter Green offered the explanation that covering the cruise had been like working down at the Boston Garden—"you're so damn busy, you don't see the fight." He'd even looked through binoculars and said he'd looked right into her face, and he thought it *was* Jackie.

The mystery woman was Pat Lawford, sister of the late president and Peter Lawford's wife. Rosalind Russell confirmed that it was Mrs. Lawford, but Roz was angry. "Don't you boys have anything more constructive to do?" she said to one of the reporters, with true *Auntie Mame* bravado.

The sensational coverage, and all the innuendo, had done their damage. The cruise had become a circus. The worst was yet to come.

The yacht sailed back to Martha's Vineyard. There one of the sailors in the crew was drowned in an accident in one of the rowboats. The death cast a gloom over everyone. The cruise had been memorable all right—for all the wrong reasons.

Sinatra ordered the yacht back to New York. Before leaving town, Frank and Mia played host to his friends at the Seafare of the Aegean restaurant, then they all went to Jilly's bar for a nightcap. Then back to Sinatra's penthouse overlooking the East River.

Newsmongers relentlessly pursued their story: Were Frank and Mia husband and wife? Close friends said no. Sinatra had no intention of marrying.

But people had learned to expect the unexpected from Frank Sinatra. The producers of *Peyton Place,* like the captains of a space vehicle, were prepared for any emergency. If Mia married Frank, the chances weren't great that she'd continue with *Peyton Place*. Very reluctantly the studio had granted Farrow a four-week hiatus from the series so that she could go on the cruise. (During that time her character, Allison MacKenzie, was in the hospital in a coma; Mia's double was used in the shots.) And if Mia and Frank tied the knot, Allison would either pass away or mysteriously disappear.

No twenty-year-old girl, no matter how sophisticated and mature, could have been prepared for the unrelenting tidal wave of attention, much of it snide and hurtful, that now surged her way.

Comedians had a new source of material, and it flooded the airwaves. Frank was almost fifty; Mia was twenty. Comedian Jack E. Leonard: "Mia doesn't smoke or drink. She's still teething." Henny Youngman: "Dean Martin sent a telegram to Frank saying, 'I've got Scotch older than she is.'" These were typical and merely the tip of the iceberg.

Mia—and Frank—cringed. After all, what the hell had they done? Who were they hurting? Frank was only fifty. Younger than Jane Fonda is today. Back then Henry Fonda was already married to a much younger woman. Cary Grant and Fred Astaire would both subsequently marry women decades younger than themselves. In the 1940s Charlie Chaplin, over fifty, had married Oona O'Neill, who was still in her teens. There are many famous May-December romances in and out of show business. But when the man is Frank Sinatra, a thirty-year difference in age opened the couple to enormous ridicule, especially during this era. One must remember this was the mid-sixties and the "flower child/hippie" revolution hadn't yet occurred. People still clung to the morals and mores of the 1950s.

The snide humor continued.

Maureen was not immune from the jokesters' harpoons. "Did you hear about Frank Sinatra, Jr.'s, torrid romance? He's going to marry Maureen O'Sullivan." The actress saw Frank Sinatra, Jr., perform at the New York nightclub Basin Street East. Owner Ralph Watkins, a Sinatra pal, was unable to shield Maureen from reporters' inquiries. She said she knew the whole Sinatra family and had wanted to see Frank junior perform and hoped the Sinatra children would come to see her children. One wisecracker said that one of Frank junior's parents was already seeing one of her children.

Stand-up comic Jackie Mason's routine about the lovers apparently rankled Sinatra the most. Mason was no stranger to controversy himself. As always his comments were penetrating, hilarious, and on the cutting edge. He discussed Frank's elevator shoes, hair transplants, and described Sinatra soaking his dentures (in fact Frank didn't wear dentures) while Mia brushed her braces; then he described Mia taking off her roller skates and putting them next to Frank's cane; and next Frank peeled off his toupee as Mia unbraided her hair. . . .

Apparently, if Mason is to be believed, as far as Frank Sinatra was concerned, Mason's biting satire had gone too far. The comedian claimed that he received life-threatening phone calls demanding that the jokes be stopped. Mason didn't exactly heed the warnings. Mia was dropped from the routine, but he continued with mild jabs at Frank. Gunshots were subsequently fired into Mason's hotel room in Miami. Mason wasn't injured, and a police investigation turned up nothing, but he was later beaten up by a hoodlum. While Mason was never able to establish a link between the beating and Frank Sinatra, he later described the entertainer—whose exquisite and moving renditions of gentle, deeply felt love songs made him the most effective and romantic crooner of them all—as a "vicious bastard."

• • •

Would Mia marry Frank? Maureen of course was further sucked into the arena as columnists tracked her down and badgered her for comments. Nothing in her long and colorful life and career had ever engendered this kind of frenetic interest and excitement. But she hadn't lost her sense of humor: "If Mr. Sinatra is going to marry anyone, he ought to marry me." She explained that Mia had been ill and in the hospital for three days and needed rest and relaxation. That was why she had gone on the cruise. And she pointed out that in all the furor a major point had been overlooked: Mia had been perfectly chaperoned the entire time, by people who were old and dear friends of hers and the family's and who were in touch with her the whole time.

Maureen's explanations were lost in the torrent of continuing publicity. But friends said that Maureen didn't think it good publicity for Mia and advised her to take a brief rest and go back to *Peyton Place.*

The adversarial relationship Sinatra had with the press didn't help matters. Certain reporters and editors held strong personal opinions about him and, truth be told, this spilled over into the tone of their coverage.

There was ample cause for ill will. There had been numerous, ugly incidents over the years, such as Sinatra's physical assault of columnist Lee Mortimer (Sinatra had to pay $9,000 in damages). Years later, after Mortimer's death, Sinatra reportedly urinated on his grave. There had been feuds with columnists Westbrook Pegler and Erskine Johnson. Sinatra supposedly once threatened to kill reporters hounding him in Mexico City. When Sinatra-admirer Dorothy Kilgallen, a top gossip columnist, provoked him with a series of articles she wrote about him, she received a gift from Frank: a tombstone engraved with her name. And in his nightclub act he referred to her ever afterward as "a chinless wonder." Frank often used his act as a forum to "punish" reporters who'd offended him.

But the bottom line of course was that a Sinatra headline sold papers, and a juicy and controversial new Sinatra romance sold even more papers.

Certainly Mia was caught between a rock and a hard place. She was new in the business and wanted to be cooperative, but now the press seemed out to get her.

There were exceptions, of course. Ed Miller, entertainment editor of *Seventeen* magazine, was an intelligent, kind man who was a veteran at interviewing young actors on the rise. He didn't go for blood. When he interviewed Mia, not long after the yacht incident, the strain she'd been under was apparent to him: "At first, Mia Farrow wears a look of despair at being trapped for an interview, a frozen look, pale, white around the eyes and mouth." It was all too clear she was a wary veteran of the press wars already, after only a year in the public eye.

She told Miller how she'd been "hurt too many times" by reporters she'd trusted ("I've been stabbed many times that way"). She explained she wasn't a kook or difficult—people who said that were wrong.

Years later she candidly admitted that all the criticism, the barbs, the ugly publicity she seemed to shrug off at the time had hurt. In retrospect it didn't matter. Her philosophy was that she was only here for a short time and had made her choice. It bothered her that people could be cruel, but she said Sinatra taught her not to care about things like that. "You live your life for the people you love."

She loved Sinatra. If, before he met Mia, he had, as friends said, felt his best years were behind him, Mia convinced him otherwise.

Chapter Seven

"I DON'T KNOW, maybe we'll only have a couple of years together," Sinatra told a close relative. "She's so young. . . . But we have to try."

To some it appeared that he tried to impress her at every opportunity, to show off for her. It was as though he were a schoolboy again.

As 1965 drew to a close, Maureen said she didn't know what the future held for Mia and "Frankie" and that she didn't think they did either. Maureen refused to hazard a guess; she observed that an outsider could never know what goes on between two people. But she was certain of one thing: Whatever relationship Mia entered into would be true and honest. Mia, she said, happened to be that kind of a girl.

Before she'd met Frank, Mia admitted she'd had no intention of getting married—to anyone. She didn't want to marry for a very basic reason: She'd never seen a happy marriage (hardly a flattering reflection on the union of Maureen O'Sullivan and John Farrow).

Before "Charlie" had entered her life—Mia called Frank "Charlie" after the famous cartoon character Charlie Brown— she was living alone and, according to her own account, drifting along, dashing out and making things happen for the sake of saying her day had been complete. She knew everyone said what a good time Mia had, but according to Mia, happiness came after Charlie.

Mia continued on *Peyton Place.*

There are many versions of a still-remembered and highly publicized incident that occurred in December of that year. The occasion: Frank Sinatra's fiftieth birthday party. It was being given by Frank's first wife, Nancy. She was held in the highest esteem by her former husband, and they'd remained on the friendliest of terms (Mrs. Sinatra was said to be waiting for that magical day when Frank would return to her). It is perhaps understandable that Nancy Sinatra, Sr., was not anxious to invite Mia Farrow to the gala birthday celebration. Yet she didn't want to offend her former husband by not doing so.

This was no ordinary party—it was almost a national event. Hundreds were invited, including President and Mrs. Lyndon Johnson and Vice President and Mrs. Hubert Humphrey (who sent their regrets). Nancy Sinatra, Sr., and her daughter, Nancy junior, decided to leave the decision to invite Mia up to Frank. He, in turn, reasoned that Mia's presence would make his ex-wife and daughter uncomfortable, so he decided Mia would stay home (he told Mia he'd join her at home right after the party).

It is understandable how a sensitive twenty-year-old girl in love would react to such a situation. If, as some said, Mia quarreled bitterly with Sinatra over it, the matter was not resolved in her favor. Everyone knew that first wife Nancy and the Sinatra children occupied an untouchable niche in Frank Sinatra's life.

Everyone in Hollywood was also certain that Mia Farrow then promptly cut off all her long, blond hair because she hadn't been invited to the party. She emphatically denied it and over the years has stuck to her story. She'd simply gotten tired of fooling with her hair, she said, and had been sick of the way she looked. Her friends voiced their own opinions. Leonard Gershe said that cutting her hair had been an act of emancipation. Garson Kanin said that Mia had simply been expressing herself, since her work in the TV series offered her insufficient opportunity to do so.

Mia told Corinne Entratter she'd done it because she had taken too much pride in her hair. Mrs. Entratter was reminded of a nun, both in what Mia said and in the way she had said it.

At a later date Mia claimed the haircut had been inspired by the film *A Member of the Wedding,* in which Julie Harris had very short hair. Mia simply got a scissors and copied the hairstyle. Others said her friend Vidal Sassoon had cut her hair for her.

Peyton Place costar Lana Wood, who was on the scene, has offered quite a different view. She said that not long after Mia had begun her romance with Sinatra, "it wasn't long until it was Mia against the producers, with Mia—not one to be tampered with—the victor."

According to Lana, Mia had asked for time off to be with Frank, was refused, and so she showed up for work the next day with her long blond hair gone and a short bob in its place. Lana recalled how Mia absolutely refused to wear a wig, and Mia's protest was the talk of the town.

Yet another version, related by Jack Haley, Jr., stated that Frank *had* intended to take Mia to his birthday party, but when he saw the haircut, he hated it and decided not to take her, that decision indicating to Haley that there was stress in the relationship. Haley interpreted the haircut as an act of defiance, a way of letting Frank know she was capable of making waves all on her own.

Salvador Dali's explanation was the most dramatic. In his opinion, by cutting her hair his friend Mia had committed "a mythical act of suicide."

Studio executives blanched at Mia's blasphemous act: Her long, golden hair had been her trademark, an important part of Allison MacKenzie's appeal.

Some say that when Sinatra returned home from the gala birthday party, the results of Mia's haircut awaited him. He told her that now she could try out for Little League, like the rest of the boys! He called her "my little boy" and "Butch." And at first he refused to be seen with her.

Not in twenty years—the last time being when Orson Welles chopped off wife Rita Hayworth's long, red hair and made her a short-coiffed platinum blonde—did a Hollywood haircut receive such worldwide attention. In Rita's case it had been for a movie; in Mia's case the haircut was the basis for dramatic speculation on her personal life. With the passing of every day Mia was proving to be like Frank in at least one regard: Expect the unexpected. Perhaps, mused insiders, she had more in common with previous Sinatra ladies than anyone had ever suspected.

Mia was always being compared to the flamboyant women Sinatra had been involved with. There were the famous ones of course. People could easily understand how he would be attracted to Marilyn Monroe, although that sad relationship wasn't public knowledge as yet. Nor was the fling he'd had years earlier with Elizabeth Taylor. Gloria Vanderbilt had been a close Sinatra friend, as had Lauren Bacall, Lana Turner, and voluptuous Swedish star Anita Ekberg. Judy Garland, Marlene Dietrich, Kim Novak, Jill St. John, Shirley MacLaine, and Angie Dickinson were among other famous actresses Sinatra had romanced. Reportedly, there had been prominent nonactresses as well, such as Lee Radziwill and Lady Adele Beatty (later Mrs. Stanley Donen).

But equally interesting, perhaps even more so, were the legion of nonfamous women Sinatra had had relationships with. People who found Frank's infatuation with Mia Farrow out-of-character simply didn't know their man's real story. Sinatra had in fact been in love with two very young women in his younger days. Both romances (one girl was sixteen, the other seventeen) had occurred while he was in his mid-twenties and still married to his first wife. One of the girls had not been unlike Mia in deportment or, relatively speaking, background. Frank had continued in both relationships for years.

Of course Frank's tempestuous years with Ava Gardner were legendary, and on the surface Ava was as different from Mia Farrow as a hot tamale from a buttercup. The passion Frank had felt for the sultry Ava, a former sharecropper's daughter from North Carolina, astonished even their intimates. After their breakup, Sinatra had at one point placed an icon of her on a wall in one of his homes, complete with candle (which he lit daily). It had obviously been Sinatra who loved the most in this relationship—and in his heart, claimed his closest friends, he would *always* love Ava. He also respected her: She hadn't caved in to his relentless onslaughts over the years, before, during, or after their marriage. It was common knowledge that the loss of Ava Gardner had taught Sinatra how to *really* sing a torch song.

The Ava era had finally ended for him, or so it seemed, only eight years previously, after she had talked scathingly about him to reporter Joe Hyams. (Mia Farrow was twelve years old when that occurred.) However, the truth was that Frank had been trying to revive his relationship with Ava as late as 1964, the year he met Mia. And Mia Farrow was not the first woman, after divorcing Ava, that he'd considered marrying.

He'd been engaged, only four years before Mia, to a beautiful young dancer from South Africa, Juliet Prowse. In retrospect Prowse's relationship with Frank perhaps bore the closest parallel to Frank's and Mia's. Prowse, too, was independent and strong-minded. She refused to abandon her career, which Sinatra had insisted upon. However, some on the scene were of the opinion that Frank's friends had a lot to do with breaking them up. The men around him didn't want an outsider upsetting the balance in the inner circle, leading one friend to comment, "With all his talents and power, I sometimes wonder who's the leader and who's being led." In any event Sinatra and Prowse called off the wedding.

• • •

The question everyone was dying to ask Mia was obvious: Had she ever been intimidated or scared by Sinatra's reputation as a great lover? Her answer was that she never thought about it. With Mia he was good and kind and gentle; she admired him and the fact that he loved life and was not afraid to live it. She felt she was exactly the same way.

Most people (including, most likely, Mia) didn't realize the true extent of Sinatra's sexual appetites. Many women have revealed his preferences in the boudoir (though the reports do vary, depending on the woman). His partners were often call girls (Sinatra was very generous financially to professionals— he didn't have to be "Frank Sinatra" with them), and he liked women of all colors and races. *Ménage à trois, quatre, cinq*—he tried it all. He was an adventurous man and as confident about his sexual prowess as he was about his singing talent.

His life was now the subject of a CBS-TV News Special (when Mia saw it, she kept repeating, "Fascinating, fascinating"). Narrated by Walter Cronkite, the show was scheduled to be broadcast in conjunction with "the world's greatest entertainer's" reaching the half-century mark in 1965. Every major magazine and newspaper had big Sinatra-celebration stories in the works. The CBS special became controversial when Sinatra blew his top because one of the conditions he'd insisted on had, in his view, been violated. There were supposed to have been no personal questions—but Cronkite had asked him about whether marriage to Mia was on the agenda, and there had been a question or two on Sinatra's alleged underworld connections. Sinatra tried to prevent the network from broadcasting the show, and his friends sent telegrams withdrawing their cooperation. The network went ahead, and when the show hit the airwaves, the public wondered what Sinatra had been complaining about: It was a valentine.

Mia and Frank were entering a crucial, and very rocky, period in their relationship. Their friends were observing trouble in paradise. Nothing major, but certainly revealing basic differences between them. For example there was the weekend, at Sinatra's Palm Springs home, when Frank hosted an informal dinner party. Mia, in sweater and slacks, sat by the fireplace under a bright lamp doing needlepoint on a cover for a stool (previous items she'd made included a pillow and a chair bottom). The guests began to arrive. It was a noisy group, and all looked forward to the charcoal-broiled steaks being prepared by Sinatra himself.

At dinnertime the guests, led by Frank, adjoined to the dining room.

According to one of the guests, Mia decided to stay put and finish her needlepoint. Time passed. Frank appeared. He wasn't angry, merely resigned to the situation. He'd obviously been through it a number of times.

"Are you going to join us, or are you going to eat that stool?" he asked.

There was no dramatic scene between them, but Mia shortly returned to Los Angeles, doubtful that Sinatra would go through with the twenty-first birthday party he'd planned for her the next week at Chasen's restaurant.

When they discussed it by telephone, Sinatra informed her the party was on—the guests had all been invited.

On the appointed date the fashionable restaurant was packed with two hundred of Hollywood's rich and powerful. The guests dined on a menu Sinatra had personally selected consisting of all the foods Mia loved best. Sinatra was always concerned about Mia's weight—he enjoyed seeing her eat a hearty meal. And he apparently derived pleasure from watching the other guests eat Mia's favorite foods as well.

The other women in the group were wearing spectacular gowns and jewels. Sinatra appreciated the trappings of wealth and power, but Mia had absolutely no interest in such things. There was no place in her ever-present Magic Box for diamonds. Her intimate possessions were totally personal and individual in nature, things that had great significance to her but that most people would have considered worthless.

For Sinatra, however, lavish gift giving was a vital pleasure, a way of showing his love and also, one presumes, of impressing the world. It was expected of him.

There was no visible tension between Frank and Mia at the Chasen's bash, although some reports had Mia at one end of the room and Sinatra on the other, with Frank leaving early because he had a recording session the next day.

The couple had been together for over a year and in fact had reached a crossroads.

They split.

One knowledgeable source described the separation as "a

'breather' in an almost constant association." The smart money was banking on a reconciliation "if somebody finds that somebody misses somebody more than *he* ever expected."

According to an account by Mia's close friend Leonard Gershe, the day Mia broke up with Frank, she left the Fox studio—just ran out. They threatened to sue. At first she didn't return their calls. Then she asked to see Richard Zanuck, head of the studio. She told Zanuck she didn't have much money but he could have what little she had (she wasn't interested in the big salary hike the studio was offering, from $50,000 annually to $100,000). She told Zanuck that Frank was ninety percent of her life, her career was ten percent, and that there was really nothing left for Zanuck.

She was hurting badly from the breakup with Sinatra. Close friends observed that the trauma changed her. She didn't flee to some remote sanctuary—she suddenly became very visible and social. Her favorite disco was the Daisy, and now Mia sometimes flirted and danced there all night. Leonard Gershe said that he viewed this as "a sort of exorcism, a testing of herself." He knew that every man in the place fell in love with Mia on these night-long revels.

It was only the beginning of what might be viewed in retrospect as Mia's plan to get Frank back by not pursuing him. The girl whose fragile beauty made her appear "breakable" was in fact a very strong soul. Close friends knew she had an unfailing sense of what was right for her.

She dated famous, eligible men during her separation from Frank, including thirty-eight-year-old Eddie Fisher. Fisher already knew Mia. He thought she was "a beautiful little girl and very smart—even shrewd—with a charm and sense of humor that were completely unique." Fisher was as fascinated with her as Sinatra was. When Fisher had first come to Hollywood, he had had a crush on none other than Maureen O'Sullivan, whom he used to see at Louella Parsons's house. Now he found himself just as enchanted by Mia. He knew she and Sinatra were having a tiff, that she was ignoring his calls, and that she was going out with Fisher and others just to make Frank jealous.

Fisher called her on it. "Mia," Fisher said one night, "what is all this nonsense? You know you're going to marry him." He recalled that Mia just smiled her whimsical smile.

One night Mia and Eddie had dinner with George Hamilton and Lynda Bird Johnson, daughter of the then president. Hamilton's mother *and* the secret service chaperoned one and all, recalled Fisher. The group saw a screening of a film, then Mia and Fisher went on to a party Polly Bergen was throwing at the Bistro. Then, Fisher has recalled, Mia wanted to drive down to Mexico. Fisher said she was always coming up with some crazy idea, so he said, "Why not?" Once they had crossed the border, Mia had another idea: "Let's get married."

"Okay," said Eddie. He wanted to see how far she would go.

Mia said she'd have to call good friend Roddy McDowall for permission.

Eddie had no objections. It was, according to Fisher's recollections, at least 3:00 A.M., but they located a phone and Mia dialed Roddy. No answer.

Fisher asked if that meant they couldn't get married.

"I'm afraid so," she answered.

"Well, ask me again later," he said, turning the car around. According to Fisher, they took their time driving back to L.A.

During this period Mia also dated friends, such as Leonard Gershe, and hot new director Mike Nichols. Nichols had recently directed *Who's Afraid of Virginia Woolf?* with Elizabeth Taylor and Richard Burton (it was Nichols's first film), and

Nichols and Mia flew to Rome to spend time with the Burtons. Mia and Elizabeth became friendly. (One wonders if Mia knew —or would have cared—that Elizabeth had once wanted to marry Frank Sinatra. According to Taylor and Sinatra biographer Kitty Kelley, their affair had resulted in Elizabeth becoming pregnant. Frank, not interested in marriage, had arranged for an abortion.)

Certainly Elizabeth and Mia had a current problem in common: They both received a lot of hate mail. Mia told Elizabeth she had never realized there were so many haters in the world. At first it had made her ill, but now she and Elizabeth began comparing mail. Elizabeth advised Mia never to open the letters—she didn't, she said. Mia supposedly took her advice.

Meanwhile Mia's jet-setting was prominently chronicled in the press. It was certainly obvious to Frank Sinatra that Mia Farrow was not going to fall into obscurity—or enter a convent —because she and Sinatra had called it quits.

Sinatra telephoned his friend Edie Goetz one evening to find out what movie she was showing that night (the Goetzes had access to the latest films before their release and screened them for friends).

But Edie hemmed and hawed; it seemed that her dinner guests that evening would include Mia, Mike Nichols, and some of their friends. Edie diplomatically suggested that, of course, Frank should come to the movie, but after dinner. Sinatra was insulted. He became angry and asked his friend Edie if she were throwing him out of her house.

However, Frank apparently wasn't insulted enough to stay home. He arrived, after dinner, and an uncomfortable situation resulted. Frank and some cronies socialized in one group, Mia and Mike in another. Edie Goetz looked tense, but Sinatra told her not to worry about it, it was fine with him—he had his group, they had theirs. He was content to keep it that way. Frank was not, however, particularly cordial to Mike Nichols when the director tried to chat with him.

Not long after this peculiar evening Frank Sinatra was once again seeing Mia Farrow. She was present at several of his recording sessions. It was apparent who had won "the test of wills," if indeed that's what it had been. An onlooker observed, in Damon Runyonesque fashion, that it had been Frank's dime that went into that first telephone call, not Mia's.

The separation had lasted about three months.

Leonard Gershe stated that when Frank came back of his own free will, it gave Mia security and confidence. Doll Face and Charlie Brown were together again.

It was apparently not a simple decision for Sinatra. He was in production on his movie *The Naked Runner,* which was being shot in London. Brad Dexter, who was producing it, recalled that Sinatra was going through a bad time, trying to decide whether or not to marry Mia.

Then an ugly incident occurred back in the States, in June 1966, involving Sinatra and Frederick Weisman, president of Hunt's Foods (he was financier Norton Simon's brother-in-law). It took place in the Polo Lounge of the Beverly Hills Hotel. Sinatra, Dean Martin, and a group of pals were celebrating Martin's forty-ninth birthday and were having a boisterous time. Weisman, who was seated with Franklin Fox, a Boston businessman, asked Sinatra and friends to please be less noisy —their comments were pretty strong for the ladies in the room.

Sinatra reportedly became hostile and insulting to Weisman, who took offense at Sinatra's personal remarks. A fight ensued. Sinatra allegedly threw a telephone. Dean Martin tried to get him out of there.

Weisman was lying on the ground. Frank Fox couldn't

revive him, and an ambulance was summoned. Weisman remained in critical condition for two days. His prognosis was not positive. Cranial surgery was required. Sinatra could not be located by police investigators. Police chief Clinton H. Anderson said the singer was in hiding but that they would get him —they wanted to find out the cause of the fight and Weisman's physical condition at the time it had occurred.

Sinatra phoned Anderson from his Palm Springs home. Mia had flown to Palm Springs to be with Frank. So had Jack and Corinne Entratter. According to Mrs. Entratter, it was the only time she saw Frank scared. For two weeks they all remained at the house, waiting out Weisman's condition. Mia and Corinne attempted to learn how to play backgammon to pass the time.

Weisman regained consciousness but remained in serious condition. The family wanted to press charges but later told friends that threatening phone calls and threats of harm to their children deterred them.

The case was closed.

• • •

A few days later Frank presented Mia with a nine-carat diamond ring, a pear-shaped gem of the finest quality. He'd bought it at Ruser's, a Beverly Hills jeweler, for $85,000.

She received the ring from Frank (which was concealed as a surprise behind a dessert he was urging her to eat) aboard Sinatra's Learjet, en route to New York. Maureen was with them and recalled how Sinatra was always coaxing Mia to eat more. (Maureen agreed that she was too thin.)

This was one diamond Mia wore, at first. She said it was a "friendship ring." Maureen had asked Frank what she should say when people asked her about the ring. He told O'Sullivan it was okay to announce the engagement, without giving a definite wedding date.

Mia wore the ring when she hobbled on crutches into P. J. Clarke's in New York, on Third Avenue and Fifty-fourth Street. She'd had a slight accident in her mother's apartment but was in great spirits and obviously anxious to show off the ring, which sparkled like a firecracker in the pub's soft lighting.

It could be seen blazing from her finger at Arthur, the town's leading disco, where disc jockey Jerry King played the hottest rock music; and at Jilly's, Sinatra's favorite New York haunt.

Frank, in Los Angeles, would telephone Mia in New York at whatever nightclub she told him she'd be visiting. One night she was at Arthur with her mother, and took a call from her fiancé. Later mother and daughter went to El Morocco, where they joined Bette Davis, Van Johnson, Rosalind Russell, and Frederick Brisson. Sinatra phoned and spoke with all of them, singing Mia's praises.

Sinatra pal Harry Kurnitz, tongue-in-cheek, said it best: "She's too old for him." The age difference, of course, was the theme constantly harped on. Everyone who knew Mia, even her mother, offered the observation that Mia had "an old soul." Even Nancy Sinatra, Jr., who became friends with Mia, concurred. "Mia was born old, like me," she said, and pointed out that Mia got along with older people more easily than she did with her contemporaries. Nancy marveled at Mia's ability to carry on long conversations, sometimes for hours, with sophisticated, older people without boring them.

Nancy junior was actually five years older than Mia. When she had first learned of her father's relationship with her, Nancy had felt that she had somehow failed her father. She thought that perhaps he was having a middle-age crisis and that Mia Farrow was his solution. But Nancy said she soon learned that her fears were groundless. During the time she spent with the couple, she "realized how good for him she was." And she found them a truly romantic couple. In Nancy's view Mia was very up-front, intelligent, funny—and quietly strong.

The news of the engagement coincided with the wedding of another famous couple, Brigitte Bardot and multimillionaire jet-setter Gunther Sachs, who tied the knot in Las Vegas. The press tied in these two very separate events because at one point Sinatra had been scheduled to make a movie with Bardot, the world's most uninhibited sex symbol. Fourth-estaters gleefully speculated on the chemistry that that teaming might have produced.

Maureen O'Sullivan was of course sought out for comment on her daughter's engagement. The actress said she couldn't have been more delighted.

At this point in time the rest of the Farrow family appeared to be doing well. Patrick was now an artist, working in California. John had recently worked as an assistant stage manager in a Warren, Ohio, theater. Prudence, seventeen, was at boarding school and wanted to become a dancer. Steffi, sixteen, had no interest in the theater. And fourteen-year-old Theresa ("Tisa") wanted to get the braces off her teeth.

Chapter Eight

"I WAS PRESENT at the great dinner party, given by Bill and Edie Goetz, at which the engagement was announced," recalls Garson Kanin. "I remember Mia was called on to speak —there were about twenty people present—it was a big, formal, fancy dinner party at the Goetzes' Delfern Drive home— and Mia got up and she very simply said, 'Now I know why I was born.' That was her whole speech. And everyone thought —we [Garson and wife, Ruth Gordon] certainly thought—that it was an extraordinarily interesting and good and healthy idea for these two to be together and to be married."

It was the summer of 1966, and the couple announced they would marry in the fall. But both Frank and Mia were now famous for doing the unexpected.

Frank was still undecided about taking the big step. Back in London, working on *The Naked Runner*, Sinatra asked his friend Brad Dexter his opinion. Dexter didn't tell Frank what he wanted to hear. Dexter didn't think marriage was a good idea: The age difference was too great. Dexter went so far as to tell Sinatra that perhaps he was confusing the love he had for his son with his feelings about Mia. Frank junior was not responding to his dad, but Mia certainly was.

Sinatra exploded with fury and almost wrecked the hotel suite. Then he telephoned Jack Entratter to arrange everything for the marriage.

Sinatra phoned Mia, the Goetzes, his lawyer, Mickey Rudin—as Dexter looked on and wondered if Frank had gone mad. In Dexter's words: "Mia's doom was sealed."

· · ·

The secret wedding date was set. On July 18, Frank had dinner with former girlfriend Peggy Connolly, and they seemed very friendly.

A few days later, not long before the marriage, Mia and Maureen were Sinatra's guests in Palm Springs. Maureen recalled that Sinatra received a telephone call from a reporter who was checking out the hot rumor concerning the imminent wedding. Sinatra was furious and yelled at the man over the phone, but used only a mild expletive. After he hung up, he was embarrassed for having used such language in front of Maureen. Maureen was surprised the language hadn't been a good deal stronger—the situation had called for it. But Maureen realized Sinatra had a strict code regarding his behavior in front of a *lady,* and Maureen was more than that—she was Mia's mother.

Back in Brentwood, Helen Berner, Mia's landlady, knew when the big day had arrived. Sinatra's security guards were out in force at the cottage. Sinatra arrived in a huge limousine, and Mia and the bodyguards emerged from the house with what seemed like tons of luggage. Mia told Mrs. Berner she wouldn't be using the cottage anymore.

On July 29, 1966, a private jet landed in Las Vegas at 3:30

P.M. Frank Sinatra was aboard. A chartered jet from Los Angeles, with Mia on board, arrived at 4:50. The couple rendezvoused at the Sands Hotel, where Mia changed into a white suit (white was now her favorite color). Mia had had her hair done on her wedding day—Frank's barber had cut it.

Minutes before the ceremony, in private, Frank told his longtime, trusted valet, George Jacobs, to get in touch with Ava Gardner (whom Jacobs has described as the love of Frank's life), to let her know about the wedding before someone surprised her with the news.

Mia Farrow wed Frank Sinatra in Jack Entratter's suite. No family members were present. Bill Goetz was best man, Edie matron of honor. Entratter gave the bride away.

Edith Goetz later said that both Frank and Mia had appeared very anxious and nervous, with Sinatra's face flushed and twitching. She also said she and her husband had nudged Frank into tying the knot. They told him to go ahead and do it —Mia was crazy about him.

The arrangements had been carried out in strictest secrecy and with awesome efficiency—wedding license (witnessed by Entratter and Henry Claiborne), judge, wedding cake, champagne. The ceremony took four minutes, and then Judge William Compton pronounced the couple "man and wife."

The triple-decker cake was sliced. Frank and Mia had one glass of champagne each, then stepped outside, where Frank introduced Mia to the press. There were thirty-seven still cameras and fourteen motion picture cameras there to capture the moment. Sinatra was simple and eloquent: "My bride."

How did he feel? "I thought I handled it pretty good." It was the most publicized romance and wedding of the decade. Old and new Hollywood had converged, and media coverage was phenomenal.

By 6:00 P.M. the newlyweds had departed on their Palm Springs honeymoon.

A few days later it was back to New York for an elegant, very private honeymoon reception and dinner at '21', hosted by Sinatra friends Bennett Cerf, the publishing giant, and producer Leland Hayward.

When the couple were chided by friends that they had surprised everybody with an early wedding, Mia stated simply, "It wasn't a surprise to us."

But in fact they had deceived their friends. On the Monday before their wedding, Sinatra and Mia, in New York, had visited one of their favorite clubs, Billy Reed's Coney Island. Sinatra deliberately said to one and all that he was going to London the following morning to work on *The Naked Runner* and that he'd be away for a couple of months.

But Las Vegas, not London, was his destination. Mia had flown to Los Angeles, and from there she flew to Vegas. If any of their friends were insulted at not being told, it wasn't evident at this gathering.

There was an unfortunate incident later that evening when Frank, after dropping Mia back at the apartment, visited his buddies Toots Shor and comedian Joe E. Lewis at Shor's restaurant. A photographer, Jerry Engel of the *New York Post,* attempted to take Sinatra's picture. According to Engel, "I went over to him and I said, 'How about a nice picture?' I hate to say what he said besides the words *parasite, creep, rat,* and he belted me—that was the last picture I could make because the camera was on the ground, my glasses were on the ground, *I* was on the ground." The "old" Frank Sinatra could obviously resurface at any time when provoked.

Mia Farrow was now Mrs. Frank Sinatra. Had it all really happened? Certainly Mia's peers were astonished. Paul Monash, of *Peyton Place,* said he'd watched with a sense of wonder and almost awe as Mia accomplished almost everything she'd set out to do. She had, in Monash's view, created a mystique about herself. Was she clever? Was it instinct? Was it *vital truth*? Monash said he hadn't the slightest clue.

Maureen offered the opinion that men had an instinctive desire to protect Mia. That was the secret. Liza Minnelli concurred, observing that people were always trying to protect Mia, "but she is stronger than all of us."

Mia's short hairdo, of course, was now all the rage. Women all over the country were cutting their hair. They wanted "the Mia look."

Not quite everyone wanted "the look." When Ava Gardner learned of the nuptials, she was blunt: "Hah! I always knew Frank would wind up in bed with a boy."

• • •

One of Mia's first visitors after she married Sinatra was hairdresser George Masters. (Masters later said he was shocked she had married Sinatra. She didn't impress him as Sinatra's type, and he was in a position to know: Masters had been Marilyn Monroe's hairstylist at the time Monroe was involved with the singer.)

When Masters arrived at the house, he and Mia chatted away up in her bedroom, when the Voice was heard from downstairs: "Who's there?"

Masters recalled that Mia grimaced into the mirror the same way she did when she was irritated with her hair or eye makeup. Mia took him by the hand and dragged him out onto the balcony that overlooked the living room.

"What's going on up there?" asked Sinatra suspiciously.

"Oh, don't worry, he's just working on me," answered Mia.

"Hi there," said Masters. The two men exchanged no further conversation. As Masters said, there was nothing else to say to a husband who pops in unexpectedly. Masters never saw Sinatra again.

Dali's wedding gift to Mia was in keeping with the artist's character. He gave her an owl, parts of a frog, and pieces of what Dali called moon rock (this was years before anyone had landed on the moon).

Mia took his word for it. After all, her friend had, by her account, taught her the world was what you make of it. Convention might be okay for the masses and to ensure an orderly society, but Mia Farrow was vocal that she didn't want it written on her tombstone that she had been a daughter of convention.

• • •

The honeymoon relocated to London, where Frank continued filming *The Naked Runner.* The couple lived in his Grosvenor Square penthouse. Those who knew them intimately at the time relate how these first few months of their relationship appeared idyllic. While he was working, Mia "played house." She shopped for the food and cooked intimate dinners for two. They spent all of their time alone. Some weekends they traveled to the south of France and stayed at Jack Warner's spectacular villa in Cap d'Antibes.

Eventually Sinatra grew unhappy in England and was very impatient to finish the picture (for which he was being paid $1 million). His temper and temperament erupted many times and, according to on-the-scene accounts, on one occasion director Sidney J. Furie broke down in tears and walked off the picture (he subsequently returned).

Finally back in the States, life for the newlyweds proceeded happily. "In the beginning they certainly seemed an absolutely devoted couple. A devoted pair," recalls Garson Kanin. "She doted on him and he certainly loved her."

The newlyweds and Kirk Douglas were both guests at the Goetzes one evening. It was a dinner party for a select group of Hollywood elite. Douglas was seated next to Mia, and he asked her what she thought of the assembled guests. He vividly recalled her reply: "She went right down the table, person by person, and gave me the most amazingly accurate character appraisal of each one." Douglas was flabbergasted. To him Mia had "always looked so naive, wide-eyed, angelic. But she was a rapier. Concise and to the point."

When they were alone, life for Mia and Frank was totally fulfilling and without artifice or pretension. Simpler and more basic than anyone would have believed, according to Mia. Frank was not lonely with her. For Mia, when she and Frank were in the house, she felt the house was full. They had each other and needed very little else. The greatest thrill for Mia was having the person she loved love her back. At this point she considered their life as normal as it could be for two people in their situation.

There were pets: Malcolm, a deaf white Persian cat; turtles; dogs; an aquarium; Samantha, a yorkshire terrier; a Pekingese, a gift from Liz Taylor (the dog was retarded and kept running into the wall); and Mia's horse, Salvador.

Frank and Mia liked to take walks. They laughed a lot. He made funny faces when she took his picture. They usually went to bed by ten and watched very late movies. They did crossword puzzles. He made spaghetti sauce. They enjoyed breakfasts together. She loved his smile. The purity of his feelings. His incredible sweetness. Her talent for creating a fantasy world enveloped them both.

Mia liked to bake cakes for Frank—which she liked to eat.

(Liza Minnelli said that Frank never really asked Mia to do anything except eat.)

In November the public got a rare glimpse of Frank and Mia in a playful encounter. Mia was the mystery guest on the national TV quiz show *What's My Line?* Sinatra was on the panel with Phyllis Newman, Arlene Francis, and Bennett Cerf. Frank and Mia seemed lighthearted and happy.

That month Sinatra performed his first singing engagement since marrying Mia. She was there opening night, escorted by Joe E. Lewis. Sinatra's comments to the audience were questionable. When he introduced Mia, she got an ovation. However, the audience was taken aback at his remark that he had "finally found a broad I can cheat on." Mia seemed very embarrassed and Sinatra sensed the strong audience disapproval. He tried to gloss over the faux pas and said he'd better sing because he was in a lot of trouble. . . .

In January 1967 Mia was Frank's hostess for a sixty-fifth birthday party Sinatra threw for Joe E. Lewis at Jilly's club in Miami Beach. (Sinatra had portrayed Lewis in the film, *The Joker Is Wild.*) It was a festive affair, and in the course of the evening Mia sat on Frank's knee. They seemed happy as lovebirds.

There was of course the matter of Sinatra's career to contend with: He was literally a one-man industry. Mia was married to a man whose product was himself. There were albums to make, club dates to fulfill, concerts all over the country—and films. The demands on his time and energy were staggering.

Mia was often ringside when he performed. On occasion she'd be with Sinatra's daughters, and he would introduce all three—his daughter Nancy, his daughter Tina, "and my Mia."

Sometimes the three girls would spend the day kibitzing in the hotel suite. When they got dressed for the evening, they'd try on each other's clothes, experiment with each other's makeup—they were almost like sorority sisters.

(Frank Sinatra, Jr., couldn't believe that his father had actually remarried, nor could he believe he'd married a woman one year younger than Junior.)

Mia was well aware of, and duly impressed by, her husband's enormous talent and breathtaking impact on audiences. He was aware that she had talent too. And he must have known that she wasn't really ready to retire before she'd even begun.

Frank wanted to indulge her. He bought her a yellow Thunderbird the color of her hair. Although the couple were living in a luxurious mansion Sinatra had rented from Anita Louise, Sinatra wanted to have a new house to share with his Mia. He asked his wife to find one for them, anything she wanted. She did—an English Tudor-style mansion. At the time the cost—$350,000—was considered fabulous. (Today the same house on the same piece of land would cost $6 million.) Mia decorated it, working with interior designer Laura Mako, in Sinatra's favorite colors, yellow, orange, and white. (Her favorite color was "rainbow.") She even designed some of the furniture. One room in the house was hers alone, a place where she could be alone with her thoughts. But she wanted this new house to be their private haven, their retreat.

They needed one. Mia acknowledged their marriage had extracted a price: Her now even greater fame was like a huge blast in the face, and she realized she didn't like fame at all. There were six-foot fences around their various houses, and they employed security guards. Mia recalled one time she and her husband were being pursued by reporters. The couple managed to make it to their house. Once inside, Sinatra joked that they were safe now. He had his gun. The gates were locked. He and Mia were alone.

Mia was surprised at his attitude. She wanted to know if she and Frank were locked in or were the reporters locked out?

Out in public, Mia said she could feel the old ladies staring holes into her. She knew her posture was bad and her fingernails were bitten down to the quick. She knew what people were whispering about.

But Frank had taught her how to handle herself in a crowd. When people start mobbing you, just walk straight ahead. Don't stop to give autographs, don't look either right or left.

Not long before her daughter's marriage Maureen O'Sullivan had made unexpected headlines of her own. Columnist Suzy stated emphatically that O'Sullivan had secretly married a twenty-three-year-old French-born rabbinical student, Henri Sobell. The story had supposedly been confirmed by Maureen's daughter Prudence, who said the two were in love and her mother was "only about twenty, emotionally." O'Sullivan was also wearing a wedding band, which seemed to confirm the rumors.

Maureen sprang to her own defense. She said she was absolutely not married (the wedding band was a prop in her current play) and that the boy in question was just a dear friend. Confronted with Prudence's remarks, she smilingly said she'd wring her daughter's neck.

The likelihood of Maureen remarrying was hardly an impossibility. As Mia often said, Maureen was still a beautiful woman, and men loved her. But this was 1966, almost twenty years before Joan Collins, *Dynasty, et al.* made older women–younger men relationships fashionable and acceptable. In any case O'Sullivan's "marriage" proved to be a false alarm, and newsworthy mainly because Mia was so much in the headlines.

Maureen observed that marrying Sinatra had put her

daughter in a somewhat difficult position. Mia was afraid of saying the wrong thing—as was Maureen—and Mia avoided personal references, even with Maureen (who said that Frank found that trait endearing).

Maureen, when she visited California, saw that Frank was very considerate of Mia. But Maureen tried to keep out of their private lives and not be a mother-in-law. She was impressed at what a proper and correct gentleman Sinatra was—and very organized. He answered the telephone himself, read the mail, dictated correspondence, and kept track of the kitchen, often ordering the food. He was very kind and respectful toward Maureen, but disapproved if she told a joke that was perhaps a bit risqué. Sinatra viewed her as his mother-in-law, and she learned to refrain from telling the "wrong" kind of joke.

One evening when Maureen was visiting Mia and Frank in Palm Springs, Mia went to bed without saying good night. Maureen asked Sinatra why her daughter hadn't said good night. Maureen felt she should have. Sinatra stood up for his wife. He replied that she needn't have said it if she didn't feel like it.

According to Sinatra's friends, Mia had had quite an effect on Frank's life-style. Everyone knew that before Mia, Frank had been an insomniac, a man who was for anything that could get him through the night—be it prayer, tranquilizers, or a bottle of Jack Daniel's.

Now that he was with Mia, Frank no longer telephoned friends in the middle of the night. For public consumption, Brad Dexter said he'd observed a dramatic change in Frank: Sinatra's old problems seemed to have gone away. Dexter noted that Frank didn't drink nearly as much as he used to. Dexter said he saw a softening in Frank's attitude, a gentleness he had rarely displayed before.

Even Frank's mother, according to friendly-to-Sinatra

sources, had noticed a difference in her son. Of course early on, Mia had been a visitor to the Fort Lee home of Dolly Sinatra, for a lavish home-cooked Italian dinner. On one such occasion movie mogul Jack L. Warner accompanied Frank and Mia.

Mrs. Sinatra, in a glowing statement, now said how much she liked Mia. She told Frank she hoped he would always be as happy as he was with her (he told her he would be), and Mama also observed that Frank appeared much calmer. Dolly Sinatra saw how young Mia was, but noted she had awfully old ideas. Mrs. Sinatra said she loved Mia dearly, especially for what she'd done for Frank. He hadn't been so carefree since he was a young boy. Now Frank was Francis again, she said enthusiastically.

However, in truth, Dolly Sinatra was, according to a close family friend, not impressed by Mia at all, but was putting on a good show for Frank. Dolly still liked Ava Gardner, who had been a big movie star when Frank married her. Dolly was impressed by that; she had never even seen Mia in a movie. And Ava had shared an easy camaraderie with Dolly; both women were at ease with each other and could let their hair down.

A family friend recalled that Dolly Sinatra had asked him his opinion of Mia. He was noncommittal, but Mrs. Sinatra wasn't. As far as she was concerned, Mia was a mystery to her: She didn't talk, she didn't eat, what did she do? In Mrs. Sinatra's view the marriage wouldn't last long and fortunately the couple hadn't been married in the Church.

However, to her own friends, and even her family, Mia seemed more mature, now that Sinatra had ostensibly taught her to be more at ease with people. Maureen, observing this new maturity, remarked that in a sense she felt younger than Mia.

Mia still liked to go out dancing—but noted that now, thanks to Frank, there wasn't that great empty moment when she got home. Mia's friend, Jack Haley, Jr., explained that when Mia got the urge to go out on the town, Frank simply accompanied her to the Daisy, which she loved but which Sinatra wasn't much interested in. (To Mia's dismay, Frank's bodyguards were always on hand, keeping an eye on her.)

At the Daisy, Frank would be very patient. Haley noticed how he would appear bored sometimes or talk to friends, but he knew Mia was having fun dancing and being around people her own age. Sinatra certainly didn't do the contemporary dances that Mia enjoyed so much. But Haley observed that Mia was free to dance with anyone she liked, so long as she knew it was somebody Frank approved of. Haley observed that these young people could never really be friends of Sinatra's but that he knew them. It was Haley's opinion that Sinatra had checked them out pretty carefully.

To others on the scene, on these excursions Sinatra appeared like an indulgent father taking a child to the zoo. Frank really didn't enjoy it, but he knew Mia did.

Ryan O'Neal has described these evenings out with Mia and Frank. He said the table was usually divided into two groups, with Sinatra surrounded by older friends and Mia with the young set. One night Frank saw Mia shiver—she was sitting under an air conditioner. He was very concerned and asked her to change places. She declined, and O'Neal said he was glad she had: What, O'Neal wondered, would he and his pals have talked to Frank Sinatra about?

•   •   •

Sinatra knew Mia's career was important to her. He loved her and had to be fair, he said. He knew Mia had talent.

They had been married about six months. Mia claimed she

had had no urge to work—until now. She wanted Sinatra to be proud of her. She knew she had a lot to learn about acting. But apparently, like her mother, she loved to act. As her friend Garson Kanin later said, Mia wanted the rainbow too.

There were, needless to say, lots of offers for her services. It was inevitable she'd go back to work. The question had been when, in what, and working with whom. (She was magically free of her commitment to *Peyton Place*.)

When queried if she wanted to star in a film with her husband, her answer was negative. Everyone would think he simply gave her the job. She didn't think a husband and wife should act together.

One of the pitfalls of returning to work was that Mia would be more accessible to the press, and this was a big problem since she gave honest answers. And according to Liza Minnelli, Mia—and Liza—*enjoyed* reading about themselves. Minnelli recalled how, earlier on, when they passed a newsstand, they'd always buy all the magazines and newspapers to see if their names were mentioned, exclaiming happily when they found something about themselves.

But few in the fourth estate had figured Mia out, whereas by now Mia felt she had figured them out. She felt reporters listened to what she said, rather than what she meant and got her all wrong. She answered what she considered dumb questions with deliberately dumb answers. For example when one reporter too many queried her on why she had cut off her hair, she answered it was because she had grown tired of ironing it.

And reporters hadn't yet seemed to catch on to the fact that Mia went through fads. She might be a vegetarian one week and something else the next.

Sinatra of course detested almost all publicity because it concentrated on his private life, rarely his work, about which he was *very* serious, totally professional and not at all averse to talking about with the press. But he didn't like to talk about the private Sinatra because he said he felt he was giving a part of himself away when he talked too much. Of course he'd already had twenty grueling years in the public eye. Mia's attitude about publicity would change in time, but for now she was still willing to play the game.

Sinatra's press agent was, for the present, handling them both. It was a form of protection for Mia, actually; some control could be exercised over what was written. When things changed, however, and she was on her own, Mia Farrow would discover that those who had been protecting her could be just as effective at embarrassing her.

Chapter Nine

THE FILM Mia decided on was *A Dandy in Aspic.* It was a thriller, to be filmed primarily in London, with some location work in Berlin. That meant Mia and Frank would be working in different parts of the globe. Not necessarily the wisest way to keep a relationship perking, especially between these two people.

Her leading man would be Laurence Harvey, whom Sinatra approved of. The men had become fast friends when they made *The Manchurian Candidate* a few years earlier, and Sinatra trusted him.

Mia joked about her pairing with Harvey. She said they were very much alike: They smoked the same kind of cigarettes, preferred white wine, liked Bogart, and loathed each other to the same degree. She also joked about how thin she and Harvey were—they would easily be the thinnest couple on the screen. They were both so skinny, said Mia, that when they danced together, it hurt.

She discussed the character she would play with the film's

screenwriter, Derek Marlowe. She had many questions about the character, which Marlowe attempted to answer. But something about the role eluded her. Then Mia told him that she once thought she'd like to have forty babies by forty of the most super men in the world, adding that she never really wanted to get married to any of them. Marlowe was delighted —Mia had provided the missing key to the character.

Mia was in fact anxious about the film. She knew it had better be good. If she failed, the thud would be heard in every producer's office around the world.

The director, Anthony Mann, was a Hollywood veteran. He minced no words discussing Mia Farrow. He said if she wanted to be a star, she could be. "But it would be nice to know if her husband will let her get to the top."

Mia flew to Paris for wardrobe fittings. Pierre Cardin would personally design the clothes, and her contract specified that she could keep them after the picture.

At the Cardin salon even the sophisticated models stared at Mia—they thought she looked about twelve years old! She wore a pale mink coat, a gift from her husband. Mia was responsible for two current Parisian trends: her haircut and the freckles on her nose (local girls were having them painted on). Everyone also took note of the fact that Mia wore no makeup —only false eyelashes.

Mia was accorded the kind of deferential treatment reserved for top-ranking dignitaries. She was welcomed to Cardin's salon by Mme. Herve Alphand, wife of the former French ambassador to Washington. Everyone knew Madame Alphand handled only Cardin's most prestigious customers.

Cardin, of course, adored Mia's size-4 frame: perfect for clothes. Mia shyly and honestly confided that she was not a clothes person and that she often bought herself inexpensive dresses in the children's department of department stores. She also said she designed her own clothes and then had them made up by two seamstresses.

Mia Farrow was not, everybody agreed, the "average" star. Furthermore the only jewelry she wore was a plain gold wedding band (the nine-carat diamond was nowhere in sight).

Pressed for details, in fashion-obsessed Paris, about her personal wardrobe, she revealed her favorite piece of clothing —one that had great value to her—was a jacket worn by her husband. It had been given to him by astronaut Gus Grissom (who had died the previous month). Mia said she and Frank had been in awe of Grissom and asked him for a remembrance of their meeting. He was, after all, a *real* hero. Grissom gave Sinatra the jacket, and Mia said he wore it all the time. In fact Mia wore it too. She said it was also her husband's favorite possession.

• • •

Production on the film began and proceeded smoothly. Mia was a total professional.

Meanwhile Sinatra was performing at the Fontainebleau Hotel in Miami Beach and shooting a new movie. There were several problems facing him. A federal grand jury in Las Vegas was seeking to question him regarding his relationship to underworld figure Sam Giancana. His efforts to elude testifying would prove unsuccessful. There were other, similar situations he had to contend with.

His new film in production was *Tony Rome*. Around this time there were many witnesses to Sinatra's sometimes rude behavior in public. And particularly to the behavior of his bodyguards and sidekicks.

Mia reportedly had a hard time with the raucous, often insulting displays of humor by these hangers-on. She said all they did was break things, tell dirty stories, bet on horses, and pinch waitress's rear ends.

When Frank's own prankster nature got out of control, which happened often—he might throw food across the table at a "pal"—Mia scolded him, telling him he was childish and could hurt someone. Once, after she'd upbraided him, he angrily stalked out of the room.

Angry that Mia obviously wanted to work rather than simply be Mrs. Sinatra, Frank reportedly had a couple of sexual interludes during production of *Tony Rome.*

There was a break in filming *A Dandy in Aspic,* and Mia took the opportunity to visit Frank in Miami. After seeing him perform at the Fontainebleau, Mia phoned a friend to talk glowingly about Sinatra's singing and she assured her friend that, contrary to what everyone suspected, everything was working out beautifully between her and Frank. She said that Frank was the one who counted, and she was prouder of his accomplishments than of anything she could ever do herself.

However it seems reasonable to believe that in view of ensuing events, the couple's future was very shaky as early as this.

Mia had to fly back to Europe almost immediately (director Anthony Mann died before production was completed, and Laurence Harvey finished directing the picture). In Germany for location work, the ever-curious young woman took a side trip to East Berlin, incognito. She was denied admittance to one of the better restaurants. She looked around the city and its ruins, with birds living in the upper stories of bombed-out buildings while business went on as usual on the street level. It was an almost ludicrous contrast, and one not lost on Mia Farrow—devastated, war-torn East Berlin and the luxurious trappings of her own life-style.

By now there were two additional films and a TV special

on the agenda for Mrs. Sinatra. To no one's surprise, one of the films had her husband's blessing—*The Detective,* in which Frank wanted Mia to play his wife. It was a hard-hitting character study/suspense melodrama about a New York City cop. Based on the best-seller by Roderick Thorp, the project had the potential for both critical and commercial success. And despite Mia's earlier protestations about working with her husband, it offered the opportunity for the Sinatras to parlay their appeal into big bucks, à la the leading husband-and-wife "team," Elizabeth Taylor and Richard Burton. The director was Gordon Douglas, who was famous for getting things done fast to accommodate Sinatra.

The other film was the one Mia's agents saw as the big break for her—*Rosemary's Baby,* based on the mega-best-seller by Ira Levin about witchcraft in New York. The director would be Roman Polanski, one of the hottest new talents in the business.

There were clashes between Frank and Mia over her involvement with *Rosemary's Baby.* Production designer Richard Sylbert has described a dinner with Mia and Frank at which it seemed clear to him that what Sinatra wanted most from a wife was her remaining at home. To Sylbert and others it seemed clear that accepting the role of Rosemary was the red flag to Sinatra. In Sylbert's view Sinatra was telling her that if she did the movie, their marriage was over.

Mia was not a person to be told what to do (any more than Frank was). This freethinking independence was one of the qualities that had attracted Frank in the first place. Ava Gardner had had it. And Juliet Prowse.

The fact is Mia signed to do *Rosemary's Baby* and then agreed to do *The Detective* immediately following it. In addition Mia had sought the role of Belinda in a TV film version of the classic *Johnny Belinda.* At first producer David Susskind, not one of Sinatra's favorite people, protested because, among other reasons, he thought her notoriety as Mrs. Frank Sinatra was no asset for the part. Finally he agreed to cast her.

For a girl who'd been busy "being a married lady," there was a lot on her plate. Many in Hollywood felt that the writing was clearly on the wall.

Mia's schedule was arranged so that she could be with Frank for two weeks in Las Vegas, where he was contracted to perform at the Sands.

•   •   •

Sinatra, too, was busier than ever.

He would play seven cities in nine days on an upcoming concert tour. A TV special and *The Detective* were on his agenda. Frank had to plan at least fourteen months in advance. How he and Mia would integrate their personal lives into their work schedules, now that Mia was working, was anybody's guess.

They tried mightily and the strain was formidable, especially for two people who liked to think of themselves as spontaneous and moment-to-moment individuals, people who liked surprises.

They celebrated their first wedding anniversary in July with a Las Vegas bash. That same month Mia's twenty-year-old brother, John, was arrested in Malibu, on suspicion of possession of marijuana. He was freed on bail, but of course the incident made headlines because John's sister was Mia Farrow Sinatra. Everything and anything Mia, or any of her relatives, did was now fodder for the media.

Consequently neither Mia nor Frank, nor anyone within their most intimate circle, dared breathe a word of a decision they (or Frank) had reached. Frank didn't want any scandal, or any more ridiculing publicity. As far as the world was concerned, the Sinatras were leading a fabulous personal life. They were "The Working Sinatras," as their PR people "sold" them, happy together and happily pursuing their individual careers. But in fact in August they agreed to a trial separation.

Sinatra wanted his wife with him, not pursuing a career. He had no hobbies. If he didn't play golf or read, he did nothing. He loved to work, but so did Mia. One would assume he could have related to his wife's feeling the same way. Work, to Sinatra, was his therapy. It would get him so charged up, he'd sleep only four or five hours a night.

One day Earl Wilson phoned Sinatra's home in Los Angeles to check a breaking story. Mia answered the phone. It was midafternoon and Sinatra was asleep.

"When he wakes up, I'll have him call you," said Mia. Wilson remembered her reply "because it wasn't evasive or tentative. She didn't say, 'I'll see if he can call you,' or 'I'll ask him to call you.' She spoke like a woman with some authority around the house!" Wilson noted that "two hours later Frank Sinatra *did* call me."

Despite the "influence" Mia wielded with Frank, and all the attention it brought her, she wasn't interested in basking in reflected glory. And simply watching her husband work was hardly a life-fulfilling prospect for Mia Farrow. While Frank might dedicate his songs to her, she understood (and so did he) that the work itself was *his*. The act of creating his performances couldn't be shared. Even with Mia he'd discuss only the technical side of his work. She realized he performed with absolute truth, from the heart, but it was quite separate—it belonged to him.

During the period with Mia, Sinatra was functioning at top level. He had absolutely no illusions about his limitations. He knew that singing, not acting, was his basic talent. He didn't consider himself a matinee idol or a leading man and would play only certain kinds of roles in movies. He thought his best work had been in *The Man with the Golden Arm,* but he liked to do musicals. Finding one was the problem.

Sinatra wanted to do a lot of unorthodox things musically —the bel canto works of Mozart; Rachmaninoff; Villa-Lobos. He felt his interpretations of pop ballads had richer meaning now. It came from living, having been married, becoming a father, trying to learn all the time. He felt a lot of the new rock groups missed the point; they didn't listen to what lyrics meant. Some shouted the music—Sinatra found that offensive. He liked the Beatles and was planning on meeting with Paul McCartney, who might write some Christmas music for him. He said he could never sing *with* the Beatles—he wouldn't know how. (He had already sung with Elvis, on a television show, and the result was remarkably good.)

Mia, who loved rock music and the new rock groups, continued to give interviews and sometimes told too much, as far as Sinatra was concerned. One anecdote she related, for example, seemed very poignant and flattering to her husband, but Sinatra hadn't wanted it told in print. The story concerned the fact that most people thought of Sinatra as the man who got into fights. But Mia said that wasn't "Charlie" at all. In England, she related, Sinatra always visited a special hospital for blind children. There was a little girl whom he grew to love. The child took him for a walk one day, in the garden, to show him the flowers she'd planted. A strong wind came up. "Don't be startled," Sinatra told her, "the wind's blown hair over your eyes. I'll pull it away." The little girl asked, "What color is the wind?" Sinatra was momentarily stunned. Then he answered, "Sweetheart, the wind moves so fast that nobody has ever been able to find out."

Obviously the very tender and personal nature of this incident revealed much more of the private Frank Sinatra than he wanted to share. He didn't want to give that much of himself away. He felt he owed the public only one thing: a great performance.

Mia filmed *Johnny Belinda* for producer David Susskind, for airing on network TV in the fall. Certainly it was a role some actresses would have turned down because of inevitable comparisons to Jane Wyman in the memorable 1948 film version, for which Wyman won an Oscar as best actress. Apparently the challenge was too exciting for Mia to pass up.

Halfway through, according to Susskind, Mia had to be hospitalized. Susskind was very worried. He considered replacing her, but then she showed up ready to work—and appeared physically battered, her body covered with bruises and welts. Susskind felt terrible for her. He told her he thought someone didn't want her to play the role. She told him she still wanted to do it and implored Susskind not to replace her. She told him she was an actress first, a wife second. The producer relented, but even with makeup her bruises were still evident in some of the shots.

In later years Mia denied Susskind's tale and all its dark implications.

· · ·

Mia began *Rosemary's Baby* in the fall.

Considering her ultradevout Roman Catholic roots, it's interesting that the theme of the picture, Satanism, didn't bother Mia at all. She observed that her Catholic upbringing had of course made a stamp on her—it was tattooed on her soul. But she didn't consider the devil (as presented in this film) evil, only a childish sketch of evil right out of a catechism book.

Director Roman Polanski's first choice for the role had been his wife, Sharon Tate's, girlfriend, Tuesday Weld. Though an excellent actress, she was not an important enough star, countered the studio. Mia was proposed. Polanski had glimpsed the Mia magic in person at the Daisy. After screening several episodes of *Peyton Place,* he gave his enthusiastic okay, no screen test necessary.

Polanski was one of the new wunderkind making movies, an *auteur* filmmaker whose films to date—*Knife in the Water, Repulsion,* and *The Fearless Vampire Killers*—had garnered excited praise from critics and stirred great interest among the younger men producing movies.

The thirty-four-year-old Polanski ("What a cute little kid," thought actress Ruth Gordon on meeting him) was born in Paris, but he'd spent his youth in Poland. During World War II both his parents died in death camps (his mother at Auschwitz).

Polanski's films offered eroticism, black humor, and horror in a blend that seemed certain to find a huge contemporary audience once the right commercial vehicle for his talents was found.

Polanski's films were provocative, and his personal life was strictly fast-lane. He was married to beautiful young American actress Sharon Tate, and the couple were very much a part of the happening social scene.

Sharon has been described by Hollywood veterans as a very beautiful but naive girl. Her reputation was that of a woman who usually became involved with the wrong man. One of her affairs had been with hairstylist-to-the-stars Jay Sebring, a diminutive but very sexy man whose own reputation in the film community was notorious. Sebring's penchant for sadomasochistic sex and drugs was well known. After Sharon's affair with him cooled down, the couple remained friends. Sharon had met Roman Polanski in London in 1966. She was directed by him in *The Fearless Vampire Killers* and found that "this small and not terribly good-looking man" knew how to take charge of things. They began living together and were married early in 1968. But friends observed that soon after the marriage Polanski "went off the deep end" and cruised Sunset Boulevard nightly, "haunting the strip clubs and picking up girls in his car." In all fairness it should be recalled that this was literally the era of "cruising," and Polanski was hardly on a solo escapade. Sunset Boulevard was very crowded.

Rosemary's Baby was to be Polanski's launching pad into the Hollywood big time, and the theme and structure of the piece were right up his alley. The story concerned a coven of witches in contemporary New York City who must find a suitable young woman to be impregnated by the devil. She will give birth to the Antichrist.

The Ira Levin novel on which it was based had already jumped to the top of the best-seller lists. Paramount had bought the screenrights for $150,000. (Novelist Levin had thought the movies would shy away from the book completely.) The producer was William Castle, a man famous for producing and directing very low budget horror pictures. Castle became ill however, and had little to do with the actual production. (Insiders joked that the filmmakers had cast an evil spell on him.)

Filming of the picture very much represented the "New Hollywood" approach, whereby the director was God in virtually every phase of the picture's production (and postproduction). It's amusing that Polanski wasn't so "new" to the system that he didn't want an old-fashioned kind of Hollywood blockbuster.

Doing interviews, he was reluctant to give away the plot, even though the novel was already published all over the world. But Polanski felt that out of 200 million potential moviegoers, perhaps only ten percent would ever read the book, so why spoil the surprise for the rest of them? Mr. Polanski was obviously a very practical kind of genius.

He was a pragmatic man, educated in art, electronics, and physics. That, he explained, was how his brain worked. And as far as the far-out plot of *Rosemary's Baby* was concerned, he thought *anything* could happen, especially in New York City.

A top cast was assembled. Actress/playwright/screenwriter Ruth Gordon (Mrs. Garson Kanin) would play Rosemary's nosy and ultimately devilish neighbor, Minnie. Offscreen Ruth and Mia Farrow became the closest of personal friends. "She and Ruth became absolute buddies," recalls Garson Kanin. "Really girlfriends. The separation of all those years between them simply didn't matter.

"Mia used to say Ruth was her 'youngest hippie friend.' She would ask Ruth for every kind of advice about everything, and Ruth, being Ruth, really gave it to her, on all sorts of things—hairdo and clothes, travel, where to go, what to do, what to avoid. They talked a blue streak. Ruth never really had a daughter. I think she sort of took on that role, became rather motherly with Mia." (The Kanins subsequently saw a great deal of Mia in various parts of the world.)

"Ruth always wore the hippie love beads Mia gave her," recalled close Kanin friend Marian Seldes. "That friendship was so beautiful and sweet."

Sidney Blackmer was signed to play Ruth Gordon's diabolical husband. Mia's actor-husband would be played by John Cassavetes (Polanski had wanted either Robert Redford or Jack Nicholson). Ralph Bellamy had a major role, as Rosemary's doctor. Newcomer Charles Grodin had a small role as another doctor, and Marianne Gordon (the future Mrs. Kenny Rogers) played one of Rosemary's girlfriends. Veterans Elisha Cook, Jr., and comedienne Patsy Kelly were also featured prominently in the picture.

Polanski had a reputation for being tough on actors (although he was greatly admired by fellow directors such as Elia Kazan and Mike Nichols, who came to the set to watch him work). John Cassavetes (himself a noted director) observed during production how obsessed Polanski was by blood and gore—to Cassavetes, Polanski behaved like a kid in a candy store. Polanski admitted that it excited him to shock other people. He said he liked to shock bourgeois audiences, who couldn't accept that other people might be different than they were.

Cassavetes felt that an actor simply tried to keep alive with Polanski, or else went under. The men had clashes. Polanski felt Cassavetes questioned every action too much—sometimes the only motivation for crossing from one side of the room to the other was simply to open the door so that another character could enter the scene!

There were no clashes between Polanski and Mia, the complete pro, although Mia had her doubts about him at first. She thought he was spending all his time fiddling with little details about the set, not worrying enough about her. But then she understood that he would stop her if she went wrong and that the reason he left her alone was that she was doing okay.

She enjoyed what she described as his marvelous, childlike enthusiasm and fantastic know-how. And she said he "jazzed" everybody. They were on the set next to the one used by the TV series *Bonanza,* and Polanski was leaping around and all excited at this, playing with all the props, wearing a holster and practicing his draw.

Polanski said he had no doubt that Mia, like him, was "nuts." "There are 127 varieties of nuts," he said. "She's 116 of them." That, he believed, might be the reason she was so charming. He said he never had trouble with her; she was sensitive, she enjoyed her work, she had a neurotic quality that was perfect for Rosemary. Polanski said that "only nuts are interesting people." On another occasion he characterized Mia as "slightly mad," but definitely a superstar of tomorrow. To Roman Polanski there was nothing more boring than normal.

Mia, working under Polanski's direction, was delivering a very powerful performance. There were some very difficult scenes as well as intimate and erotic ones. The husband-wife relationship between the Mia and Cassavetes characters was depicted in a very contemporary fashion, and in the morning-after-the-rape scene, in which Mia wakes up in her own bed with Cassavetes and has scratches all over her back, she most definitely is nude from the waist up (she cups her hands over her breasts).

Her love scenes with Cassavetes were very sexy and effective. It's fascinating to note that some of the dialogue in the picture could have been lifted from Mia's real life: a line about "Liz and Dick" at the beginning of the film; Rosemary saying, "I was brought up a Catholic—now I don't know." Some other dialogue, referring to the pope and Catholicism, would have had John Farrow, were he alive, running for the hills. The dialogue was typical of the new freedom in movies—at one point Rosemary even talks about having her period.

Mia obviously contributed personal touches to Rosemary's physical surroundings. For example the character has her own Magic Box, in this case a Louis Sherry tin can, in which Rosemary keeps things that have special meaning for her.

Off camera, Mia gave her new friend Ruth Gordon a Magic Box, shocked that the older actress had never had one (maybe she did, countered Gordon, only she didn't call it that).

As in Mia's real life, in the film Rosemary's friends are all older people—however, Rosemary is forced into this situation. At one point, desperate and at wits' end, Rosemary throws a party for her young friends to which Ruth Gordon and the others are not invited: "It's a special party," Rosemary angrily tells them. "You have to be under sixty to get in."

The picture was a long, hard, emotionally draining shoot, and Polanski was a perfectionist.

To relieve the tension there were occasional trips by helicopter from Paramount to Disneyland. While they were filming in Los Angeles, Mia was in a serious auto accident driving her white Jaguar. Incredibly she escaped injury.

Sources on the set at Paramount claimed that it was evident that Mia was being physically abused by Sinatra during this period. And he phoned the set constantly. Others could clearly hear him screaming at her as she held the phone.

The couple still socialized publicly. Close Sinatra buddy Sammy Davis, Jr., and other stars, including Tony Newley, had invested in an exclusive members-only discotèque-restaurant, the Factory (it was in fact a converted warehouse), on Santa Monica Boulevard. Frank and Mia were there one night when Mia ran into her friend Judy Carne, the actress who would shortly begin work on the *Laugh-In* television series and gain national popularity as the "sock it to me" girl.

Carne had been standing alongside Sinatra at the bar (his back was to her). She overheard a drunk ask Sinatra if he had any "grass" (marijuana) on him.

"Yeah, pal, I got plenty of grass," Sinatra said. "It's all at home—on my *lawn*."

Sinatra's bodyguards immediately hoisted the stranger away.

Judy Carne had decided not to introduce herself to the Legend, and mingled back into the crowd when she heard Mia's familiar voice calling her. Mia made her way through toward Carne.

When Judy greeted Mia, she noticed that Farrow "seemed unusually nervous." Mia quickly led her to the ladies' room and confided, "It's Frank. I can't seem to get away from his bodyguards. They're watching every move I make. I'd love to smoke a joint. Do you have one?"

Judy said she did, but "we can't do it here."

They went outside to a fire escape "and lit up," said Carne. The women recalled the fun they'd had when Judy and her then-husband, Burt Reynolds, used to visit the *Peyton Place* set.

The two women talked about what they were currently doing, and Mia admitted to her that *Rosemary's Baby* had taken its toll on her personal life. "I didn't have to ask her what she meant by that," said Carne.

Mia told her she was excited about the trip she was planning to India, telling her, "My brother and sister are coming along, as well as Mike Love, of the Beach Boys." She invited Carne to join them (her debut on *Laugh-In* would prevent the actress from taking Mia up on it).

Meanwhile Mia and Judy had to return to the disco—but the fire escape door had locked behind them! "We were both quite stoned," said Carne, "and I saw terror wash over Mia's face, afraid of the reaction she was likely to get from Sinatra."

Judy took Mia's hand, and "we slowly groped our way down the fire escape and around to the front of the club, where we made a giddy reentrance amid a blaze of flashbulbs."

The outside starting date for Mia's scenes in *The Detective* was fast approaching. Mia was doing the best she could to complete *Rosemary* on schedule, but that was Polanski's responsibility. *Rosemary* was *his* baby.

Certainly he was getting results. All the performances were working. One scene required the pregnant Rosemary to crave raw chicken livers, which she voraciously devours. A variety of items were substituted, but Polanski was unhappy with Mia's performance. It wasn't truthful enough for him, perhaps because Mia was having to fake her reaction.

Mia got the message and offered to try the scene eating actual chicken livers. Needless to say the cameras captured a very real moment as Mia ate the uncooked livers and retched with genuine disgust. Polanski was delighted.

Sometimes Mia's concentration on the set was so intense that she could endure no distractions. Once, when important studio corporate executives visited the set, Mia refused to work until the set was cleared.

One scene, filmed on location in New York, called for Mia, her character pregnant and in a daze, to stumble across Fifth Avenue. The traffic wasn't organized at all. They simply *did* it. Polanski said nobody would hit a pregnant lady, not on Fifth Avenue.

For the scene where Rosemary gets a blood test in the doctor's office, the procedure was graphically photographed. Mia later said it had been her suggestion that it should be *her* arm. Her doctor was there and took blood for a test of his own. Mia said she would do almost anything if there was a good enough reason.

• • •

There was finally a strong indication to the public of deep trouble in her marriage in October, when Paramount issued a press release stating that after production on *Rosemary's Baby* Mia would be taking off a month in January to travel to India and meditate with the mystic Maharishi Mahesh Yogi.

That same month she had taped a segment for a TV special, *The New Generation,* in which Ryan O'Neal interviewed her. She'd talked about Sinatra as though they were the happiest and most compatible couple in town. But when the show was aired in November, her remarks about Sinatra had been excised at her own request.

There is some confusion about the ensuing chronology of events. Columnist Suzy, a close Sinatra friend, later reported that the divorce was supposed to have taken place before Mia's journey to India, but Mia wanted to take the trip first. Suzy, previously very flattering in her reportage of Mia, now suggested in print that the actress gain weight and let her hair grow ("at least as long as the Maharishi's"), and Suzy advised Mia, now that she was no longer a teenager (and drifting swiftly out of Sinatra's protective orbit) to become less of a sprite and more of a woman.

There is evidence that Mia's trip to India was supposed to have taken place after she completed *Rosemary's Baby* and *The Detective,* which seems logical. There was a lot of money to be made from a picture toplining Sinatra and Mia.

Rosemary's Baby was over schedule, with important scenes remaining to be filmed or refilmed. Suddenly a deep crisis existed for Mia Farrow. She was slated to begin *The Detective* with Frank immediately. Sinatra damn well expected her to be there. He had been in production situations similar to Mia's and walked out. He was already shooting *The Detective* on location in New York, and the company had shot around Mia's scenes.

But by now Mia was so totally immersed in and consumed with *Rosemary's Baby* that she simply couldn't—or wouldn't—walk out on it. In any event Paramount supposedly wouldn't release her, despite Sinatra's badgering phone calls.

Richard Sylbert has said that Mia was determined to complete the picture. He went so far as to say it was too important to her to give up, either for any other role or for her marriage. In Sylbert's view her choice was clear.

Frank couldn't believe it—and couldn't live with this development. To make matters worse, on the eve of the day he'd delivered his ultimatum to her to walk off the picture, she'd gone to the Factory disco and danced with Sinatra's archenemy, Robert F. Kennedy. There were other reports that while at the Daisy, Mia had danced with and palled around with Peter Lawford. Lawford was out of Frank's orbit now, no longer in favor, and some say that Mia knew this and saw Lawford to assert her independence of Sinatra.

Frank was enraged and exasperated. He lost his temper. And rather than delay *The Detective* any further, Sinatra asked that his wife be replaced in the picture.

During this period Sinatra reportedly telephoned Mia at night and told her he couldn't live without her while during the day he planned their divorce.

Production on *Rosemary's Baby* ground on. For the nightmare sequence Polanski instructed all the actors to "strip." John Cassavetes, amused, asked Polanski if he didn't know that Mia was married to Frank Sinatra. Did Polanski want the ceiling to fall in on all of them? asked Cassavetes. Cassavetes also commented on how he'd never allowed his own wife (the actress Gena Rowlands) to do a nude scene. And here Cassavetes was, naked!

Mia didn't go nude, nor did Ruth Gordon or Patsy Kelly. Kelly said they'd worn flesh-colored garments.

This was for the scene in which Rosemary is raped by the devil, while the rest of the coven chant and observe. The scene called for Rosemary to be in a dreamlike state, but in fact Rosemary hasn't taken the drug she was fed and was awake. "This is really happening!" she cries out in horror at a climactic point. Mia enacted every emotion for this sequence, including orgasm.

Polanski was fanatical in getting the performances he deemed crucial. He, along with the cameraman and soundman, hovered closely over Mia as she writhed her way many times through the graphic scene.

Afterward the actor who portrayed the devil got up off the bed and politely introduced himself to Mia Farrow Sinatra. He called her Miss Farrow and told her what a pleasure it had been working with her. Mia couldn't believe it—he had certainly, albeit inadvertently, relieved the built-up tension, and Mia enjoyed telling the story afterward.

Actually *Rosemary's Baby* had an awful lot in it to offend Frank Sinatra's sensibilities, assuming the couple had remained together. Word had certainly seeped back to the Sinatra camp that Mia was involved in making one very avant-garde and kinky movie.

By now, though, Sinatra had implemented his decision. Mia received the official news one afternoon in her Paramount dressing room.

According to Garson Kanin, Mia was "shattered. And for reasons best known to Frank, he hadn't even told her. He sent his lawyer to see her and tell her."

Roman Polanski has recalled they had been ready for a take when Milton ("Mickey") Rudin, Sinatra's lawyer, showed up. He said he had urgent documents for Mia, and Polanski delayed filming.

When Rudin left and Mia was summoned to the set, there was no response. Polanski entered her dressing room—she was "sobbing her heart out." Polanski said she felt she'd been treated like a servant who'd been fired. She couldn't comprehend the contemptuous, calculated cruelty of the act.

Ruth Gordon was on the *Rosemary's Baby* set that day, and she comforted Mia and took care of her.

There was still a difficult scene to be filmed that very afternoon. No one in the company other than Polanski and Ruth knew what had just occurred, so a shaken Mia went out and went to work. Patsy Kelly recounted how she played the bedside scene with Mia, who was black and blue after the witches had pushed her, shoved her, kicked her, shook her, and pinned her onto the bed at least twenty times. Mia's attitude, recalled Kelly, was no-nonsense. At one point Ms. Kelly touched Mia's forehead and felt a high fever. She told Polanski they'd better get Mia to a doctor. Mia kept right on working.

Once the official announcement of the Sinatra-Farrow separation was released—and the cagey PR people waited until Thanksgiving weekend to divulge the news, knowing the public would be occupied with other things—there was nonetheless an explosion of publicity.

Sinatra's press agent issued a statement that the couple had no comment. A reporter had somehow obtained the private telephone number of the Bel Air mansion and reached a maid on the premises. Mrs. Sinatra had gone upstairs to her room, reported the maid, and hadn't had anything to eat all evening. Mia was in seclusion in the house, which was surrounded by Sinatra's bodyguards. A strict no-visitors policy was in force. Sinatra was in Palm Springs.

Hollywood sob sisters had a field day speculating on what had happened and what would happen next. Some said that one of the couple's disagreements concerned whether or not to have a baby (in view of Mia's future actions in this department, these rumors were not farfetched).

The press couldn't claim that either party was involved with anyone else, although Sinatra insider Earl Wilson claimed the crooner had not lacked female company during this difficult time.

Halfhearted attempts were made to link Mia's name romantically with Leonard Gershe and Roddy McDowall, both of whom were strictly close buddies of the actress's. Laurence Harvey's name came up too—definitely no romance there, admitted insiders. Quotes attributed to Mia at the time she had made *Dandy* in London had her stating that she'd never really been lonely until she got married and that it was awful to be given something marvelous and then have it taken away. But of course she'd been referring to the temporary separation necessitated by filming in London while her husband worked in the United States.

Things had changed. The quote had a totally different connotation now.

The marriage, while on the rocks, was not yet over. Not as far as Mia was concerned and apparently not for Frank either.

Chapter Ten

ONE EVENING late in 1967, in London, there was a party. Many film people were present. Andre Previn was a guest and the party was as deadly as he'd feared it would be. At one point, standing in the crowded, noisy, and oppressive room, he felt he had to get a breath of fresh air and stepped outside. Another person at the party had had the same impulse and she was outside too. Previn turned around and there she was. Mia Farrow.

They'd met before, several times over the years. Mia's godfather, George Cukor, had even introduced Previn to Mia, she later recalled. Their paths had crossed on the Fox lot, when Mia, nineteen, was making *Peyton Place* (it was around the same time she'd met Sinatra).

On this occasion Previn said hello to her and she remembered him. He asked her why she was leaving the party so early and she said because she couldn't stand it in there. He said that was interesting, because he couldn't stand it either. He invited her to have dinner. She accepted. They went out to dinner. According to Previn, that's all there was to it. Nothing further occurred.

Previn, sixteen years older than Mia, was one of the most creative and successful composer/arranger/conductors in the business. (He had won four Academy Awards, for his musical direction of the films *Gigi, Porgy and Bess, Irma La Douce,* and *My Fair Lady.*) He had enjoyed a brilliant career in Hollywood and was currently concentrating on a recording career in London, as well as on his duties as principal conductor of the Houston Symphony Orchestra back in the United States. He was also a married man. His current wife, Dory, was an extremely talented but troubled woman. The couple had recently collaborated on the theme song for the film, *Valley of the Dolls,* which was recorded by Dionne Warwick. It sold over a million copies. Dory Previn, who wrote the lyrics, said the song was taken directly from her own experience as a woman hooked on pills. She was, by her own account, wary of many things, including travel. Her husband's career demanded a great deal of travel. She wasn't willing, or able, to accompany him and the two were often apart.

At this juncture it appeared that Mia Farrow still harbored hopes, however slim, for a reconciliation with Frank Sinatra.

After Mia and Frank separated, she had bought a camper and driven from Los Angeles up to Carmel, California, to join friends. She announced that she planned to study with the Maharishi Mahesh Yogi, and learn his theories of Transcendental Meditation. Sinatra hadn't been pleased with this development. But it hadn't been, as people thought, a sudden, impulsive act on Mia's part. She had been into the study of Zen Buddhism for years. She was always open to improving the quality of her inner life.

Mr. and Mrs. Sinatra's mutual friend, Eddie Fisher, had encountered the Maharishi and offered an interesting and hard-edged opinion on the so-called guru or holy man. Fisher had met him on a flight to Los Angeles. The guru, noted Fisher, was traveling with a personal manager, and they were en route to an appearance at the Hollywood Bowl. Fisher introduced himself to the Maharishi and wanted very much to discuss some pressing personal problems with the renowned teacher. After all, the Maharishi was being avidly consulted by prominent show business stars, including the Rolling Stones; Shirley MacLaine; Donovan, the English folk singer; and the most popular singing group of all time, the Beatles, who had put him on the map.

The Maharishi knew who Eddie Fisher was, but thought it the wrong time and place to talk with him—it was too noisy on the plane, and there were too many distractions.

But Fisher persisted, and the Maharishi began discussing Transcendental Meditation with him. Fisher noted that as the guru spoke, he was also making notes of some figures on a menu. When they reached Los Angeles, Fisher looked at the Maharishi's menu. He recognized the numbers: admission prices, seating capacity. The guru had been calculating what his gross would be from the upcoming Hollywood Bowl appearance.

The Maharishi was in fact a well-educated former factory worker whose father had been an unimportant official in the Indian government. The Maharishi had graduated from the University of Allahabad in the early 1940s and worked in a factory for several years. But around 1947 he heeded an inner call to head for the hills to become a holy man. In the late 1950s, he returned to civilization and established the International Meditation Society. When the Beatles turned on to his teachings, he became a star himself.

Mia and her sister Prudence had first met the Beatles in London, just before filming began on *Rosemary's Baby*. The young men were impressed that Mia and Prudence weren't impressed by them (that of course was one of the perks of being Mrs. Frank Sinatra—very little impressed her as far as celebrity was concerned). The Beatles were particularly taken with Prudence, according to one version of events, and subsequently recorded a song ("Dear Prudence") inspired by her. It was Prudence whom the Beatles introduced to the Maharishi, and she in turn told Mia about him.

In any event, no matter how she met him, as far as Mia was concerned, he had much to offer.

She was at a crossroads. According to her own very candid account, she was overwhelmed. She felt she had cut off her freedom, closed off her privacy, and made her face a stigma. She had nothing, she felt, just the remnants of a marriage. She had no work. The all-consuming *Rosemary's Baby* was over— and suddenly she realized she had to go somewhere. She thought she had brought everything on herself, but what should she do? Where should she go? She said it had almost reached the point where she had nothing she wanted to live for. That was the frame of mind that caused her to go to India.

She'd been staying in her soon-to-be ex-husband's house and realized that that kind of lostness, that kind of unhappiness, was so destructive, and so bewildering that she latched onto what seemed to be the nearest hope. It *wasn't* a whim; her life was crumbling, her marriage was gone. She'd been looking at all the Western religions, and as far as she was concerned, they'd all seemed to stop at a crucial point.

Mia's interest in the Maharishi's teachings seemed almost intentionally misunderstood by the outside world. He was in fact opposed to drugs, including LSD, and his method of meditation strove to achieve a hidden source of strength that he called "pure thought." He was *not,* as Mia tried to explain, practicing or teaching some new religion. It wasn't that at all, she said. One could remain in one's own religion, whatever it was, and benefit from the discipline—*meditation*—out of which, Mia said, all sorts of wonders came.

Mia was always searching for the something big that was happening, that would add to or enhance her life and her being. The Maharishi was espousing a theory that appealed to her. It seemed full of promise and made good sense. She had first followed it out of curiosity, more than anything else, and also out of a sense that it offered something higher. She said she attacked it with a terrific amount of hope. It hit her as true, and for Mia that was enough incentive to pursue something new.

However, if she had hoped that the media would not pursue the guru and his followers on his home turf, she soon learned that India was not exempt from an onslaught of paparazzi. On arrival in India, she was dismayed and frightened to find them swarming everywhere. Like rats and locusts, they were on the ground and even in the trees.

But she was traveling light: Everything she owned was on her back. She could be remarkably inconspicuous, and she loved it. The world was her home and her feet were her vehicles.

She later told a close friend that the experience had been different from what she thought it would be, but she hadn't been disappointed, except a bit in herself. It had been scary in the Himalayas, but she admitted she was scared of just about everything at that time.

One account reported that Mia left the Maharishi's compound before the arrival of the Beatles. Another report said she was at the airport to greet them. By far the most bizarre and ludicrous account described John, Paul, Ringo, and George as "absolutely scandalized when they saw the great master Maharishi Mahesh Yogi making a pass at Mia on the banks of the Ganges.''

It seems that she left before the Beatles arrived and embarked on yet another adventure. She didn't know where she'd go next. She joined an American hunting party, but left when she realized they were not only inept, but were actually going to shoot a tiger.

She spent some time with a gentle, friendly group of beggars, who, it turned out, were lepers. Mia scrubbed herself red in the sacred Ganges.

She wandered and hitchhiked. She actually traveled for hours on the back of a cart carrying sugarcane. At one point she had to cross a bridge that had caved in over the Ganges. The water was only several feet deep, and Mia placed her few belongings on top of her head and strode across. Her belongings included a small camera, a book by Aldous Huxley, some clothes, and a bottle of soda. She was drenched when she finally reached a rural restaurant, where she encountered a friendly group of European hippies. They were en route to the island of Goa, which they described to her as a paradise.

She didn't accompany them, but proceeded to travel there on her own. For a while she lived alone on the seemingly endless beach and then sent for her brother, Johnny. The feeling of freedom was incredible.

She thought a lot about remaining in Goa. But she discovered she was too committed to what was happening in the world. She said she couldn't divorce herself from the problems facing so many people—the civil rights movement, the situation in Greece—and, she honestly admitted, she couldn't simply turn her back on her own personal problems. The easy way would be to remain on the island and create her own utopia. To escape.

But Mia never took the easy way.

• • •

Frank Sinatra hadn't been pleased with Mia's affiliation with the Maharishi. Mia, when asked what she thought Sinatra's opinion was regarding the whole thing, said she didn't know his opinion but she knew he was very interested in everything.

Eddie Fisher described Sinatra at this time as being close to the end of his patience with Mia. Fisher and Frank talked for hours about Frank's personal life, and Fisher's too. Eddie was embroiled in a rocky relationship of his own with actress Connie Stevens, who was pregnant with his child. Sinatra told Fisher he had to live up to his "moral obligations" and marry her. Sinatra even lent the couple his private plane so that they could fly to Puerto Rico to be married (which they did). The point of the story was that while Sinatra was telling Eddie to live up to his "obligations," Fisher felt that his pal Sinatra, the marriage counselor, then took a different course of action regarding his own life. When Mia flew to Miami in March for a summit meeting with Frank, he refused to see her. Fisher noted that apparently no reconciliation was on Sinatra's "obligation" agenda.

Frank was much more candid about his situation with Sammy Davis, Jr. Davis was having his own marital problems (his wife at the time was May Britt) and met with Frank to ask his advice. Sinatra admitted he and Mia were having problems, too, and told Davis they were breaking up because of a dispute over their careers.

Mia, always cognizant of what is in her best professional interests, continued to grant interviews (*Rosemary's Baby* was due for a June release), and the impression one came away with was that everything between Mia Farrow and Frank Sinatra was just great.

She went so far as to say that perhaps she and Frank would have a few children of their own, but they'd adopt lots of them—Vietnamese kids, who would have had a hard time without them. (She made good on this promise, but not with Frank Sinatra as the father.)

She admitted, however, that the thought of supporting and caring for kids was a bit overwhelming. She couldn't presume to take care of anyone right at the moment. She didn't have a road map for herself, let alone anyone else.

She still considered herself Mrs. Frank Sinatra. She admitted that there was no point in discussing her marriage because things were in a state of change. (But there was in fact now going to be a summer summit meeting with Sinatra. A lot would be decided at that time.)

An interviewer noted that Mia struck her as "one of those few extra-brilliant people walking a tightrope between madness and sanity, clinging to her fantasy life with one hand, to the real world with the other."

· · ·

Andre Previn has described the time he was spending with Dory, during this period, as increasingly like a patient/nurse relationship. Dory was mentally ill and required frequent stays in a sanatorium. She was a schizophrenic. The illness was a heavy burden for both of them. But their marriage was working on important levels, and Andre tried to keep it alive.

In Houston Previn was working on an updated version of *Peter and the Wolf.* He wanted to attract young people to the Symphony, and this seemed the perfect vehicle with which to do it. A narrator for the piece was required. Previn suggested a lady he said he didn't know all that well, and he wasn't certain she would do it, but he did know she was a hell of an actress: Mia Farrow.

Mrs. Frank Sinatra?! The Houstonians were not only delighted but, one assumes, greatly impressed. Mia agreed to do it.

Within a short while the Hollywood grapevine was buzzing with rumors about Mia and Andre.

• • •

Before the June release of *Rosemary's Baby,* Mia was in London at work on her next film, *Secret Ceremony,* in which she was starring with Elizabeth Taylor and Robert Mitchum. The director was Joseph Losey.

Elizabeth was portraying a whore, and Mia a confused girl whose fantasy life and real life blend in her mind. She believes the whore is her mother, and the convoluted plot—a strange one indeed for a "major" movie—seemed to revolve around what was real and what was imagined.

Losey hadn't been thrilled at the prospect of working with Mia, and at first, according to Losey, they had some personal problems. His early reaction was that she was "an hysterical amateur," but then he saw *Rosemary's Baby* and the dailies of Mia's first scenes with Elizabeth Taylor and he dramatically revised his opinion about her. He felt she was probably a genius.

Before coming to London to start the film, there had been a brouhaha in Rome involving Mia and the paparazzi. Mia had hoped to spend some time in Rome with her mother, but the newshounds had made it impossible, and Mia and Maureen met in London instead. There was some sort of a skirmish between Mia and the photographers as she was about to leave Rome, and Mia was made out as the heavy. She later said she'd simply been walking quickly and that the photographers were so oafish that they'd tripped over each other. A molehill was subsequently built into a mountain by ensuing coverage.

Anything involving Mia was news, and she was about to become even more of a headline lure.

She had been terrified about the reception *Rosemary's Baby* would receive. The film meant a great deal to her, both privately and professionally. More than anyone knew. She realized her future was at stake and knew she had put herself on the line. With *Rosemary's Baby* she was in effect saying this was it, this was what she could do. She was only human—insecurity and uncertainty have always been a universal affliction in the community of actors.

Rosemary's Baby became a stunning success, critically and commercially. Even the ad campaign—"Pray for Rosemary's Baby"—was a classic. The film raised Mia Farrow to the level of first-rank movie star. *The New York Times* review, by Renata Adler, said, "Mia Farrow is quite marvelous, pale, suffering, almost constantly on screen in a difficult role that requires her to be learning for almost two hours what the audience has guessed from the start."

Farrow's personal reviews were glowing. The impressive trade-paper reviews had begun appearing during the early days of filming *Secret Ceremony*. But then a disaster occurred, back in America, that was so devastating that production halted momentarily on the picture—everyone was too upset to work.

Robert F. Kennedy had been assassinated. Mia and Elizabeth funneled their frustration and rage into some positive action. They arranged for full-page ads in *The New York Times* and the London *Times* demanding more effective gun control. The actresses obtained the signatures of Charlie Chaplin, Barbra Streisand, Marlene Dietrich, and many other superstars in their efforts to ignite some action in the corridors of government.

Mia was more than willing to do her share, feeling that something constructive had to come out of the murderous act.

Maureen O'Sullivan on the set of *Tarzan and His Mate*. (Photofest)

John Farrow and Maureen O'Sullivan get married at last, 1937. (Photofest)

The Farrow clan: John, Maureen, baby Prudence, Michael, Patrick, Mia and John. Stephanie and Tisa were yet to be born. (Photofest)

Teenaged Mia poses with her mother on the *Peyton Place* set.
(Photofest)

With Ryan
O'Neal in
Peyton Place.
(Photofest)

The courtship of
Frank and Mia. At
the 1965 World
Series. (AP/Wide
World Photos)

At a formal affair.
(Photofest)

Forty-nine-year-old Frank Sinatra and twenty-year-old Mia Farrow wed, 1966. (Photofest)

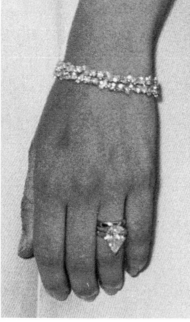

Mia's nine-carat diamond engagement ring and diamond bracelet. (AP/Wide World Photos)

In *A Dandy in Aspic*. (Photofest)

Mia with Ian Bannen in *Johnny Belinda*. (Photofest)

With Ruth Gordon in *Rose-mary's Baby*. (Photofest)

Playing the role
of proud parents-to-be
with John Cassavetes in
Rosemary's Baby. (Photofest)

With Tony Curtis and
Roman Polanski on the
Rosemary's Baby set.
(Photofest)

Elia Kazan
pays a visit.
(Photofest)

Signing
autographs.
(Photofest)

Mia, nearly unrecognizable in a brunette wig,
with Elizabeth Taylor in *Secret Ceremony*.
(Photofest)

With Dustin Hoffman in *John & Mary*. (Photofest)

Celebrity flower child: Mia with the Maharishi Mahesh Yogi. (AP/Wide World Photos)

Mia and Andre Previn during their courtship. (AP/Wide World Photos)

The first of Mia's children: twins Sascha Villiers and Matthew Phineas in England. (AP/Wide World Photos)

Seven years later, the children number six. Here Andre holds Fletcher while Mia sits at the piano with Summer and Lark. (AP/Wide World Photos)

Mia plays Daisy Buchanan to Robert Redford's Jay Gatsby in *The Great Gatsby*. (Photofest)

With son Matthew on the *Gatsby* set. (Photofest)

With Danny Kaye in a Hallmark TV production of *Peter Pan*. (AP/Wide World Photos)

Mia in *Death on the Nile*, with Simon MacCorkindale, Jack Warden, Maggie Smith, and Bette Davis. (Photofest)

In the forgettable *Hurricane*. (Photofest)

With Anthony Perkins during rehearsals for the play *Romantic Comedy*. (Photofest)

The start of a long collaboration: Mia and Woody Allen in *A Midsummer Night's Sex Comedy*. (Photofest)

Mia impressed the critics with her portrayal of a Mafia moll in *Broadway Danny Rose*. With Woody Allen in the title role. (Photofest)

With sister Stephanie in Allen's *The Purple Rose of Cairo*. (Photofest)

Mia with Barbara Hershey and Dianne Wiest in Allen's critical and commercial success *Hannah and Her Sisters*. (Photofest)

Maureen O'Sullivan, right, appears in *Hannah*, playing Mia's mother opposite Lloyd Nolan, center. (Photofest)

With Woody Allen in *Crimes and Misdemeanors*. (Photofest)

With Denholm Elliott in Allen's *September*. (Photofest)

With the children in 1985. Left to right, front row are: Fletcher and Lark. Rear row: twins Sascha and Matthew, Soon Yi, Mia holding Misha, with Summer Song at her right elbow. (AP/Wide World Photos)

With Woody Allen and their adopted child, Dylan. (AP/Wide World Photos)

That meant talking to reporters, but she was leerier than ever at the prospect. She wondered how interviews could mean anything when she didn't "know" someone even if she'd known them for a number of years, so how could it be any use meeting a reporter for an hour? She claimed that if she didn't say something interesting or sensational, then it was all made up for her and was all wrong.

This was a somewhat inaccurate allegation on Mia's part, considering all the authorized interviews with major magazines and newspapers she'd assented to over the years. In virtually all these instances the writers had been carefully screened by Mia's PR people as to their disposition to Mia Farrow and what they had written about her in the past. These in-depth pieces were very balanced in how they presented her. It was strictly the tabloid press that was guilty of sensationalism and mis-quoting.

She continued to give interviews. And one leading magazine journalist, Jack Hamilton, described her as "cagey."

While making *Secret Ceremony* she telephoned Sinatra, back in the United States, all the time. She loved to play his "Strangers in the Night." In London she lived in his apartment. She added a few touches of her own to the decor: some pop-art posters and a blowup of a newspaper article that claimed she was an agent for the CIA and was using the Maharishi's headquarters as a base of operations!

Sinatra was constantly on her mind. One evening Mia was dining with the Burtons and Robert Mitchum and his wife, Dorothy. Mia had a thought: She'd send Frank a postcard and they'd all sign it. However, one of her dinner partners would have to mail the card; she was worried that if she was seen mailing it, the postcard would be read.

Mia and Elizabeth Taylor got along famously. They worked well together on the set. They talked about everything, but very little about the roles they were playing. They didn't do much rehearsing. Everything seemed to work perfectly well without it, according to Mia. Both actresses seemed to function in the same instinctive way.

There was a strong sex scene in the script, between the characters played by Mia and Robert Mitchum. Joseph Losey and the writer, George Tabori, were sure Mia would do it (look at what she had done in *Rosemary's Baby*). They probably didn't believe that a body double had been used in certain scenes of *Rosemary*. It was currently very fashionable to have a nude scene in a film. Major actresses were doing them. That may have been a major reason why Mia, never one to emulate others, wouldn't do it. Also, the world seemed to think she'd already done one, so why do it again? And there was the practical Mia; she had learned from *Rosemary's Baby* that nudity offended a lot of people, and being offensive was hardly a smart career move.

Mia's gut instinct, regarding what she could and couldn't do, told her no. She charmed her way out of it. She said that that kind of scene was all right for the Burtons. They were older and had been married for a long time. But Mia said she just couldn't do it—and she didn't.

Mia was impressed with the relationship the Burtons appeared to have. Mia was working only with Elizabeth, but she said that working with one Burton was working with both. She admired the way the couple always contrived to be close to each other, arranging their work schedules so that they'd always be in close proximity. Mia thought Elizabeth seemed very happy and fulfilled.

Mia's social life was in frenzied high gear. She danced all night in her favorite London clubs with pals like Mike Nichols, Peter Cook, and David Hemmings. Sleeping was a waste of time, she said, a person only lived once. She figured she'd lived longer than most twenty-three-year-olds because she'd stayed up longer.

Not everyone was charmed by Mia Farrow. An English model, a very beautiful girl, was apparently jealous that her boyfriend was showing a great deal of interest in Mia. The model told a journalist researching a story on Mia, "Don't ever be taken in by Mia's act, that little-*boy*-lost routine of hers. You've only got to clock how bloody uncomfortable she is around other women to know how phony she really is."

Mia had to have developed a somewhat thick skin regarding catty social companions. A writer "friend" had this to say: "She looks innocent. She sounds innocent. But you just know she can't be Shirley Temple. Marriage to a guy like Sinatra, even such a *brief* marriage, doesn't leave a woman totally naive, completely unshrewd. She's got to have more angles than a Meccano set."

In any event Mia certainly knew how to have a good time. And somehow, after a night of partying, she was on the *Secret Ceremony* set, promptly at 8:00 A.M., lines memorized and ready to go, looking none the worse for wear.

Mia wasn't certain what her next film project would be. She said she wanted some time to put her life in order.

• • •

If Mia was a superstitious soul, there were all sorts of bad signs in the air. She was staying with her mother in Weybridge, England, and their house was ransacked by burglars. They were searching for the $85,000 engagement ring Sinatra had given Mia.

Farrow, one assumes, had by now reluctantly, grudgingly accepted the inevitable as far as her marriage was concerned. All her efforts at reconciliation had failed, and on August 16, 1968, a Mexican divorce was granted, on grounds of incompatibility "due to intolerable arguments." She'd refused to charge him with mental cruelty. She said she didn't seem to be able to please him anymore. She had her maiden name legally restored. The divorce was accomplished on a Friday, so that newspaper coverage would appear in the United States on Saturday, a low-circulation day.

First Civil Court Judge Lorenzo Holguin Asneros granted the divorce in Juarez, after a thirty-minute appearance by Mia. She looked different, somewhat like a hippie, with her hair dark brown, longer, and less severe than she'd been wearing it. Sinatra, needless to say, was not present.

According to his daughter, Nancy junior, Frank had been very sad and feeling empty over the whole affair. He was hurting, and he felt it would be harder for Mia because of her age. He knew the years had hardened him to withstand such emotional blows.

Sinatra received the news of the divorce after taping had wrapped on the dress rehearsal for a TV special. His close buddy Jilly Rizzo told him attorney Mickey Rudin had called: It was over.

Sinatra asked Don Costa, his musical director, if the tape had been okay from the orchestra's point of view. Assured it was, Sinatra then told the producers of his show to use the dress rehearsal; he couldn't do the show again.

He didn't snap out of it overnight. During production of *Lady in Cement* in Florida Frank was not exactly fun to work with. In addition to his other woes, he caught pneumonia. Frank summoned Ava Gardner, who flew to his side, but only for a short while. Many other female friends, old and new, were available to nurse him back to health. Mia kept telephoning his suite, but Frank wouldn't take her calls. She flew to Florida, but wasn't welcomed.

Frank junior was quoted as saying if the family could make it through Mia, he guessed they could endure anything.

• • •

Not long after the divorce Mia stated that perhaps it bothered Frank, not being young. She perceived that he felt things getting away from him. Her friends from India would come into the house barefoot and hand him a flower. In Mia's opinion that made him feel "square" for the first time in his life.

Sinatra had been shocked that Mia had requested no financial settlement. She'd said she wanted only his friendship. He would have been far more sanguine if she'd insisted on a million (which he'd been prepared to pay).

According to certain sources, after the divorce Mia was very lonely. She'd confided to one woman that she'd had a miscarriage, and the actress described Mia as "a real sad little girl, the walking wounded . . . she was terribly lonely."

When Sinatra telephoned to see how she was getting on, Mia asked him if she could come back. He told her he'd invited a couple of dozen pals to the house in Palm Springs for Christmas, and if she didn't object to the company, he'd be delighted to have her join them. She later said she would have taken the offer even if thousands of people were going to be there.

The whole "crowd" was there—the Goetzes, the Brissons, the Cerfs, the Hornblows, the Haywards, Harry Kurnitz, the Kanins. . . .

Sinatra was a happy man that weekend. Mia later said she'd never seen him that happy. But there was no reconciliation on his agenda.

There was a bizarre postscript to the Sinatra-Farrow saga. Mia was at the Daisy the night before the final decree was granted. According to one account, George Jacobs, Sinatra's trusted, longtime valet, was there with a date. Mia danced with Jacobs. When Sinatra learned of this, via a news item delivered by Rona Barrett, he was enraged. Jacobs was out of the fold. The man was later quoted as saying that Sinatra's henchmen had told tales to Sinatra, who should have known better than to believe them. It was a cruel blow for Jacobs, who couldn't believe Sinatra would do that to him, after all they'd been through together. Jacobs had been with Frank through many rough times.

As was the case with Mia and the divorce, the death blow, so to speak, wasn't delivered in person. The task again fell to Sinatra's lawyer to tell Jacobs he was fired.

● ● ●

Many years later Mia reflected on the Sinatra years and admitted that the age difference had finally mattered. She'd been too ill at ease with his remoteness and unable to fathom his complexities. She realized in retrospect that she'd been immature, and though she knew how much he needed it, she was not capable of being enough of a friend, however much she wanted to be. Mia acknowledged, too, that they had lacked understanding in everyday life as well. (Incredibly, she remained on speaking terms with Sinatra.)

Her friends were wondering how a person not accustomed to failure was going to adjust to a major defeat. According to Robert Mitchum, Mia was a fighter. She didn't linger on yesterday or the day before, an invaluable character trait if one is to survive.

Chapter Eleven

THE MIA-SINATRA DIVORCE was grist for Johnny Carson's nightly monologue on *Tonight*. He observed the occasion by commenting that there had been trouble in the Sinatra household when Mia dropped her Silly Putty in Frank's Poli-Grip (poor Sinatra—all the denture jokes when he didn't even wear them). At least there were no subsequent reports of Carson receiving any threatening phone calls.

Financially one would have thought Mia was in the big leagues by dint of her own star-salary. That, people assumed, was how she could afford no settlement from Sinatra (although reports claimed she'd kept the jewelry he'd given her, plus another gift—a magnificent sterling-silver service for forty-eight).

The trade press said Mia's price per picture was now $400,000 (big, but not near the $1 million-per-film, plus a percentage of the gross, that the Burtons and a select few others, including Frank Sinatra, commanded). However, Mia not only denied that she had much money, she said she was still working off her old 20th Century-Fox contract, signed years earlier.

The financial details of her marriage to Sinatra are also surprising. The couple had always kept separate bank accounts, and Mia had never used (nor did she take with her afterward) any of the money that had suddenly become available to her when she became Mrs. Sinatra. She hadn't thought of that as her money, she explained. It was his money. She reasoned that since she didn't really have money of her own to speak of, she had no fear of being broke. The idea of being alone was Mia's fear—"the dangerous loneliness"—not a lack of funds.

In movie-star terms Mia may have been on the low end of the financial totem pole, but her assets were sufficient for her to buy three hundred acres of land on Martha's Vineyard.

After *Rosemary's Baby* the Kanins were on their way to the Vineyard, where they were renting a house. "Mia came along with us," recalls Garson Kanin, "and it was on that trip that she was so besotted by the island that she immediately saw that she wanted to buy some property there.

"She immediately took off and went around all over the island, looking here and there to buy property. She wasn't too crazy about Edgartown—too 'towny.' She wanted much more open space. She wanted to be on the water.

"She eventually found a place—an enormous place, three hundred acres," relates Kanin, "a lot of it on the sea. She bought it on the spot. It didn't have much of a house. It belonged to a Boston clergyman, who was selling it. The best she could do was to begin adding to it." (Kanin adds, "I don't think she ever completed her dream of having a really lovely house put on the property.")

But Martha's Vineyard was a perfect place for Mia Farrow. She was left alone there. Her privacy was respected. It certainly was a place where she could contemplate and unwind. If and when she wanted excitement, she could return to her home in London.

• • •

In retrospect, she considered her breakup with Sinatra nobody's fault—except, perhaps, "the system's." But she also admitted she'd finally been carrying more than she could handle.

Mia and Peter Sellers, who had just ended his passionate, strife-torn marriage to Britt Ekland, found brief consolation with each other. They met through mutual pal Roman Polanski, who considered the couple to be true "soulmates." (Ekland found the teaming ironic since it had been Mia who'd replaced her several years earlier in the film *Guns at Batasi,* from which Sellers had forced Britt to withdraw.)

After Sellers, Mia dated John Phillips of the Mamas and the Papas. According to Phillips's autobiography, he and Mia once took mescaline together. "While tripping, Peter Sellers, who had dated Mia and was still in love with her, dropped in. He was upset that we were so stoned," wrote Phillips. And he remembered Sellers saying angrily, " 'I'll get you down from that drug if I have to pull you down by the pubic hairs.' "

Mia spent time with Phillips at the Joshua Tree Inn, a desert retreat. And according to the singer-songwriter, "We shared an intense passion." But Phillips concluded that Mia was a person with a deep, untouchable soul—a part of herself "that belonged only to Mia." John Phillips soon reconciled with his estranged wife, Michelle Phillips.

Back in Britain, a provocative incident involving Mia occurred in a London municipal court. There are several versions of what happened. In essence, the following transpired: Mia was in court because she'd allegedly told two police officers

what they could do to themselves as they tried to escort her
and several friends, including a black model, out of a nightclub
(described in some accounts as racially biased). The officers
had been summoned because of Mia's "boisterous" behavior.

Confusion reigned in court. According to one account,
when the magistrate instructed Mia to come forward, she
asked if she could first take off her clothes. This seems highly
unlikely. If Mia wouldn't take off her clothes for Roman Polanski or Joseph Losey, for the sake of art and the camera, it
wouldn't be in character for her suddenly to become an exhi-
bitionist in court. Mia later said she'd asked if she could take
off her *coat*.

After order was restored in the courtroom, the magistrate
asked Mia if she'd used foul language in front of the police
officers.

She stiffened with righteous indignation and wanted to
know what constituted such language. *War* was a foul word in
her vocabulary. Did he mean that?

The judge refrained from losing his temper. He meant
"obscene language."

"Dirty?"

That was correct. Mia, the consummate actress, had been
given her opportunity. A look of innocence radiated from her
countenance, as she asked if the word in question was *fuck,*
which was surely not a dirty word, explained Mia, since she
said it would be the nicest thing she could wish the judge. She
was upset that lovemaking, which she described as the very act
everyone owed their existence to, had been made a gutter word
to be put at the bottom of a trash barrel and stomped around
on.

This was the era of protest by discontented young throughout the world, and Mia was in the vanguard. Her efforts to
change the world made the usual headlines.

She and Andre Previn frequently made the London social scene together. Previn was a very trendy dresser, Mia a unique one, and the couple were highly visible everywhere they went. They had a constant companion with them at virtually all times: her notoriety. The press wouldn't leave her alone. Her private life had captured the imagination of the world. Like it or not, it was a situation Mia —and now Previn—and, back in the United States, Previn's wife, Dory—had to contend with.

Obviously Mia Farrow was a relationship-oriented person, and so was Andre Previn. He certainly wasn't intimidated by her celebrity (or anyone else's). He was quite a celebrity himself. His whole life had put him in close, creative contact with celebrities. He'd even worked with Sinatra, in his MGM days, and subsequently on a few occasions as pianist and arranger. The men hadn't become social buddies. Previn said he found Sinatra's kind of "power play a bit overwhelming." (After Previn became involved with Mia, he came off Sinatra's Christmas-card list.)

Secret Ceremony was literally raced through postproduction and into release in record time, hitting theaters in the United States by November, less than six months after it had gone into production. The studio wanted to take fast advantage of the pairing of Elizabeth Taylor and Mia, who was still on screens in *Rosemary's Baby.* But the studio also knew the picture was neither good nor, truth be told, commercial. It was, in effect, what was then termed "an art film."

Mia agreed to publicize the picture back in the United States. In appearance off screen Mia was very much into her flower-child period and was anxious to voice her intense feelings about what was going on in the world. What better way to accomplish this than to do a publicity tour, all expenses paid?

Universal had obtained a suite for her at the Plaza Hotel in New York (the O'Sullivan-Farrow apartment on Central Park

West must have been full-up), plus a full-time chauffeured limousine.

First on the agenda was a select press conference for Mia, arranged by the Universal publicity department, in one of the private dining rooms at the exclusive Laurent restaurant on East 56th Street (coincidentally, one of Salvador Dali's favorite haunts). Phyllis Schwartz, who worked with New York advertising and publicity chief Jerry Evans, recalled that when Mia first entered the room, "I wondered who the hell the girl was dressed in a sheet! It looked like she was wearing a flowing, king-sized white sheet." Mia, in fact, was dressed in her flower-child robes, and it appeared to be the first time that many of New York's movie reporters had encountered a flower-child celebrity in person.

During the next week the schedule went smoothly (Mia canceled only one appointment). The interviews were one-on-one, and Mia gave each journalist a rose carnation. She was interested in talking about things that mattered to her: Sally Trench and that amazing woman's work with the poor in the slums of London; the war in Vietnam; atomic weapons. She wanted to be a voice for what she termed the voiceless generation—the activists, the protesters, the dropouts who, one interviewer wryly observed, actually seemed to be making plenty of noise and with a very loud voice. One couldn't blame Mia for trying; but it was hard for some to accept social conscience from one who could, if she chose, return to either a plush sanctuary or the cocoon of a soundstage.

In the studio-provided limousine, en route to another interview, the car passed the Sutton Theater on New York's East side, where *Secret Ceremony* was playing. Mia glanced up at the theater, where her name and Elizabeth Taylor's were emblazoned on the marquee. Mia said, in an enigmatic voice, "Poor

Elizabeth." What exactly she meant by that has remained her secret.

Back in the suite she received a call from Frank Sinatra. It seemed, to an outsider at least, that she sounded friendly but guarded. She could have been speaking to an aunt or uncle.

Mia had gotten wind of a pending story about her that one of the major newsmagazines was working on. She didn't want the story to run—and got to work on accomplishing just that. It was obvious how direct and efficient Mia Farrow could be; no PR man or woman could have been more effective (or *as* effective, under the circumstances). She got on the phone herself, right through to the managing editor of the magazine, and discussed the matter with him. She was very blunt, but not discourteous. She spoke in very practical terms and pointed out that there was no point in running the story because certain facts would be missing; if they waited, she promised to cooperate with them at a later date. Mia was persuasive and the story was canceled.

Despite the massive publicity campaign and the presence of two top stars, *Secret Ceremony* flopped. In the film Mia had worn a long, black wig. It was not the look she had sported in *Rosemary's Baby,* a look that had caught on all over the world. But, as the world would discover, Mia would look different in *every* picture.

Mia's career was not tarnished by the box office failure of *Secret Ceremony.* She had signed for *John and Mary,* and would costar with Dustin Hoffman. It was a contemporary love story (the lovers attempt to get to know one another *after* they've spent a night in bed), and how could that miss? (famous last words). Hoffman, after *The Graduate* and *Midnight Cowboy,* was the hottest young male actor in the country, and Mia's star was still firmly in orbit as the grosses on *Rosemary's Baby* continued to roll in.

Andre Previn's career was in high gear. In June 1968, nearing his fortieth birthday, he'd become the official conductor for the London Symphony Orchestra, and it was to prove both an exhilarating and a stormy relationship. It was the first time an American conductor had been signed to head a major British orchestra.

As his star had risen in England, it fell in Houston. Previn's "pop life-style," his headlined romance with Mia, was blamed. Supposedly the Houston Symphony's staid board of directors had sternly disapproved.

Previn subsequently dismissed that as nonsense (although, tongue-in-cheek, he admitted it was a good thing he wasn't running for Parliament). He said the Mia publicity had had nothing at all to do with his problems with the Houston Symphony. Previn, like Mia, was a rebel. There had been a personality clash between Previn and the board. He wanted to tour the orchestra in the provinces, make it available to the less affluent. He wanted to launch a TV program in Houston, to expand the audience for symphonic music and draw in young people. The Houstonians were aghast. They couldn't have cared less, however, about his personal life. Probably they found it titillating. Mia, newly divorced, and Andre, still a married man, were openly sharing hotel rooms. In a few months they'd begin living together.

• • •

Early in 1969 Andre was in London working with the London Symphony. Mia was shuttling between London and New York, where she was filming *John and Mary*.

The film's director, Englishman Peter Yates, asked Mia if all the press attention heaped on her had ever brought on an identity crisis. So many opinions about her had been expressed in print. Her answer was to the point: no. All the hoopla never clouded what she was to herself, only to others. She said that most accounts were so opinionated and so biased and so righteous that some of the writers, in Mia's opinion, had created a completely fictional person and not her at all. She said it didn't affect her all that much now. She thought she had gotten over all that hurt.

Yates, like most everyone who met Mia, was taken by her. He said he was convinced she had only just stepped out of a convent, all scrubbed and holy and chaste. It was sometimes a shock to remember who and what she really was.

It was the height of the flower-child revolution. It seemed that almost everyone was experimenting with drugs. In her trailer dressing room on location shooting in Manhattan at Thirty-first Street and First Avenue, Mia kept a marijuana plant. She watered the plant frequently and remarked to a visitor that it needed a lot of love. The plant had been a gift from the film crew.

One day some flower-children friends of Mia's visited her in the trailer. She was very happy to see them and put them at ease with some white wine, which she served in paper cups. When someone noticed the marijuana plant, he tried to make a reefer, but the leaf he'd picked was either too green or too moist, he complained. Unsuccessful attempts were made to roll a joint, as a friendly, unsuspecting policeman stood guard outside the trailer keeping the public from intruding on the movie star.

Mia continued to fly to London at every opportunity. In London Mia and Andre were photographed together often. He met her flights at the airport. They frequently attended the theater and were seen embracing backstage after a Festival Hall concert.

Andre was protective of Mia. He said that because of the way she dressed and behaved and the things she talked about, she was perceived as some sort of freak (as compared, for example, to all-American Debbie Reynolds). But Andre emphatically stated that as far as he was concerned, Mia was the straight one and Debbie Reynolds was the freak.

Reporters in the United States pressed Mia for information on when they were getting married. She answered that marriage or no marriage, she'd been spending time in London with the one man she felt she could live with for the rest of her life.

Chapter Twelve

As EVERYONE KNOWS, there are at least two sides to every story.

Dory Previn's version of events concerning the breakup of her marriage to Andre Previn paints Mia Farrow as a calculating, selfish young woman who knew Dory was an insecure and neurotic person and knowingly took advantage of her weaknesses and stole her husband. As far as Dory was concerned, she regarded Mia as a femme fatale in flower child's clothing. (Dory subsequently wrote a hit song about it all, "Beware of Young Girls.")

Mia, on the other hand, has said that Dory's version of events simply wasn't true. Period. And she described the song Dory wrote as "tasteless." (Dory was indignant at this response. She felt that if anything the song deserved more discussion.)

Dory Previn has recalled Mia's entrance into the lives of the Previns, not in London, as Mia and Previn have remembered it, but in California. According to Dory, Mia had been visiting with their next-door neighbors, director Alan Pakula and his wife, Hope, and came all the way across the patio to meet the Previns. Dory was flattered and impressed. Mia was indeed glorious-looking, luminous, and youthful with a voice "gently buffed by good schools and privilege." She described Mia as "lace-curtain Hollywood," "second-generation MGM."

Mia wanted to be their friend, and Dory was more than eager, although Andre, as she recalled, seemed less impressed.

The Previns socialized with Mia. Dory has remembered an evening at a restaurant—she, Andre, Mia, and Mike Nichols. In so many words Mia proclaimed to Nichols that she'd be a wonderful Peter Pan. She said she'd been to Never-Never Land a number of times.

Andre's annoyed reaction to her statement surprised Dory, who wondered why Mia always irritated him, although Dory admitted to herself that she was pleased at this. Dory was over forty and she found twenty-four-year-old Mia's physical perfection threatening.

She recalled two times Previn had seen Mia less than perfect—once, when the young actress drank too much at the home of composer Leslie Bricusse and the Previns had to drive her home; and at another party, at Adolph and Phyllis Green's. That evening Dory was pleased to observe that Mia wasn't a graceful dancer; she was dancing to rock music (Dory was embarrassed that she herself couldn't do any of the current dances) and her movements reminded Dory of a stork.

Dory Previn has also recalled she had once been invited to Mia's home when Mia was still Mrs. Sinatra. Andre was away, with the Houston Symphony, and Mia had asked Dory why she wasn't with her husband. Dory explained she was terrified of flying. Of crashing. (Dory not only feared flying but also taking trains.) Mia's reply would have been no surprise to those who knew her well; she said the following to Dory, in effect: "So what if you crash? It's your only life. Live it *now.*" Dory reflected on how easy it was for a twenty-four-year-old to think that way. She proceeded to confide her innermost fears to the intelligent, sympathetic, and articulate Mia Farrow—that Andre wasn't happy being alone in strange hotel rooms. Dory's nightmare, she revealed to the younger woman, was that one day someone would hold a hand out to her husband, "and out of loneliness, he would accept."

She later recalled that the last time she saw Mia was when the actress came to the Previns' home with Mia's then best friend Liza Minnelli. It was one of those evenings out of an MGM movie, with Andre at the piano and Liza performing. He knew all the obscure songs Liza wanted to sing, and Dory was not charmed by Liza's enthusiasm and effusiveness over Andre's talent. Nor did she like the way she kept touching him. Through it all, recalled Dory, Mia was on the sidelines, quietly observing. When the two young women finally left, Dory recalled that she resolved that it was Liza who would not be invited again.

• • •

In early 1969, when Oscar nominations were announced, Dory Previn was in the running for the song she had written with Fred Karlin, "Come Saturday Morning," for the film *The Sterile Cuckoo.* The movie, starring Liza Minnelli, was a box-office dud, but the song was a hit.

In a real surprise development, Mia Farrow was not nominated as best actress for *Rosemary's Baby,* while costar Ruth Gordon was nominated (and won) in the best-supporting-actress category. Apparently nonconformist Mia, her success and celebrity notwithstanding, wasn't too popular with her peers.

Mia subsequently revealed that not receiving a nomination had been a blow. She said it was the shock that helped her to put everything else in her life in perspective. There had been a rumor circulating that Sinatra had been against Mia receiving an Oscar nomination. Mia said she'd never heard such a rumor. It was in fact ridiculous since it implied that any one person could prevent or cause an Oscar nomination which, as Steven Spielberg can well affirm, is simply not true.

Andre Previn, in Europe, wrote to Dory congratulating her on her Oscar nomination. Dory received the letter in the mental hospital she had been admitted to in Culver City, California. According to her recollections, the letter included a request for a divorce, and it was the first time, according to Dory, that the matter had been brought up.

Andre Previn later emphatically denied that anything regarding a divorce had been mentioned in the letter. He cited Dory's confused state at the time and claimed he discussed a divorce with her in person.

Around May 1969 Mia discovered she was pregnant. Dory learned of the situation from an erstwhile friend, a columnist who had tracked her down to tell her the news and to see if Dory had any comment. Dory's marriage to Previn, as everyone knew, had been childless.

Dory seethed with anger. A few weeks later, in a desperate state, she told her doctor that she needed a pass to leave the hospital in order to attend an important recording session. The request was granted.

Unknown to her doctors, Dory (whose fear of flying was legendary) had booked herself on a flight to London. Even in her condition she was determined somehow to salvage her marriage. She telephoned her husband to meet her at Heathrow Airport. After all, she reasoned, he met Mia frequently at the airport, according to the newspapers. Previn replied he'd have their mutual friend Robert Carrington meet her.

Dory never made it to London. She became hysterical and behaved irrationally on the plane before it left Los Angeles. She tore off her clothes and ran bare-breasted down the aisle. She shouted threats at a fellow passenger (a priest, no less).

It seems hard to believe, but this low point in Dory's life, in retrospect, was said to be the beginning of a turnaround in her condition. From this point she would very slowly begin to improve. Her hostility and outrage had a focus—Mia's pregnancy—and she initially told herself Mia had intentionally become pregnant in order to steal Andre away. The hate she felt for Mia, for Previn, and for herself apparently had a cathartic effect and somehow enabled her to get through her ordeal and on the road to recovery.

Certainly Previn felt deeply guilty about Dory's total breakdown. It took a heavy toll on him, although to the outside world this wasn't evident. One of Dory's doctors, according to Previn, actually helped him by telling him he had to decide whether he was going to be one lady's male nurse or another lady's husband. He made his choice. But Previn was too intelligent and too sensitive not to have been deeply troubled and guilt-ridden by the traumatic breakup of his marriage, regardless of whose fault it was—or wasn't.

Many years later, looking back, a recovered Dory Previn was not unsympathetic to Previn's dilemma. She realized and admitted her own shortcomings in relation to her former husband. She acknowledged that she had been suffering an identity crisis all along and had willingly lived in his shadow. Dory actually wondered, ten years after the fact, how Andre had been able to stay with her as long as he had (ten years). Dory theorized that long before Mia had entered the picture, she'd abandoned a world of reality for her own inner world, one that Andre, understandably, could neither share nor relate to. But it took many years for the breach to heal.

In 1969 the press had a field day reporting the "shameless, open" affair between Andre Previn and Mia Farrow. The couple traveled "brazenly" from England to the United States, where Previn was collaborating with Alan Jay Lerner on the new Broadway musical *Coco,* based on the life of Coco Chanel.

Mia Farrow was having an out-of-wedlock baby. She was the first big star to do this since Ingrid Bergman had defied convention in 1949. Would Mia, like Bergman, be vilified? Would she be banned from films—and branded an outcast?

At the same time Mia's name was in the news because of a bizarre and shocking tragedy that occurred in August 1969. The horrible Manson murders were committed in California, and the world was stunned. *Rosemary's Baby* director Roman Polanski's beautiful and pregnant wife, Sharon, was slain, along with her former lover Jay Sebring and other friends who were at the home the Polanskis were renting from Doris Day's son, Terry Melcher. (Insiders speculated that Sharon's baby was in fact Sebring's.) Polanski wasn't there that night and escaped the horror.

The press made much of the speculation that *Rosemary's Baby* appeared to the superstitious to have been a jinxed endeavor that was pouring ill luck on all who had been associated with it.

• • •

Katharine Hepburn was making her musical debut in *Coco* and was very nervous about it. The young Michael Bennett was choreographer. (He would eventually take over the whole production, replacing the director, Michael Benthall.) The producer was Frederick Brisson, Rosalind Russell's husband. (The Brissons had been Mia's companions on the Sinatra-chartered yacht fiasco only four years earlier.)

As the opening of *Coco* approached, Andre and Mia were

living together in New York. Mia was very conspicuously pregnant. But cohabiting and illegitimate children were almost chic at this point in time. Unmarried couples were commonplace. And a phenomenon called Woodstock had occurred only a few months earlier—the gathering of hundreds of thousands of hippies, flower children, and believers in a new order of things, coming together peacefully in a small town in upstate New York and luxuriating in a total communal experience. They were there to celebrate life, to make music, make love, and in some cases take drugs.

Mia Farrow was certainly a vocal member of the Woodstock generation, and sometimes some of her ideas clashed with those of her older friends.

Garson Kanin has told of a friendly but emotional discussion he had with Mia about marijuana. The day after an evening when Kanin and his wife, Ruth Gordon, had left one of Mia's parties early, Mia wanted to know whose idea it had been to leave early, Kanin's or Ruth's. Mia pressed him for an answer, and he admitted they had left early because Ruth had become dizzy (although Ruth hadn't known why). Kanin thought he knew why. He told Mia it was because his wife "was beginning to pick up a bit of a contact high, wasn't she?" (A contact high results when someone, who is not smoking, inhales the smoky air at a pot party.) Mia didn't agree with Kanin, but even if it was so, she said, did it matter?

Kanin became angry. He didn't feel prepared to enter into a debate with Mia on the pros and cons of marijuana. He said he didn't know whether *she* did or not, and didn't want to know, because it wasn't anybody's business, but he said that some of those at the party really "blew that room out," with one of the guests "closing doors and windows and plugging crevices, so no wonder Ruth began to—"

It was Mia's turn to express anger. She pointed out that

while pot was illegal, hard liquor, which was every bit as dangerous and potentially deadly, *was* legal.

Kanin, of course, didn't disagree, but two wrongs didn't make a right. As far as Kanin was concerned, the real highs in life came from turning on *to* life—music, books, lovemaking, nature. His point was that artificial turn-ons diminished one's capacity for the real ecstasies.

Mia got the point (she didn't say whether or not she agreed with it) and loved and respected her friend for debating it with her.

Maureen O'Sullivan's attitude on pot produced no clashes with daughter Mia. Maureen was both downright liberal and one-hundred-percent commonsense in her approach to it. She was in favor of legalizing marijuana. She felt the most dangerous thing about it was that it was illegal. If it were legal, she pointed out, young people would never fall into the hands of pushers who put them on hard drugs. And she admitted she had tried pot but didn't like it. She found it terribly overrated. She preferred a cocktail.

She had some advice for parents: Instead of having "this horror of the idea of marijuana," they should try it. Then they would know what their children were doing.

Maureen said she had tried meditation too. At one time she had a regular weekly session with a swami, without ever having to leave New York City. He was located nearby, on West End Avenue. While she was cheerfully philosophical about meditation, she had found she simply didn't have the patience.

She dismissed all the gossip and innuendo swirling about Mia during this time, and said she found all the talk boring. She was very proud of Mia; her daughter had guts. She took life and wrung what she wanted out of it. How else, wondered Maureen, should a human being live?

Maureen was no slouch in the guts department. She was back on Broadway, in a revival of *The Front Page.* She said it took guts to go out there on stage every night. A woman had to have guts to stay in the mainstream. And a woman, said Maureen, in a statement not likely to have endeared her to the women's-lib movement, should have a man. Maureen was not of the going-out-with-the-girls persuasion. (She was reportedly having a romance with her *Front Page* costar, Robert Ryan.)

Maureen pointed out that widows of celebrities dined alone, which was fine before 5:30 in the evening, but after that, Maureen repeated, a woman should have a man.

She said she knew a dozen women at home at that very moment without a man, and according to Maureen, they were trapped. Many restaurants wouldn't serve a woman alone, or else the waiters made her feel uncomfortable, she observed. She'd rather stay home and make her own scrambled eggs.

Her eighteen-year-old daughter Tisa was living with her at the time in her Central Park West apartment. Mia often dropped over, and there were heartfelt discussions among the family on what was happening in the world, in the country, in New York. Mia was miffed, indeed offended, that a march for peace, involving thousands of people, would get modest coverage in the press while her own inane opinions often ended up on page one.

Tisa Farrow was a beautiful, blue-eyed brunette, a soft-spoken, gentle girl. Her resemblance to Mia, facially, was very strong. Her figure, however, was voluptuous; she referred to herself as the fat one in the family. Tisa was an individualist just like Mia—and definitely a member of the Woodstock generation (they were "the dirties, the weirdos," she joked). She had seen Stanley Kubrick's *2001* thirty times and was a high school dropout. She had attended college for a day. She had been a waitress and enjoyed it because she liked pleasing people (and had already spent all the money she'd made waitress-ing).

Her current boyfriend, Doug, was coming out of a bad period. At one point he'd gone out on the ledge outside the apartment window, eleven stories up, and wandered from window to window. Fortunately that crisis was over.

Tisa was going to pursue an acting career. She recognized the pitfalls of being the sister of a celebrity. She said she couldn't help but feel she had something to live up to. Comparisons would be inevitable. She'd be either as good or not as good as Mia. The prospect was not going to deter her. If she turned out to be a lousy actress, she could always return to waiting on tables. (She had worked at a Schrafft's, a Mexican restaurant in Greenwich Village, and an Indian restaurant on the West Side.)

Maureen seemed totally comfortable with her children's life-styles. (Years later, however, when Mia Farrow's kids were in their teens, Maureen remarked on how they weren't putting Mia through what she had suffered when her kids had entered adolescence.)

When *The Front Page* closed, Maureen intended to visit with her son Patrick and his wife in Vermont. O'Sullivan said she didn't want to lean on her children, but she always wanted to communicate with them, and thought she did.

She was an active lady. In addition to performing, she was contemplating writing her memoirs and was an executive with Wediquette, a wedding consultant firm (although formal weddings were hardly de rigeur at this time).

• • •

All the negative publicity Andre and Mia were receiving was actually about to result in a positive career break for Previn. It was a frantic time for him, but sandwiched in between emergencies regarding *Coco,* he received a visit from one Herbert Chappell, a television producer for England's BBC. The producer realized the publicity Previn had been getting proved he was of interest to the public, and he wanted Previn to helm a series of TV broadcasts featuring the London Symphony Orchestra along the lines of the highly successful TV specials hosted in the United States by Leonard Bernstein. Previn accepted. If these shows were successful, it would greatly enhance his earning power and he was determined to provide a comfortable home for Mia and their imminently due child. He was also determined to make their relationship work.

On December 18, 1969, *Coco* opened amid an explosion of publicity but received only mixed reviews, as far as the book and score were concerned. Katharine Hepburn, of course, was the attraction and she ensured the production's commercial success, at least as long as she remained in the cast. (Everyone wondered why Frederick Brisson hadn't cast his wife in the role. Roz Russell had proven her value as a huge Broadway draw in *Wonderful Town* and *Auntie Mame.* One version claimed Coco Chanel hadn't wanted Roz to portray her. In fact Ms. Russell had cancer, and her health didn't permit taking on such an arduous assignment.)

Previn and Mia were slated to return to London after *Coco* was launched. First Andre supervised the recording of the cast album. It was reportedly a disagreeable experience. The chief recording engineer and Previn were at odds, and according to one account, "there was so much music on the record that it was squeezed down too tight and played a trifle too fast. The result was that Katharine Hepburn sounded rather like Donald Duck." The entire record had to be done over.

Finally Previn and Mia returned to London to await the birth of what now appeared to be twins, and to await Andre's divorce.

They rented a house in Belgravia, from super-model Jean Shrimpton. The rooms were tiny, and there was only one bathroom. Quite a contrast to the lavish Sinatra abodes Mia had been accustomed to (but a lot more comfortable and luxurious than what had been available in India). But the couple didn't mind the house. It was the sudden appearance of the paparazzi that alarmed them. The house was ideally located for easy access by the horde of fourth-estaters that now descended— and remained—virtually in the backyard, the front yard, and on the streets.

The couple felt like prisoners. They literally couldn't go to a food store without being followed by photographers. Things got worse. One morning Previn spotted a photographer who had actually climbed into a tree, his camera equipped with a telephoto lens, and pointed inside the house.

Unlike Frank Sinatra, however, Previn had no desire or ability to wage war with the press. A practical man, he very cleverly contacted a leading public relations lady, Wendy Hanson, who gave him very good advice: hire a photographer, pose for him, then let him sell the photos to all the newspapers. Previn wisely followed the advice. Top lensman Terry O'Neill got the assignment and shot a series of Victorian-style photos of Mia and Andre (with Mia's bare toes visible in some shots), which were then sold and circulated worldwide.

In some of the shots Andre's hand rested on Mia's tummy ("Our Twin Babies," ran one newspaper's caption), and one of the stories pointed out that the couple were "members of the set that practices a new kind of morality. Where love is more important than marriage." (John Farrow would have had to go into seclusion after this—or on a very long retreat.)

But the ploy had worked. The press no longer patrolled the premises and the couple could once again resume a social life and go to the theater and out to dinner.

Mia gave birth to her boys, Matthew and Sascha, in February. Seven months later Andre's divorce from Dory became final. On September 10, 1970, Andre and Mia were wed.

There were matters to settle back in Los Angeles now that Previn was divorced. Dory got to keep their valuable collection of paintings, but Previn could sell the Bel Air house and would use the proceeds to buy the house of his dreams in England.

Real estate agents assumed the renowned conductor and his film-star wife would only consider the most lavish and ostentatious of estates. Previn, in fact, was not one for ostentation (he drove a modest car), nor was Mia. They were both quality-oriented, of course, and he was not opposed to many of the luxuries of life. He patiently searched for exactly the right place. There was one feature Previn was insisting on: There had to be lots of trees.

He finally found their dream estate in Surrey, outside of London. It was located between two small towns, Dorking and Reigate. The main house was seventeenth-century, a former tavern. There was a smaller thatched cottage (only about fifty years old). Trees (including one three-hundred-year-old oak, "alive when Mozart was alive") were in forestlike abundance on the twenty acres of grounds. There were streams and deer. Mia was ecstatic. The couple named their new sanctuary the Haven.

Amusingly, neighboring villagers anticipated a very high-profile family (the publicity had of course reached into the hinterlands) and were pleasantly surprised to discover a couple seeking peace, quiet, and privacy. The Previns were not only liked but protected by the local townsfolk. If a journalist turned up in the town pub asking how to get to the Previn house, the response was, "No idea how to get there." And if a reporter actually located the Haven, Andre simply phoned the local policeman, who would come over and inform the intruder that his camera might be irreparably damaged if he were to be an uninvited visitor a second time.

Previn's career with the London Symphony soared. In addition to his enormous musical talent, taste, and sense of showmanship, Previn was a real diplomat at dealing with the musicians, and they respected him and responded to him. His television shows for the BBC became tremendous successes and established Previn as a genuine personality. His sense of humor was a great asset, too, and he subsequently hosted a successful weekly talk show, *Andre Previn Meets* . . . (Mia was a guest one week.)

Mia certainly proved to be no phony in her claim that she was family-oriented, and now that she was a mother, she did not abandon her new twins to a nanny (although the babies did have a nanny during the week) and grab a hot new film role back in the States. Contrary to later reports, though, she continued making films. ("It wasn't as if she was sitting around the house," Maureen O'Sullivan remarked, recalling these days.)

Mia and Previn worked together twice, the last time in February 1971. She read the title role in Arthur Honegger's *Joan of Arc at the Stake,* with Previn conducting the London Symphony and a huge chorus. (Ingrid Bergman had performed the part years earlier.) Mia found speaking in time to the music somewhat difficult, and she wasn't thrilled with the final results (nor were critics). She hoped she and Andre would have an opportunity to do it again (they didn't).

She said she loved the prospect of appearing in a musical that Andre might write for her (this never materialized). She also said Previn knew what was best for her professionally and that she adored her agent but would take Previn's advice over his anytime. She admitted, however, that if Previn and her agent advised her against tackling a role she wanted, she'd do it anyway.

When the subject of Frank Sinatra came up in interviews, as it inevitably did, Mia usually clammed up. But she did reveal, on one occasion, that Sinatra often called Maureen to find out how Mia was getting on. And Mia said that Frank would be welcome at the Haven anytime, although she couldn't immediately imagine any reason he would want to come.

Mia got a taste of what it was like to have to contend with "another woman" in *her* husband's life. Previn, hardly conventionally handsome or physically imposing (one critic described him as "gnomish"), was considered a very attractive man by many members of the opposite sex. Previn considered himself far from handsome, but allowed that perhaps talent was an attraction in a man just as good looks were in a woman.

Women who were writers seemed to be attracted to Andre Previn. His first wife had been a writer. And so was Gillian Widdicombe, a beautiful young music critic for the London *Financial Times*. Her initial reviews of Previn's concerts with the London Symphony were not enthusiastic, and she even politely ridiculed him regarding his penchant for attracting publicity.

However, according to Previn's biographers Bookspan and Yockery, once she got to know Previn the man, her reviews of his work became quite enthusiastic.

Reporters on other newspapers were not unaware of, or reluctant to call attention to, the "close friendship" that existed between Previn and Widdicombe, who were "frequently seen out together." Ms. Widdicombe parried queries from fellow journalists with the aplomb of a seasoned movie queen. She didn't make any outright denials of anything.

Previn and the London Symphony toured a great deal. Gillian Widdicombe was one of the critics who traveled with them on a highly publicized and very successful tour of Russia in 1970. Mia had had to remain in Surrey, since one of the twins was ill.

Even before she had become acquainted with Andre, Ms. Widdicombe had not written favorably of Mia Farrow Sinatra Previn. She had described her as "his unusual wife who comes to concerts."

As Gillian Widdicombe's friendship with Previn developed, so apparently did the hostility between Gillian and Mia. Andre, on occasion, invited both women to certain musical happenings—recording sessions, for example. Some observers found the situation "bizarre," with, according to one source, "his wife and girlfriend in the hall at the same time. To everyone's relief, they just avoided looking at each other."

One cannot help but comment that Frank Sinatra would never have orchestrated such a situation, certainly not in public.

More drama was in store.

At one London Symphony concert at Festival Hall Mia was seated directly behind Gillian Widdicombe and, according to observers, seemed delighted at the opportunity "to make life uncomfortable for her rival. Mia slumped down in her seat so that she could dig her knees into Gillian's seatback." At intermission "both women went backstage and staged a shouting match over which of them should or should not be admitted to the conductor's dressing room."

One can imagine how gleefully Dory Previn might have reacted to this purported scene, which was observed by many members of the company, but the payoff was that "none of it seemed to have any adverse effect on Andre's conducting." Previn obviously had the ability to keep his personal and professional lives totally separate.

In time the Andre-Gillian situation simply seemed to fade

away. Previn's marriage to Mia would in fact endure, and apparently flourish, for a few years.

"Mia was tremendously proud of him and at least at times appreciated what he did," observed their friend Adolph Green. But Previn understood that Mia's interest in music was "passive, not active."

Chapter Thirteen

IN THE SUMMER of 1971 Mia, Andre, and the twins journeyed to the United States. Previn was conducting a concert in Los Angeles at the Hollywood Bowl, and Mia was going to star in a movie-for-television, *Goodbye, Raggedy Ann*. It was a property about a struggling young actress that 20th Century-Fox had supposedly bought for her back in the *Peyton Place* days. She loved the script and, over her agent's objections, made the movie. (Although some thought Andre was opposed to her working, it was through Andre that the script got into Mia's hands.)

Gossip at the time implied that Mia had agreed to do the picture so that she could take a vacation from Andre. She had admitted she'd planned to come to the United States anyway, but with Previn and the babies by her side, so much for the gossip. The couple rented a house in Beverly Hills for the duration of their stay.

Once again, and hardly for the last time, Mia said she would give no interviews, complaining that every time she said something, she destroyed herself. She didn't care what people wrote, but she had grown weary of contributing to her own destruction.

As usual, she gave several interviews. She downplayed her "star" status and stated she had always wanted to be a character actress like Angela Lansbury. Mia had never been driven to become a star. Her mother had been a star (one could dispute whether Maureen had been a bigger star than Angela Lansbury). Mia wasn't impressed by stars. She pointed out she'd seen them all her life and was more impressed with the Farrow's old family cook, Eileen.

Mia was strictly interested in getting better at her craft, not being a "star." But when she spotted Marlon Brando in the studio commissary, she became a fan and asked to meet him. The young character actress and the legendary superstar had a very strong common ground. They commiserated about the unflattering, unrelenting publicity they both received.

Goodbye, Raggedy Ann proceeded on schedule. Mia liked the role. She emphasized that she would never do a part she didn't like—she'd rather be a waitress or librarian.

She also noted that if she weren't an actress at this point in time, she'd be in an asylum—she was sure of it.

Certainly during production of the TV movie, which co-starred the great Hal Holbrook, Mia was treated by producer-writer Jack Sher and director Fielder Cook as though she were a crown princess. And for a girl who had to be the most self-effacing and modest superstar in the business, she never seemed uncomfortable at the deferential treatment.

The character she was playing in the movie was described by director Cook as basically a silly adolescent, and he made the point that he saw no resemblance whatever between that character and the actress portraying her. He described Mia as a mature woman.

Whereas movies-for-TV were shot in two weeks in those days, in this case the schedule was considerably longer. And people were once again impressed with Mia's take-charge attitude. When it was learned that the network planned to censor the film, editing out a key scene, they watched as Mia phoned the head of the network and told him she'd leave the picture if the scene was cut. The scene remained.

It was family day on the set on more than one occasion. Hal Holbrook's wife came to the set with their fourteen-month-old daughter. Another actress in the cast, Marlene Warfield, brought her three-month-old infant. Mia brought one of the twins. And Andre visited the set frequently.

Mia couldn't wait to visit her property on Martha's Vineyard. Her brother John was currently staying there, living in a camper, becoming a writer. Mia looked forward to spending time there.

She and Andre visited the Vineyard as often as feasible over the next few years. And the couple "seemed always to be *extremely* close," relates Garson Kanin. "Ruth and I used to see them on the island a lot.

"The odd thing about life on Martha's Vineyard is that most of us who live there, who go there, we all have our own lives and there isn't all that fraternization. It's not a social place at all, the way Long Island is, or Southampton. Everybody goes to the Vineyard to be away from it all, and everyone respects that."

The Kanins usually encountered Mia and Andre in the town of Vineyard Haven. "We'd run into them in a shop or on the street. They seemed to be wholly, *entirely,* loving and compatible and happy. The island was new to him, and he seemed to like it very much."

• • •

There had been considerable interest when sister Tisa Farrow finally made her film debut, in a picture called *Homer,* released the previous year. Tisa made the point that she had won the part not because she was Mia Farrow's sister but because the coproducer, Steve North, had wanted a girl who looked like Tisa Farrow.

Controversy was not passing this Farrow by either. In the film, in which Tisa portrayed the girlfriend of an alienated farmer, she had a nude scene. Far more "shocking," however, was the fact that Tisa had done a nude pictorial for *Playboy* magazine (modestly revealing by today's standards). Major stars were doing it, and Tisa certainly had the figure, but for a girl whose strict Roman Catholic upbringing and education had made her terrified of changing clothes in gym because the nuns had taught her it was wrong to show her body, this was quite a breakthrough, of sorts.

Far more important, at the time of *Homer*'s release, Tisa had given birth to her first child, Jason. Terry Dene, the twenty-nine-year-old coproducer of the picture, was the father.

Tisa said that making movies was what she really wanted to do. She said she'd dreamed of it her whole life and wanted to direct a great horror movie before she died. She'd shoot it in New York, with vampires and Central Park in it, and she would be the star.

As far as Tisa was concerned, she'd had no advantages coming from a famous family and supported this view by pointing out she had spent a long time going around town trying out for commercials and didn't land one. She would always run into some career woman who disliked her right away because she didn't like her sister Mia.

The other Farrows, at this time, were scattered and active. Patrick, now twenty-six, was married with two small children. He was an artist and worked in a ski lodge in Vermont. John, twenty-three, was now producing movies in California. Sister Steffi was considered the prettiest—and funniest—in the family. Prudence, twenty-one, had recently married and was working with the Maharishi Mahesh Yogi in India. (Tisa referred to Prudence as the strange one, the spiritual one, probably the only Farrow who continued to practice Transcendental Meditation.) Prudence's husband was the Maharishi's head initiator in New York.

Mia had become disenchanted and distanced herself from the whole Maharishi movement when it appeared to her that his organization had, in effect, become far too commercial. She would not rejoin the fold.

The Indian influence had lingered for a while in the decor of Mia's New York apartment. But Mia no longer needed the Maharishi in her search for inner strength. She said she drew psychic strength from positive elements in her life—like a phone conversation with her dear friend Ruth Gordon. And Mia's relationship with Dali. He was always ready with advice for her, and perhaps Mia was one of the very few who could benefit from the artist's prismatic view of life and his exotic solutions to its problems (for example, wear your right shoe on the left foot and vice versa, he once advised Mia, and she would emerge from whatever rut she felt she was in. She tried it and said it had worked).

Mia's interest in the Maharishi had created a potential business problem for her, and she had had to reassure producers *et al.* that she hadn't deserted the "real world." She attended a lot of industry functions and parties so that all could see she was in good mental shape and willing and ready to work. Some feared she had gone off the deep end. Little did they know what a survivor Mia Farrow was.

After *Goodbye, Raggedy Ann* Previn and Mia returned to England, where she made films locally. There was Peter Shaffer's *The Public Eye,* directed by Carol Reed. And a thriller, released in the United States as *See No Evil,* in which she played a terrorized blind girl. The picture opened in New York at Radio City Music Hall, and hopes were that it would be a hit along the lines of a similarly themed film, *Wait Until Dark,* which had starred Audrey Hepburn. Mia's film didn't make it. There were other pictures she made at this time that weren't even distributed (or that found only limited distribution) in the United States. Among them was a film for Claude Chabrol, *High Heels,* costarring Jean Paul Belmondo, in which Mia spoke fluent French.

She'd reportedly agreed to play Hannah Senish, an Israeli freedom fighter, in a film that had no definite starting date. It was around this time that Andre reportedly asked Mia to put her film career on hold. She did. There would be outlets for her other than films. Like her mother, Mia wasn't limited in this regard. Her plan, once the twins were a bit older, was to join a repertory company.

• • •

The Haven welcomed houseguests on occasion. Andre Previn's fourteen-year-old daughter, Alicia (from his first marriage to Betty Bennett), was one. The family's life-style was informal, and Mia was no gourmet cook. Food was no big deal at her home, and that was fine with Mia. She disliked cooking and was a vegetarian at the time, and said that Andre liked very simple dishes and would eat anything. But the couple were looking for a good housekeeper.

Mia drank Guinness to keep her weight up, and she ate constantly and said that everybody hated her because no matter how much she ate, she never weighed more than one hundred pounds. Previn said all he had to do was walk past an Italian restaurant and he put on two pounds.

Mia admitted that she missed the States, at times. She cared very much about what was happening there but realized one had to become involved where one was; she was in England and said Andre believed they'd live at the Haven forever. But they were keeping their American citizenship, and Mia was glad their sons had dual citizenship. She said she was still a pacifist, without enough time to be a good one. She still went to rallies and did what she could.

Mia and Andre, throughout the mid-seventies, appeared to enjoy their life, and the couple lived like English gentry on their sprawling old estate. It was indeed a haven, an oasis of beauty, peace, and tranquility that welcomed them after an exhausting tour or after a superhuman workday.

The fraternal twins, who were very attractive children, called Andre Papa. Mia, however, was known to them as Mia, and she was a very "hands-on" mom. Contrary to her own upbringing, the children didn't have a separate wing or a separate life from their parents. Mia and Andre did their best to give the children as stable a life as possible.

During this period Andre and Mia became chummy with some of the leaders of British government. This came about largely because of Edward Heath, then prime minister of England, who was a former chairman of the London Symphony's board of trustees. The Previns were frequent visitors to both 10 Downing Street and Chequers, the prime minister's country home. The main topic of conversation was usually music, and the very clever Andre Previn invited Mr. Heath to conduct the London Symphony for a benefit performance. The resulting publicity, and positive attention focused on the Symphony and Andre Previn, was a remarkable coup for Previn. Sense of humor at the ready, he remarked that it was untrue that he was aiming to be prime minister for fifteen minutes.

Previn's career continued to demand constant travel, and

sometimes Mia felt "a little lonely—stranded." She began to do theater close to home. She made her British theatrical debut in 1972 in the play *Mary Rose,* in Manchester.

It had been years since she'd appeared on stage, and Previn was concerned. The theater was so different than films and required a whole different vocal technique. An actor had to be heard in the last row. Previn needn't have worried. After he saw the play, he noted that Mia "could be heard in Yankee Stadium without a microphone."

It was in fact a personal triumph for Mia, and the play went on to London. She realized her ambition to join a repertory company when she was invited to join the Royal Shakespeare Company. The prospect made her very nervous since she couldn't simply be a minor player. That, all agreed, was ridiculous. She'd have to, as fellow actor Ian Richardson later said, jump right into the deep end. Richardson also recalled that at first she appeared like a very frightened little bird.

David Jones, a Royal Shakespeare Company director, noted that Mia was more nervous about being with the company than the company was about working with her. He noted that there was absolutely no trace of "film star" in her behavior. Jones said, after working with her, that she was a director's dream. She just drank up every direction he gave her, making life easy for a director. He observed that she had an immense emotional truthfulness, a quality of sincerity. In performances she was fresh each time. She played in the present tense. Obviously she could, if she wished, perform on the stage for the rest of her life.

It was true that she put the children first, recalled Mia's mother. Maureen said she didn't know how Mia did it when she was doing a play every day. She'd be up with the children, get their breakfasts, be with them until she'd go off in the car around four, do the show, come home.

And the shows were not exactly lightweight. Mia, working with people like Richard Pasco and Paul Rogers, was doing the plays of Anton Chekhov, Federico García Lorca, and Tom Stoppard. In 1973 the Previns adopted a child. Andre had been deeply moved, several years earlier, by a visit to an orphanage in Korea. The children there were victims of the Vietnamese war. Mia had been talking of adopting Vietnamese children when she was still Mrs. Sinatra.

The two-month-old infant who joined the Previn family was named Kym Lark (later called Lark Song). Previn has recalled the incredible moment when he and Mia first saw the baby. There had been mountains of red tape, but finally a telegram had arrived informing Andre and Mia that a Belgian nun would be conveying twelve orphans from Saigon to Paris. The Previns went to Paris to meet her. It was an unscheduled flight, and the couple waited almost twenty-four hours for it to arrive. When it finally did, a planeload of children and babies emerged. Bringing up the rear was a tiny Belgian nun, Sister Pascal. She recognized the Previns and walked toward them carrying a little plastic basket. In French she said, "Mr. and Mrs. Previn, here is your baby." She handed them the baby, and Mia burst out crying. They were looking at the tiniest two-month-old baby they'd ever seen. Her papers were pinned to her blanket. Andre and Mia looked up and the nun was gone, as though, Previn later recalled, she thought they might change their minds.

Adopting was a deeply meaningful experience for Mia. She became active in an organization named Friends of Children, which aided people in adopting children.

Just as their family was expanding, a stunning career opportunity presented itself to Mia, and she decided to take advantage of it. According to later accounts, she'd hoped that with their growing family, Previn would remain home for longer stretches, but she learned that wasn't to be. His schedule simply wasn't flexible (not unlike Frank Sinatra's)—concerts, recording sessions *et al.,* like those of any highly successful professional musician's, were booked more than a year in advance. So Mia decided to make herself available for another film.

• • •

Paramount was producing a new film version of F. Scott Fitzgerald's *The Great Gatsby.* The studio's head of production, Robert Evans, had initiated the project for his then wife, Ali MacGraw. This was to be a top-budget, prestige project. Evans signed David Merrick to produce. Merrick negotiated for the rights to the novel, which belonged to Scottie Smith, Fitzgerald's daughter. The price was a then-whopping $350,000.

The role of Gatsby, of course, was a plum, but the leading actors that Evans wanted to cast—either Warren Beatty or Jack Nicholson—wouldn't play opposite Mrs. Evans. They agreed with many in Hollywood that Ali MacGraw would be out of her depth in the role of Daisy.

Evans tried to sign Marlon Brando, who was in fact twenty years too old for Gatsby. It wasn't his age that prevented a deal —it was his asking price. Evans's next choice was Robert Redford, who wanted the part and had even tried to buy the rights to the book himself, as had producer Ray Stark. A deal with Redford was negotiated.

The search for the right director was equally troublesome. Mike Nichols, Peter Bogdanovich, and Arthur Penn were each highly desirable and at the top of their form—but there was, as far as each of them was concerned, a stumbling block: the fact that Ali MacGraw was playing Daisy.

Jack Clayton was eventually signed. This didn't appear to

be a brilliant choice, since *The Great Gatsby* was a quintessentially American tale, and Clayton was British; and it had been years since Clayton had made a movie.

The next hurdle was the script. A Truman Capote version had been commissioned, but the final product was turned down. (Capote sued, and the case was settled out of court for more than $100,000.) Francis Ford Coppola, fresh from his *Godfather* triumph, was signed to write a new script, which was accepted. Producer Merrick was not discreet about crediting Jack Clayton with having helped a great deal on the script; he claimed Clayton should have received coauthor credit.

Then, in true Hollywood fashion, a new and totally unexpected development occurred: In the considerable time it had taken to finalize all the elements, Ali MacGraw had become romantically involved with Steve McQueen, and her marriage to Evans was on the rocks.

Evans resigned as executive producer of *The Great Gatsby.* Merrick became producer. But Evans, as head of studio production, was still involved with the picture.

Suddenly Merrick heard from Freddie Fields, Steve McQueen's agent: McQueen was interested in playing Gatsby. (McQueen had just starred with Ali MacGraw in *The Getaway,* a big hit at the box office.) But Merrick was happy with Redford, who was already signed. Freddie Fields suggested Merrick give Redford another role in the picture, because that was the only way Ali would do the picture—McQueen wouldn't let her be in the film unless he played Gatsby.

It was, as far as Merrick was concerned, out of the question. Ali MacGraw was released from the picture.

Enter every other major actress in Hollywood. It was like the battle for the role of Scarlett O'Hara, thirty-five years earlier. David Merrick now insisted on screen tests for all the potential Daisies, just as Selznick had insisted on screen tests for Scarlett O'Hara.

The role of Daisy was a difficult one to cast, because of the character's complexities and the way she had to look. If Grace Kelly had been twenty-eight, she would have been perfect casting. Or Elizabeth Taylor, as she had been at the time of *A Place in the Sun.*

Natalie Wood was offered the role of Daisy, on the condition that she test. The chemistry between Natalie and Robert Redford had been exciting in two films to date, *Inside Daisy Clover* and *This Property Is Condemned* (even though both movies had flopped at the box office). Unfortunately Natalie, a star her whole life, was insulted at the "condition"; she refused to make a test.

Faye Dunaway, Katharine Ross, Candice Bergen, and others did test. The role remained open. The story goes that Bob Evans now received a communiqué from Mia Farrow: "Dear Bob, may I be your Daisy?"

Jack Clayton was of course familiar with Mia's recent work in the British theater. She was well liked, she wasn't temperamental, and as David Jones had said, she was a director's dream. There had been so many problems up until now that they knew they had to have an actress who wouldn't cause unnecessary delays.

Clayton felt Mia's vulnerable quality, which made men want to protect her, made her the right Daisy. And he noted that in Mia's vocabulary, there was no such word as *can't.* She was, as far as Clayton was concerned, the most real and suitable Daisy—someone who had the class; someone who was incredibly feminine, aware that men found her infinitely attractive; someone who made men aware that an extremely beautiful woman was sitting next to them.

Furthermore, since Clayton has been described as a somewhat macho individual, one assumes Mia's extreme femininity presented no threat to the director's authority down the line if and when disagreements arose.

Clayton directed Mia's screen test for *Gatsby* in London. (She ran a temperature the day she tested.) The test supposedly played very well for studio executives back in the States. David Merrick thought she had the necessary aristocratic look, and Evans (instrumental in the production of *Rosemary's Baby*) of course liked her too. As far as the Paramount money men were concerned, on their books Mia Farrow was a very big box office star. *Rosemary's Baby* had been a blockbuster, and the fact that her ensuing pictures (none of them for Paramount) hadn't clicked didn't even enter into the picture. Mia got the part. (Francis Ford Coppola disagreed loudly with the decision.)

From Mia's point of view, since much of the picture would be shot at England's Pinewood Studios, she'd be close to home much of the time.

Amid a tremendous amount of publicity, shooting began in Newport, Rhode Island. The film had an arduous eighteen-week shooting schedule, and soon production coincided with a far more important development in Mia's life: She was pregnant. David Merrick was outraged—her scenes would have to be filmed before her condition showed. There was no alternative: It would cost a fortune (and appear disastrous) to replace the leading lady after the picture was several weeks into production. Filming proceeded as scheduled.

Mia later admitted that when she played Daisy, she had found the role difficult and elusive. She kept losing the character because the director's vision of Daisy was not clear, and neither was her own. She pointed out, too, that Daisy was harder to play than people thought. Scott Fitzgerald had written very little description of her.

Interest in the picture escalated to Olympian heights. During its production and before its release, *The Great Gatsby* was, from late 1973 through 1974, almost an equivalent of what *Gone With the Wind* had been in its era. *Gatsby* was dovetailing into, indeed reflecting, the nostalgia craze that was sweeping the country and everything about the picture—the era (the 1920s), the clothes, the music, the look—was of intense interest.

Before the picture's release it appeared that Mia Farrow would once again be the hottest screen actress in the world. And Robert Redford *was* currently the hottest actor—*The Way We Were* and *The Sting* had both opened while *Gatsby* was being filmed.

Unfortunately there was no great chemistry on-screen between Redford and Mia. She was quoted as saying that while he might look like the perfect superstar, he was in fact—and enjoyed being—extremely ordinary. She said she thought he was intimidated by famous actors and described him as starstruck, if the way he kept mentioning Barbra Streisand's name was any indication. (Streisand was Redford's costar in *The Way We Were.*)

A British newspaper printed a story purporting to express Mia's negative views on Redford, headlined: "How Do You Kiss a Man That You Can't Stand?" In the piece she was quoted as saying that every time a love scene came up, she had to bite her tongue. The quotes were picked up by *Newsweek,* which quoted Mia as saying that Redford thought he was the world's greatest actor, was a know-it-all, and that everyone else, especially women, were inferior.

These quotes were certainly questionable, not at all Mia Farrow's style. In almost ten years she had never come out and blasted a fellow actor. It would seem most peculiar to begin at this point, on the verge of a major comeback. Mia sued the

British paper and was awarded several thousand dollars in damages.

The expectations were so great for *The Great Gatsby* that Paramount's sales department had been able to demand huge nonreturnable advance money guarantees from exhibitors, ensuring a profit for the film before one ticket of admission had been purchased. This practice turned out to be the only reason the picture was profitable, because the film was a critical and box office disaster. Redford had dyed his famous blonde hair brown for the role, so fans were getting a different, and not necessarily better-looking, Robert Redford; and Mia was miscast as Daisy. She was adequate but hardly memorable. Her reviews were mixed. Some were good. But others, like Jay Cocks's of *Time* magazine, thought the movie didn't work *because* of her: "[Mia Farrow's] characterization—on which so much of the movie depends —is a catastrophe. She works up a mannered creature with bulging eyes and squeaky voice who never suggests Daisy's strength, her greed, or even her gaiety and charm."

Far more important to her than the hit or miss of any film was the birth of a healthy son, Fletcher, who was blond and looked just like her. One assumes Mia's commitment to and concern for her family, the fact that her career was not *the* most important thing in her life, were what kept her focused and functioning after the *Gatsby* disaster.

Previn was truly relishing his role as papa. The twins were robust and fun-loving, and Mia and Andre were elated as tiny Kym Lark began gaining weight and relating to her new parents and stepbrothers.

That the Previns loved children and parenting is incontrovertible. The next year they adopted two more little girls: Soon-Yi, a Korean, and Summer Song (later called Daisy), a

Vietnamese. There were now six children residing at the Haven.

The adoption of Soon-Yi had, by necessity, brought out the activist in Mia. In fact Mia Farrow almost single-handedly succeeded in having a U.S. federal law repealed as a result of her determination to adopt this child. It all started when Mia discovered that American law forbade a U.S. family from adopting any more than two foreign children. Mia had had her heart set on Soon-Yi, a six-year-old who had spent her entire life in an orphanage in Seoul, Korea. As many people in the entertainment world had already learned, when Mia Farrow was determined to do something, she did it.

First she made certain that nothing could go wrong in adopting the child even if Mia couldn't get the law repealed. Certainly the people she had met, via Andre, who were high up in the British government, were helpful. The U.S. Justice Department granted "people status" to young Soon-Yi, which meant that Mia was permitted to bring the child into the United States. Once this was accomplished, Mia felt she had a good chance of having the law in question changed.

The next step was for her to find a congressman who would sponsor the necessary legislation. Massachusetts's Michael Harrington was the man. He sponsored the special bill that repealed the old law. Congress passed the bill, and Soon-Yi was adopted by Mia. Mia flew to Seoul, where she aided in the arrangements necessary to send Soon-Yi, as well as many other children in the orphanage, to the United States.

• • •

Some say that around this time, when Andre returned from a long tour, Mia demanded that he spend time with her and the children. Previn sometimes acquiesced, and engagements were canceled, but he couldn't make a habit of canceling, or his career might suffer badly.

Previn and the London Symphony received a singular honor in 1974, which Previn was able to share with Mia. The orchestra had received an invitation to perform at the highly prestigious Salzburg Festival. It was a first for a British orchestra, and in Andre's world this was a momentous occasion. Mia not only accompanied her husband on the jaunt, the couple also gave a joint news conference. It was a glittering and warm occasion, with many overtones on both a professional and a personal level. It seemed to forge a closer bond between Previn and the London Symphony and to reinforce the commitment Previn and Mia had to each other.

Mia had a health scare in October of that year. In great pain she had to be rushed to the hospital. She was frantic about leaving the children alone in the house and adamant, regardless of her pain, that one ambulance attendant remain with them before she agreed to leave.

At King's College Hospital in London it was discovered she'd suffered a ruptured appendix, and her condition escalated into a life-threatening crisis. Several operations were necessary. At one point doctors feared she was lost. Even in a delirious state, her concern for the children was all she spoke about. Maureen flew to England and took over at home in her daughter's absence. Andre, on tour, returned at once. Fortunately Mia recovered; her recuperation took several weeks.

Incredibly, the British tabloids interpreted the ordeal as having been a possible suicide attempt "in response to Previn's purported infidelities." Those close to Mia were loathe to dignify the reports with any kind of response. They knew that Mia, with her sense of responsibility to her children, would never even consider such an act. And as far as her husband's "dallying around" was concerned, that would not push Mia over the edge and cause her to try to take her own life.

History did, however, seem to be repeating itself insofar as Previn's comments were concerned. He was a big star in England, and journalists tracked him closely. Around 1975 a familiar lament was attributed to always-on-tour Andre: that he hated to come back to an empty hotel room. A stewardess for British Airways was mentioned in these reports.

• • •

While Mia had created no stir in *Gatsby,* Previn's success continued to grow. His work, home, and family were all in England. But Previn, like Mia, could be unpredictable. In March 1975 he acted on an offer he'd received from the Pittsburgh Symphony Orchestra, back in the United States. It was an offer he simply couldn't refuse. His English cronies were shocked, and the governing board of the London Symphony made a decision of their own: They gave him his two years' notice. They subsequently coated the announcement with a thick icing of verbiage, along the lines that Previn had already outlasted any previous conductor of the LSO and "it was never intended for Andre Previn to be conductor for life."

Previn's decision, at least in part, was certainly prompted by the fact that Mia missed the United States (she'd returned on many occasions to spend time at her place on Martha's Vineyard), and to an extent so did Previn. And they wanted their children to know the United States.

(It's amusing to note, in view of Previn's alleged womanizing, that one member of the search committee for the Pittsburgh Symphony had been affiliated with the Houston Symphony in the days Previn had been making headlines with Mia. That person now expressed misgivings about possible pitfalls awaiting in Previn's future private life. Orchestra manager Seymour Rosen successfully nipped this objection in the bud, pointing out in so many words that he personally knew that Previn was no runabout; why, Andre had only recently gone out of his way to avoid the blatant come-on by none other than a very beautiful and wealthy member of the board of the Pittsburgh Symphony, a lady known to many of the search committee members.)

Music was a vital element in the home life of the Previns. The children were strongly encouraged to play any and all instruments and to develop tastes in music. Small tape recorders were in abundance at the house, and classical music was favored. The twins loved Handel and Haydn.

As far as Previn was concerned, and Mia avidly supported his belief, music was a second language that unlocked amazing doors for children.

Frank Sinatra appeared in concert in London around this time, and Sinatra invited Mia to the event. She attended, and some observers reported that she cried. Maureen, when queried, said she had no idea why Mia would have wept—she was happily married with a lovely family she adored.

There is no doubt that the Previn family's home life was, for the kids, rich, rewarding, and real. Author-journalist Mel Gussow spent time with the Previns at the Haven around this time. He was researching a magazine article, and Gussow, not a journalist known to pander or fawn, observed a happy, functioning family situation and a real and genuine romantic relationship between Andre and Mia. There was a sense of humor. Previn had had a mock bookjacket printed: *All I Know About Mia Farrow.* When she first saw it, there was a momentary panic attack, then the joke sank in.

There was an actual railroad caboose in the middle of the Haven's woodsy grounds, which had been a present to Mia from Andre. The couple sometimes slept in it so that they could wake up on a train. Mia loved to arise at dawn and walk in the woods. She loved to look at the stars, and Andre had bought her a telescope.

Mia's and Andre's relationship with the children was heartwarming. The kids were a part of their parents' lives. Previn often encouraged one or more of them to sing for him. Mia made puppets and put on puppet shows. She took the kids on picnics, and when a couple of the tykes got cow manure on themselves, Mia didn't yell or berate—she laughed and cleaned them up as though it weren't an unpleasant task at all.

Gussow noted, however, that the longer Mia lived in England, the more deeply she felt about being American. Rather prophetically Gussow also observed a crucial difference in the personalities and careers of the Previns. Andre planned years ahead, whereas Mia didn't know what she was going to do tomorrow.

Her theater work didn't seriously interfere with the time she had to spend with the kids; she worked at night, was always home in the morning, and the brood often didn't realize she'd been gone. And Previn noted that if, for some reason, they had to be punished (one got the feeling this was rarely the case), the worst deprivation was taking away their time listening to music. As for Mia, Previn acknowledged that while she wasn't flawless in all areas, in the area of motherhood and maternal instincts she was.

She had finally achieved her desire to play *Peter Pan,* but not on the big screen. It was for television in the United States, a Hallmark Hall of Fame project costarring Danny Kaye. Mia sang her songs herself (at first alternative singers were considered; then, as was the case with the lullabye sung over the credits in *Rosemary's Baby,* Mia's voice won the day).

One thing about Mia Farrow: She wasn't afraid to re-create

roles that had been memorably played by other actresses. First Johnny Belinda and now Peter Pan, in which Mary Martin had scored a phenomenal success. In neither instance did Mia surpass (nor make one forget) the other actresses, nor did she make a fool of herself.

Her kids loved her Peter Pan; when one of them asked her at home to please fly around the room, her reply was not a predictable "It was only make-believe, darling." Mia knew, from her own experience, that a child's fantasy world was precious. Mia's reply was quintessential Mia Farrow: She told the child, "Not tonight. It has to be a special occasion."

The activist Mia had again surfaced in February 1976 when she presented an antiabortion petition at the House of Commons. She was there on behalf of the Society for the Protection of Unborn Children, a conservative English group that was "pro-life." (She had become involved with this group a few years earlier, after the birth of her twins.)

But in addition to all her other activities, and despite whatever disenchantment she was experiencing in her marriage, Mia wanted to make movies.

It wasn't so simple to find suitable roles for Mia in films. She wasn't a Streisand-like powerhouse, then in fashion; she wasn't a sidekick for the leading man, also in fashion (as were men's vehicles); she knew she couldn't yet play mature women —and she didn't want to play whores.

She was rarely idle, and there were outward signs of inner turbulence: She still smoked heavily (sometimes cigarillos), and her fingernails were bitten to the quick. People who knew her wondered what Mia's next move would be. She was, after all, a *very* resourceful lady.

Chapter Fourteen

MIA REACTIVATED her film career without spectacular results, but she was a name, there were roles, and her price per picture was around $250,000. One of the films she made in the late seventies was Robert Altman's *A Wedding,* a very interesting and effective movie that died at the box office. It was hot and uncomfortable filming the picture in Chicago, but stars loved working with Altman—the director encouraged them to stretch, risk, and improvise, a challenge right up Mia Farrow's alley.

In *Death on the Nile,* another physically uncomfortable shoot, this one in Egypt, Mia was one of a group of stars assembled for the latest Agatha Christie-based whodunit. Her old friend and ally Bette Davis (now seventy years old) was in the cast, but the slickly made picture, which opened in the fall of 1978, came and went, creating no special stir at the box office.

Avalanche costarred Mia with Rock Hudson, but the movie was simply awful. Apparently everyone connected with this one had done it for the money.

The work had taken her away from home with more frequency and for longer periods. Sometimes she took all, other times only some of the kids with her. She was miserable if separated from them.

She later stated that these films were best forgotten, and she'd done them for very bad reasons. Previn had very negative feelings about Hollywood films and didn't want Mia working in them because they were usually dreadful. He made her feel ashamed to be doing them. Yet on the other hand, he was constantly traveling, leaving her "very lonely, sitting at home in the drizzling rain of England without my friends or family."

• • •

Unfortunately Mia's and Andre's marriage did not stand the test of time. Apparently Mia could look the other way for just so long. It was very upsetting for her to read about Andre's "dabbling" in the newspapers. "The clamor of the rumors about Andre's infidelities became too much for Mia to ignore," observed writer Denise Hall.

The break with Previn was gradual, and Previn subsequently said in all seriousness that he thought England was to blame for their rift. He said that Mia had always felt vaguely alien in the country, whereas he felt he had at last come home. And while Mia loved the Haven, she didn't really enjoy being in England and over the years had grown restless there. He pointed out there was no British film industry to speak of, and once Mia was back on the filmmaking scene, she had decided she could no longer tread water with her life.

According to Thomas Kiernan, Roman Polanski's biographer, Mia and Polanski had a brief, secret romance in London and "looked forward to renewing it in more tropical surroundings." Polanski was to direct a multimillion-dollar remake of the 1937 disaster epic *Hurricane,* and Mia would be the star.

However, Polanski was arrested in Los Angeles in March 1977 for "unlawful intercourse" with a minor (a thirteen-year-old girl), and the scandal sent tremors through the entertainment community. Hollywood wags cruelly joked that the girl may have been thirteen, "but she looked eight." When Polanski subsequently went on trial, he had character references submitted to the court by many of his friends. Mia was one of them.

Polanski withdrew from *Hurricane,* but Mia went ahead with the film. It was filmed on the South Pacific island of Bora-Bora and was a trouble-plagued production, with difficulties of every sort in abundance. At one point Mia reportedly got into a fight on the set with costar Timothy Bottoms and ended up needing stitches. She was physically injured on another occasion, knocked around in a rowboat. On a personal level, she reportedly became romantically involved with Sven Nykvist, the Swedish cinematographer (then fifty-five years old). The indefatigable British press subsequently suggested that Mia had become pregnant by him, necessitating a public denial from Mia's PR people (such an announcement, between the lines, also told producers that Mia was available for further films).

Her marriage was definitely over. She wrote Andre (who was involved with English beauty Heather Jayston) asking for a divorce. The marriage had lasted eight and a half years.

• • •

Jasper Parrott, Previn's manager in London, subsequently commented on his famous client's marriage. In Parrott's view it had been "sort of an insoluble conundrum, two people with such strong personalities." Parrott had felt the marriage was doomed. Andre and Mia couldn't both function in the same place; Mia never really understood the demands of a concert career. Nor, according to Parrott, was Mia the sort of successful conductor's wife who provided constant coddling and cosseting (but then again Andre, according to Parrott, wasn't looking for that). The sadness of the marriage, observed Parrott, was that the couple had reached an impasse: Andre would not have been happy, could not have functioned, living on her terms, and she apparently could not function living on his terms.

Ronald Wilford, Previn's manager in the United States, was typically direct and blunt in his observations. He said he could never figure the couple out. He'd sit there and listen to them tell him how much they loved each other and think, They're writing a script.

There was no acrimony or bitter fighting. The parents had joint custody. As it turned out, Andre would have the twins for most of the year. The two boys loved England and the Haven and their school chums. The four younger children remained with Mia in the United States, but there would never be a problem as to which kids would spend time with which parent and when. Previn had already been through a broken marriage where children were caught in the crossfire. Both Andre and Mia were determined that their kids would feel secure in the knowledge that they had two parents who needed them and loved them and looked after them and in whose lives they were a stable necessity.

They succeeded to a remarkable degree.

Once again Mia returned to acting on the stage. Only this time Broadway was the venue and a new play, *Romantic Comedy,* the vehicle. This would be her Broadway debut. The plot of the play was rice-paper thin: Old-maidish schoolteacher falls in love with married playwright. Like *Same Time, Next Year,* it covered a period of years. It was a comedy, which appealed to Mia a great deal—what a pleasure, for a change, to hear people *laugh.*

Old friend Tony Perkins was the leading man. With Farrow and Perkins the producers had two still-youngish, former big names in the movies who would undoubtedly pull in crowds to see them in person. The playwright, Bernard Slade, joked that it was indeed a strange package: the stars of *Psycho* and *Rosemary's Baby* in a *comedy*?

However, the fact that neither star would be signed to appear in the subsequent movie version indicates that thirty-four-year-old Mia and forty-six-year-old Perkins's standing in the movie industry was cold indeed.

For Mia *Hurricane* had been a disaster on all fronts. She had retreated to Martha's Vineyard for months, rebuilding and strengthening her inner resources. She was very self-sufficient. Weeks went by when she didn't speak to another adult. She didn't like strangers in the house, and without outside help, looking after six children kept her busy indeed. She cooked, played house, was a mother, and drove the Jeep to school on the long, rutted Martha's Vineyard roads. She listened to Bach and Mahler, read *War and Peace* (which took three months). She loved Martha's Vineyard and never got tired of walking and looking and listening. She loved her big gray house.

She went back to work because she needed the money. She said she wasn't career-driven the way a lot of people were. With Mia, her personal life came first. She found it very satisfying, and fascinating, trying to understand children, to discover what fulfilled them and made them happy. It brought something out of her that, she said, she probably needed to give.

But she felt especially strong at this point in her life. She said she was a survivor, and she was.

She had divorced Previn in March 1979 (she flew to the Dominican Republic to get the decree) and by November was performing for the first time on Broadway. And she was adding to her family: She was adopting another child. This one, a two-year-old Korean boy, was physically handicapped. Mia later said she'd decided to adopt the child when she moved to New York. She talked it over with the other children first, and together they decided they could do it. The child wore a leg brace and had some weakness in his side, but all the children helped with his exercises, and the four older ones took turns doing his therapy. "It's been wonderful for all of us as a family," observed Mia.

She spoke to Andre practically every day (one recalls that after her divorce from Sinatra she spoke with him frequently on the phone), and Andre was all for the adoption. She and Previn were still very close. Mia denied that any formal reconciliation was on the horizon, but she acknowledged the strong bond between them, wryly adding that she often told him, "Why fool around with a woman with seven children?"

Romantic Comedy proceeded smoothly. It had a mildly controversial aspect: It was the first Broadway play to have a star do a nude scene. But it wasn't Mia—it was Perkins, and the only one who didn't see the nudity was Mia, whose character is embarrassed and looks away.

Rarely did two stars function as well off and on stage as Mia Farrow and Tony Perkins. Neither had the kind of ego that got in the way, and, in fact, to ignite some chemistry, they went out on a "date" together (they saw a play and had supper).

In fact Mia hadn't been playwright Bernard Slade's first choice for the role. Fortunately the director, Joe Hardy, had worked with her in the past and sang her praises. Nobody regretted this decision.

The play opened in Boston, and Mia brought several of her children with her to stay at the hotel. After the successful Boston tryout, Slade happily observed that Mia had the "sunflower syndrome," whereby an actor finds the audience responding to him (or her), which in turn makes her respond.

Obviously if Slade had seen any of Mia's work on the British stage, he wouldn't have been so surprised.

Maureen O'Sullivan was back on Broadway, in the revival of Paul Osborne's play *Mornings at Seven.* At sixty-seven she was more accomplished on stage than ever. The world was impressed that mother and daughter were performing successfully on Broadway at the same time. Maureen appeared blasé about it all, but she really considered it miraculous, and Mia was openly delighted and excited about it. There was talk of the two costarring in a play, but the project never materialized.

Mia and Maureen were sharing the big Central Park West apartment, but it was not a conventional arrangement. The sprawling dwelling had been enlarged (a total of eleven rooms) and turned into two separate apartments, with two kitchens.

Looking back, and with benefit of hindsight, did Maureen regret that she herself had retired from the screen to raise so many children? Not at all. She didn't feel she'd abandoned any great career. She hadn't been Bette Davis or anything exciting, in her view; she felt lucky that she hadn't been stuck with that kind of star status, and besides, she now said, she always knew she'd come back to acting.

Her other children were all doing well at this point. Patrick was a sculptor, living in Vermont; John was a screenwriter, who also managed a construction company in Washington, D.C.; and Prudence was working for the Maharishi Mahesh Yogi in Florida. Tisa and Stephanie were actresses. Maureen had recently taped a TV special with Tisa for Public Broadcasting. Titled *One Who Was There,* it had a religious theme. Maureen played Mary Magdalene, and Tisa played the younger Mary.

In the apartment Maureen's three-room "world" was elegant and peaceful. When she wanted to be alone, she simply put up a Do Not Disturb sign on her door. Mia's quarters included three children's bedrooms, filled with bunk beds, an assortment of toys, and a huge, stuffed Easter rabbit. All seven kids were on the premises. The twins, now ten, were visiting from England, and the place was undeniably noisy. (As the kids grew older, quiet reigned.)

But Mia claimed her life was peaceful. She said she had time to herself. She had a baby-sitter and another woman who came twice a week to help with the cleaning. She described her children as particularly understanding and undemanding. There was a communal atmosphere. The older ones cleaned and cooked and helped with the younger ones. Mia was proud of all of them. She said she'd observed other children, and she didn't think any could hold a candle to hers.

Nor did she think it was her own upbringing and family that had inspired her to have such a large family. None of her own brothers and sisters wanted a large family. Mia simply loved children; she explained it was an ambition of hers, one as strong as any other she'd ever experienced. It was a real drive, and where it came from, she didn't know.

The children often came with her to the theater. She usually took one (if not more) every night, and at the Sunday matinee all were there, playing and wandering around. Mia had named the youngest child Misha, after her late brother, but later the child was called Moses.

As to what Maureen thought about it all, Mia thought her mother probably thought she was crazy, even though she had done it all herself. But of course, as far as Mia was concerned, there were major differences: Maureen had had a big house, a lot of help, a yard, and she was a devout Catholic.

Mia's kids had a healthy respect for *all* religions, and they had a concept of a God, but they were not being raised as

Catholics. As far as Mia was concerned, Catholicism hadn't brought the Farrows anything but problems.

An outsider overhearing a conversation Mia had during this period with Andre Previn on the telephone would never have suspected the couple had been divorced. She called him Toots and inquired after his health and concluded the call with "You, too, I love you." She said she and Andre spent a great deal of time together, and it was time well spent.

Previn said, about his relationship with Mia, that it had worked out.

The kids had certainly absorbed his love of music. Lark Song and Matthew were taking piano and violin lessons; Sascha, the trumpet; Summer Song (Daisy), the piano. Mia encouraged them to listen to classical music at bedtime.

Mia was in a Broadway hit, but she was committed to the children first and fit a career in on the side, according to her. Interestingly it was her opinion that most likely she enjoyed her work more than her mother did; she felt that none of it was very serious for Maureen. While Mia didn't characterize herself as ambitious, she admitted she was much more ambitious than her mother had ever been.

Mia was certainly a colorful character, despite all her protestations to the contrary. And she was very aware of the value and importance of publicity if her career was to sustain as she matured. While, as usual, all topics remained off-limits to interviewers—no questions about Sinatra, or about Previn, or their rumored possible remarriage, and so on—she broke her own rules frequently. Some interviewers were lucky, others weren't.

The mother-daughter duo of Maureen O'Sullivan and Mia Farrow made all the papers when Mother's Day rolled around in 1980. There were photo layouts on the whole family enjoying a glorious day out in Central Park. Maureen even rode down a sliding pond with Lark Song, and Mia carried Misha (Moses) on her shoulders, and all gorged themselves on ice cream.

Maureen said that she'd already received a Mother's Day gift from Mia and was expecting phone calls from her other kids. She said she was lucky, observing that a lot of mothers were forgotten by their children, but that maybe that was because they weren't as much fun when they were older. She had some advice: Children should be *reminded* of their duties to their mothers. (Maureen, like her daughter, was also a very colorful character.)

Mia's good-fortune leprechauns were never far from her shoulder. A new man had entered her life, and while he wasn't a latter-day icon/former bobby-sox idol or a world-renowned composer-conductor, he was a genius, he was rich, and he was famous. And he was relationship-oriented.

As the song lyric goes, "Who could ask for anything more?"

Chapter Fifteen

WOODY ALLEN'S BACKGROUND is as diverse from Mia Farrow's as salami from crepes suzettes. He was born Allen Stewart Konigsberg on December 1, 1935, in Brooklyn, New York, to Martin and Nettie Konigsberg. His family, and his home life (fictionalized, of course), have been the bedrock of his humor. He was the only male in a family of many women. He had a sister, female cousins, and a mother with seven sisters. He was always surrounded by women, and his later work would exhibit an understanding and uncanny perception about the way women think. In his films Allen has very rarely thought in terms of male characters, except for himself. And Allen has said that he sees himself in most of his female characters.

A contrast of the Woody and Mia upbringings could result in a very humorous sequence in a Woody Allen movie. Suffice to say there was no separate wing for the nursery in the Konigsberg household, nor were there nannies for the kids. There was, however, plenty of *tsouris* (a Yiddish word for aggravation and trouble), enough to call on for an entire career.

Allen attended Midwood High School in Brooklyn and

very early in life began writing jokes. One-liners were his specialty, and he sent them to press agents and newspaper columnists, who not only used them but requested more. As a teenager he was signed for representation by the William Morris Agency and was eventually earning $1,500 a week writing gags.

Allen's formal education was a dud (he flunked out of NYU and CCNY), but his career rose as fast as the fictional Esther Blodgett's in *A Star Is Born.* He wrote sketches for stage revues and began writing for top TV shows, including the Sid Caesar show where he joined such top-of-the-liners as Mel Brooks and Larry Gelbart.

In 1954 nineteen-year-old Woody married for the first time. Harlene Rosen was his bride, and the marriage lasted six years. A much longer marriage (one that endures to the present day) took place in 1958, when Allen left the William Morris Agency and signed with agents Charles Joffe and Jack Rollins (they were his manager-agents and later produced his films).

In the 1960s Allen was a regular on the comedy-club and college-campus circuit (where he met his second wife, Louise Lasser). He was a success, but had to contend with the perception that concert bookers, club owners, agents, and producers had of him—that he was basically a New York act, whose appeal and material wouldn't play out of town. He had to fight that myth constantly when he started as a cabaret performer. When he performed in downtown Manhattan, everybody said it was fine but that it was strictly Greenwich Village. When he performed at the swanky Blue Angel, they said it was fine but that it was uptown. Then he began performing all around the country, and finally they said he was an American phenomenon. But Allen contends that he never thought of himself in those terms. He was simply doing his routines.

He appeared on the leading TV variety shows of the day, such as *Tonight* and *The Ed Sullivan Show*. He found that doing his stand-up routines for television wasn't too different from performing in clubs. If anything, he found it a bit simpler, although Jack Paar, then host of *Tonight,* and Ed Sullivan were both edgy about Allen's material, which to them seemed at times too explicit. (Allen never became buddies with Jack Paar —he barely knew him. Allen has recalled that when he first appeared on the show, Paar was taken aback by the material, but after enthusiastic audience response Paar was extremely nice to him.)

The material Allen wrote and performed in those days remains contemporary and hilarious. Example: Allen confided to the Reverend Billy Graham that honoring his father and mother was his least favorite commandment. He confided to William F. Buckley, Jr., that a liberal was a girl who would neck with him on the first date.

Allen's writing was not confined to the show business arena. *The New Yorker* magazine published satiric pieces he wrote.

It's not generally remembered, but Allen did two TV specials: *Woody Allen Looks at 1967* for NBC, and *The Woody Allen Special* for CBS. But Allen didn't enjoy the medium of television, because suddenly he was recognized in the streets; it wasn't a comfortable feeling, as he'd been an anonymous writer for years. He gradually stopped doing television and later said he didn't miss it at all.

In 1965, a big year for Mia Farrow with *Peyton Place* and her relationship with Sinatra, thirty-year-old Woody Allen married his second wife, Louise Lasser, who had begun establishing her own reputation as a leading comedienne-actress. Ms. Lasser was from a prominent Jewish family; her father, J. K. Lasser, was one of the leading tax experts in the country.

Allen was already a hot show business property. He'd written (and played a supporting role in) the hit movie *What's New Pussycat?* There was intense demand for his services in the movie industry, but Allen, guided by Rollins and Joffe, moved cautiously.

He was offered the opportunity to salvage a Japanese adventure film. He devised *What's Up, Tiger Lily?* dubbing a new, funny soundtrack and narration over the cheap imitation of a James Bond movie. Louise Lasser was one of the voices. Woody would also feature Louise in his 1971 film comedy *Bananas.*

Allen's talent was not limited to writing films, live performing, and movie acting. He was also a playwright.

Garson Kanin observes that he's known four people in his lifetime to whom he'd apply the word *genius*—and Woody Allen is one of them. "If he were nothing but an actor—if that's all he did—he'd be celebrated. If Woody did nothing but write, he'd be celebrated. If he were only a director, we would know him. How many people can claim that distinction? It's remarkable."

Don't Drink the Water, Woody Allen's first full-length play, became a Broadway hit in 1966. In 1969 Allen hit again on Broadway with *Play It Again, Sam,* in which he costarred with Diane Keaton and Tony Roberts.

He divorced Louise Lasser in 1969 after four years of marriage. That was also the year of his *auteur* film debut as star, writer, and director of *Take the Money and Run.*

Allen's cult following was building. He was hailed as the new generation's Marx brothers and W. C. Fields, but as far as Woody was concerned, every time at bat was like the first time. His burgeoning success appeared to bring him neither satisfaction nor confidence. He simply forged ahead, always focusing on the next project, the next challenge.

He began a long relationship with Diane Keaton and wrote some of his best scripts for her. He has explained that when he knows an actor intimately, he can write nuances and subtleties into a character for the actor to portray. Allen felt he could do a lot better writing for an intimate than he could writing for a total stranger. He's always found it an advantage to work with friends (Charlie Chaplin, to a great extent, had functioned the same way). And Allen has also used Diane, his own sister, and a couple of select, close friends as sounding boards for his ideas. It was, for Allen, a very effective way of shaping his work, as Mia Farrow would discover.

Woody Allen's personal and professional relationship with Keaton flourished in the early and mid seventies. She costarred with Woody in the 1972 film version of *Play It Again, Sam* (Woody didn't direct the picture), *Sleeper* (1973), and *Love and Death* (1975).

Woody had totally given up live performing to become a filmmaker, but he continued to use the same universal themes in his films as he had in his stand-up comedy routines. These included his obsessions with sex and death ("Sex and death—they both only come once in my lifetime. At least after death you're not nauseous"), love ("The heart is a very, very resilient little muscle"), and the question of the possible nonexistence of God ("To you, I'm an atheist—to God, I'm the loyal opposition").

Through the seventies Allen continued to mold a character for himself on-screen that people naturally assumed was Woody Allen offscreen—a nebbishy but honest little man diffusing the seriousness of his neuroses with one-liners. Whether he was playing Fielding Melish (in *Bananas*), or later, Alvy Singer (in *Annie Hall*), he was always the not-quite-attractive ethnic runt longing for the all-American prom queen.

But like most of the great "funny men," Woody Allen is a

very serious man. People who have worked on Woody Allen's films note that Allen's trademark humor is usually nowhere in evidence off-camera. Like Chaplin, Woody Allen the filmmaker is also a businessman. Actors who have worked for Allen, including the eminent Kitty Carlisle Hart and the delightful Mae Questel, have commented on his frugality.

Although his films, throughout the mid-seventies, had been successful, he'd yet to deliver a blockbuster. But then came a picture that drew heavily on Woody's own past and on his relationship with Keaton: *Annie Hall.* (Keaton's real name is Diane Hall.)

This 1977 release was an artistic and financial smash, winning Oscars for best picture, best actress (Woody had won a nomination as best actor), best director, and best original script (an honor Woody shared with coauthor Marshall Brickman). The movie even had a strong influence on fashion (women began dressing in what became known as the Annie Hall look), and it established Keaton as a first-rank, bankable star. (She has yet to find another vehicle to equal *Annie Hall*'s success.)

The couple's romantic relationship didn't endure, but their friendship has continued to the present day. Keaton, by her own admission, is the kind of woman for whom falling in love is difficult. Just letting herself be vulnerable to somebody and open to the possibility of what it is "to really fall in love and have dreams about some kind of life you're going to build together where you'll be happy together—all that is *not* what I imagine myself falling into *at all.*"

For Diane "happily ever after" was an impossibility—for anyone, in her view. She didn't think life was like that and didn't believe that's what love was at all. She thought it was work, and being able to make compromises and all those practical things.

Nor was Diane one to look on the "up" side. And she considered marriage, for her, as remote as living in outer space. But she believed in falling in love, and after Woody there was Warren Beatty and Al Pacino.

Mia Farrow appears to be the exact opposite of Diane Keaton in all departments. She's a woman for whom it is the most natural thing in the world to make a commitment—and to make every attempt to stick with it.

Some of Allen's work in the late seventies, prior to his becoming involved with Mia, had explored the darker side of his psyche: *Interiors,* a Bergmanesque psychodrama, and the Felliniesque *Stardust Memories,* in which many people from his real life were easily identifiable (although fictionalized of course). Most of the characterizations in *Stardust* were not only highly unflattering but downright mean-spirited. And Woody's own character in this epic, a film director heavily weighed down by all his success, was unhappier than ever. (One is reminded of the late Arthur Bell's comment on Paul Newman, who was complaining about press coverage he was receiving: "Poor Newman. If only he were broke and a nobody.")

It's interesting to note that in *Stardust Memories* Woody's character is involved with a neurotic movie star but is attracted to a waiflike other woman. In one memorable movie-within-the-movie sequence Woody is trying to transplant the brain of the kind of woman he always falls for—the waiflike intellectual—into the body of the woman he always obsesses over, the gorgeous neurotic. But of course even after the transplant he falls for the wrong woman.

Moviegoers thought they were peeking into Woody and Diane's private life while watching *Stardust Memories.* In the film Woody's pal, actor Tony Roberts, played an actor named Tony Roberts who tells the Woody Allen character, "Yes, she [the girl friend] is fantastic four days a month, and the rest of the time she's a nut." The intense, gaunt Charlotte Rampling gave an excellent performance as the neurotic movie star.

During this period there had also been *Manhattan* (in which Tisa Farrow had a small role), which was not the derivative oeuvre the other two films had been. It was, along with *Annie Hall,* some of Allen's best work; it was very favorably received and a hit.

• • •

Mia Farrow had first met Woody Allen years ago at a party in California, which she'd attended with Roman Polanski. Woody was then involved with Diane Keaton. Mia was not at liberty, and no bells went off for either of them.

Their next meetings were in New York, once at a mutual friend's house and another time at Elaine's restaurant. Mia had come from a performance of *Romantic Comedy* and was having dinner with Michael Caine and his wife. Woody was there, and Mia talked with him.

He phoned her the next day and invited her to have lunch. They went to Lutèce (one of the finest and most expensive restaurants in New York) and conversed at length. And then, according to Mia, they became friends.

It was a "courtship" conducted out of the glare of the spotlight but under the noses of insiders comprising the elite of New York's show business community. Mia was front-and-center at a 1980 New Year's Eve bash hosted by Woody at Harkness House. "Mia Farrow is so charming and such a beauty," noted fellow guest Andy Warhol, who was in his element among such celebrities as Mia, Woody, Robert DeNiro, and Mick and Bianca Jagger. Warhol considered Woody's parties the best in town (although he couldn't stand "Woody Allen movies").

There were aspects to Woody's and Mia's personalities

that did not seem, to the outside world, to be compatible. Mia was surrounded by children and pets and loved nature—the countryside, the woods *et al.*

Allen, as everyone knew, was a devout Manhattanite. He was a sports fanatic, and the only television fare that interested him was sports events. He followed his favorite teams avidly.

While they both loved music, Mia's tastes were eclectic. Woody, however, was devoted to jazz. He played the clarinet (Woody practices at least an hour or two every day) every Monday night at a New York restaurant-bar, Michael's Pub. In fact to this day he still jams with the boys every week, although, interestingly, musicians who've played with him over the years state that Allen is very remote and doesn't socialize with his fellow musicians.

In their first year together, as far as the press was concerned, Woody and Mia were an extremely discreet twosome around town—no easy task for two easily recognizable celebrities in New York City (the couple literally ran from newsmen).

Was Mia going to marry Woody? asked their nosy friend Andy Warhol, one of the few who could get away with bluntly posing the question. Mia told him she really didn't know, and Warhol told her he was only kidding, he didn't care anyway.

It was over a year before an in-focus shot of Mia and Woody together was captured by a news photographer. The enterprising cameraman caught the couple in the lobby of Mia's Central Park West apartment as they were emerging from the elevator. This time the duo made no effort to escape —they politely smiled and posed, but explained they were late, en route to the theater (Woody's new play, *The Floating Light Bulb,* was set to open in the spring of 1981 at the Vivian Beaumont Theater in Lincoln Center).

Mia had obviously found a man whose sense of fashion was in tune with her own. Allen was clad in an army fatigue jacket and corduroy pants. Mia wore slacks, a sweater, and a knit hat with faux eyeglasses embroidered on it.

One wonders why Allen, who claims to crave anonymity, would wear such an outfit to a Broadway play in the evening, where he was bound to stand out amid an audience filled with men in jacket-and-tie. But that, of course, is part of the enigma that is Woody Allen.

The couple didn't cab it to the theater that night; they rode in Woody's cream-colored Rolls-Royce.

To try to avoid the paparazzi, who would continue to plague them, Mia convinced Woody that they should do what she and Previn had done in England: pick one photographer and let him take "official" pictures. Woody, though uncomfortable with this idea, went along.

The couple had started work on their first film together, *A Midsummer Night's Sex Comedy*. Mia later said that the prospect of working with Woody had terrified her; she was afraid she would disappoint someone who was a friend and whom she cared about. She kept asking him if he was sure he wanted her —didn't he want another actress? She was fearful she wouldn't be good enough and that he would inevitably be disappointed in her. (Mia's insecurities were certainly not unlike those of a "typical" Woody Allen cinema heroine.)

But Woody had no doubts about Mia. From the start he was confident she was someone who could do comedy and wanted to work with her because he liked working with people with whom he was emotionally involved. He enjoyed writing for someone he knew intimately—it was an advantage that brought out the best in him.

A Midsummer Night's Sex Comedy is very revealing of their budding relationship. Woody's character in the film is married to another woman but is irresistibly attracted to Ariel, Mia's character, an ethereal, spritelike creature who has reentered his life.

While to some observers Mia and Woody offscreen appeared an odd couple indeed, their relationship made perfect sense to anyone who knew each of them well. It was as though all of Mia's diverse experiences with the major men in her life had prepared her for Woody. There was no big age gap, although Woody was ten years Mia's senior (Sinatra had been thirty years older; Previn, sixteen years).

Mia was no longer ill at ease if a man was sometimes remote (as Sinatra had been and certainly as Woody Allen could be), and she was now better equipped emotionally to fathom a creative, artistic man's complexities.

She was no longer immature. She was capable of being a friend to a man when he needed that. Not only were she and Woody in tune on the major, deeper themes, but most importantly they could deal well with each other on a day-to-day basis. Part of this was because they did *not* live together. She was quite content in her role as Mama Mia living in her own apartment and managing her own children. He was quite content living in his own luxurious Fifth Avenue penthouse and visiting her and the children as frequently—or infrequently— as he wished. Woody was impressed with Mia's ability to deal with both the children and a career.

Before she met Woody, she'd been lonely; in Woody she'd found a man who was as faithful in relationships as she was. She'd found a soul mate.

Mia had great respect for his talent and said she was awed by the fact that he could act in a film while directing it and still watch what she was doing—how he did it she didn't know; it was beyond her.

She enjoyed Allen's sense of humor (one didn't have to be Jewish to appreciate it, although one might joke that it helped). Their relationship flourished because there were none of the hindrances that had intruded in each of her marriages. One could present strong arguments that Sinatra and then Previn had driven Mia away, not vice versa. Now she was working at what she loved doing and was doing it with a man she cared for.

Unlike the situations that had existed with Sinatra and Previn, Woody was rarely away or out of town. Furthermore home for Mia was not a remote area in England or a fortresslike compound in the Palm Springs desert. Mia was smack in the center of New York City with entree to all its best features. If she wanted country life, she had her place in Martha's Vineyard and had bought a house in Connecticut for occasional weekends away. She was relieved to be permanently back in America and felt the children would have far more opportunities available to them.

While *A Midsummer Night's Sex Comedy* was not one of Allen's better films (again, it was highly derivative of Ingmar Bergman's work), nor was it a box office success, the actor-writer-producer would hit an enviable stride with his next efforts; four films in four years, each starring Mia Farrow. It was the beginning of a dazzling creative arc for Woody Allen and his new star.

The subject matter of the ensuing films obviously parallels their own lives. In *Zelig,* a hilarious send-up of pretentious documentary films, Mia Farrow's character is the only person who understands Zelig, Woody's character. Mia plays a brilliant, loving, attentive, sweet, stubborn—and strong—psychoanalyst who cures Zelig of his inability to be himself. An important element in this film (photographed primarily in black and white and structured like a documentary) was the special effects, which enabled the actors to be integrated into old news film with a totally realistic result. Consequently the character of Zelig is present at some of the greatest moments of history.

While some critics observed that the film seemed in part a tribute to Mia and Woody's real-life relationship, and commented on her "ethereal" quality, Mia said *she* didn't see herself as ethereal and didn't experience life that way. She admitted she used to be a daydreamer but pointed out she hardly had time to daydream anymore, not with seven kids and a revived film career.

Mia was able to juggle family and career successfully because in effect she'd become part of Allen's unofficial repertory company, making films that were shot in New York and on a schedule compatible with her life-style. She didn't have to go on location and leave her children, a fact that was extremely important to her.

As far as working with Woody, who was a *very* strong-minded person, Mia was in her element. Allen's knowing-*exactly*-what-he-wants trait (Polanski had had it) didn't intimidate her, it made her feel much more secure as an actress. With certain roles she'd played before, it had literally been a shot in the dark at "finding" the characters; she'd had to go on hunches, and some were wrong. If a director's vision of a character wasn't clear, Mia's wasn't either. Woody didn't allow that; he kept actors on a steady course and didn't let them wander away from *his* view of things, which was usually explicitly presented in his scripts.

Woody was thrilled with Mia's talent and professionalism, which was, as director David Jones had said, a director's dream. Allen dismissed past descriptions of her as wispy and incapable and pointed out that she ran a home, had seven children and took them wherever she went, cooked and cleaned, and still looked beautiful when she went out in the evening. Anyone who could do that possessed a remarkable strength and independence.

In Mia he'd found a person whose outlook on life encompassed a broad spectrum. She wasn't the typical neurotic actress totally obsessed with herself. Mia had certainly opened up a new world for him; Allen realized that children could be integrated into his life. Judith Crist notes, "Mia certainly did bring Woody into a new awareness of family and children." Mrs. Crist also observes that Allen's artistic collaboration with Mia had a positive effect on his performances; as an actor she'd found him slipping into a rut.

By now Mia and her brood had the entire Central Park West apartment to themselves. Maureen O'Sullivan had married "a younger man," sixty-six-year-old businessman James Cushing, in 1983. (Maureen was seventy-two.) She joked that miracles were plentiful in life, she was living proof. Cushing was wealthy, and the couple divided their time between his several residences throughout the country.

Zelig had been an enormous critical success and big box office in New York and Los Angeles. All the influential critics had talked and written about it, and Allen had begun work on a new project for him and Mia, *Broadway Danny Rose.*

Again, elements in their personal life were included in the script. The story concerns the quintessential New York Jewish talent agent (Woody), who is also a comic. He meets a woman, in this case an Italian-American gun moll, who's totally different from him. They seem to have absolutely nothing in common, but by film's end they have found some common ground. Interestingly the agent character had been touched on in Woody's autobiographical play, *The Floating Light Bulb,* which wasn't a success. But when he combined the agent character with Mia's character, the elements worked.

As the start of production approached on *Broadway Danny*

Rose, Mia got cold feet. It loomed as a very dramatic departure for her—she'd never played anything remotely like it. The prototype for the character had been a woman who worked in a restaurant Mia and Woody frequented. Mia had told Woody she wanted to play someone like that, and through the years Woody and Mia had each known similar women. The couple discussed the role before shooting began and arrived at the look and voice. Preparing for the part, Mia had also spent time with office secretaries and their friends, who talked like Tina Vitale did, and she also listened to a tape of *Raging Bull.*

Tina was a tough-talking Broadway dame, the kind Bette Midler or the late Judy Holliday could have played (and then been labeled "typecast"). Woody later recalled that it was a part Mia felt she could do until he wrote it for her and then she started to feel differently. Mia admitted that Tina was *too* different for her and that she was scared—until the first day of production. Then she realized she *could* do it.

Woody admired Mia because she was such a pro. She learned her lines. She possessed two distinctive and invaluable qualities: It was impossible to photograph her looking anything less than beautiful—she was blessed with a beautiful face; and she had a great sense of believability. He could give her anything to do, and she would make it real. In Allen's opinion she'd always been a perfectly fine and talented actress, she just hadn't taken acting seriously enough after she'd been married and started raising children.

Woody and Mia were on a roll, both creatively and personally. *Broadway Danny Rose* was another critical hit (a triumph for Mia), although obviously her Hollywood "friends" were still not true fans of her work, since the picture received Oscar nominations for both original script and direction but not for best actress.

While Woody and Mia remained out of the Hollywood

mainstream, they were *the* New York couple, with lots of press attention as they continued ostensibly to try to be "private people."

Arthur Schlesinger, Jr., has commented on the Woody paradox: "the man consumed by shyness who nevertheless eats at conspicuous tables in conspicuous restaurants." When Schlesinger first met Woody, "he seemed like a scared rabbit, head down, eyes darting this way and that, as if he wished he were anywhere else but trapped in conversation." In subsequent encounters, however, Schlesinger found him far more relaxed, "especially relaxed perhaps when in the company of the lovely, gifted and generous-hearted Mia Farrow."

The couple were seen at all the right hangouts—Elaine's, where they'd usually be accompanied by a couple of the kids, and the Russian Tea Room, with a couple of more kids. Mia viewed the children's interrelationships as very different from those that had existed in her own family. The Farrow clan, back in the forties and fifties, had been typically active, brawling, and loving. But Mia's children, according to her, had more understanding at their age than she ever did. She attributed this to their disparate backgrounds and to the fact that she consulted them so that *all* of them together could decide on daily activities and the like. She wanted them to feel they had input. She was a hands-on parent, saw the kids off to school before she went to work, and was home by five or six to take charge of them.

She acknowledged that the kids missed Andre, and obviously it would have been better if they'd had two parents, but they were close to Woody, and Mia was delighted. He was a good father substitute, there for them in important ways. He spent time with them, took them to the park, played ball with them, and took them around the city. He was always available whenever they wanted to see him.

Woody found them wonderfully pleasant, companionable children and wryly noted that of course Mia did all the heavy work, while he skimmed off the cream since he saw them at their best. (The kids weren't exactly "civilians" with just an average mix of friends. For example, Sean Lennon, son of John Lennon and Yoko Ono, lived nearby in the Dakota apartment building and often played with Mia's children.)

Mia was more relaxed about her life and often cooked dinner at home. She was a believer in health foods, so red meat was scarce at the Farrow table; bean soups, fish, and chicken were plentiful, and when Mia felt ambitious, a soufflé was on the menu.

The kids, as they reached appropriate ages, were enrolled in coed private schools. A housekeeper came in daily and kept Mia's sprawling premises in order.

Mia had family nearby. Two of her sisters and their children lived in the neighborhood. Her brothers and their families visited frequently from Maryland and Vermont, and in the summers Mia and the brood went to the house in Connecticut. (They went there once a month in the winter.)

Mia and Woody argued about spending time in the country. Woody didn't object to a few hours or a day, but he didn't like staying overnight. He was at a loss in the country. He did everything there was to do in a fraction of the morning—fishing, ball playing—and then he was at loose ends before noon. Mia said that he wouldn't dream of going swimming—there was only a lake to swim in, and Woody said there were living things in the lake. (One ought to have heard the way he said it, recalled Mia; to him it wasn't a joke.)

Evenings in the country were no better. Allen would begin to think of the Clutter family (from Truman Capote's *In Cold Blood*). He talked about the possibility of deadly serpents in the lake and thought longingly of Elaine's and the Russian Tea

Room. It was so quiet in Connecticut, Mia said, she could almost see his point.

• • •

Mia and Woody were continuously gossiped about. There was a chic New York party one evening, "and they all talk about Jews trying to be WASPS and they were all talking about Woody Allen and Mia Farrow and really putting down Mia," wrote Andy Warhol in his diary in April 1985. If Mia was aware of the talk, it certainly didn't faze her.

Woody was approaching his fiftieth birthday and was reaching new heights creatively. He continued writing scripts with Mia in mind, and their next film project was *The Purple Rose of Cairo,* which some critics feel is Woody's most challenging and fascinating script.

In *Purple Rose* Mia plays Cecilia, a waitress in a small New Jersey town in the 1930s. (Mia's sister, Stephanie, now thirty-six, was cast in a small role as a fellow waitress.) Cecilia is a sweet, innocent young woman trapped in a miserable marriage and a miserable job at the height of the Great Depression. She goes to the movies to escape, and at the peak of her troubles a leading man in one of the sophisticated movie comedies she adores literally jumps off the screen and into her life. The film is a realistic fantasy (and, one would assume, an Allen homage to the Hollywood genre of classic screwball comedies). Woody of course wrote the screenplay and directed, but he did not costar in this film.

The role of Cecilia called for Mia to look very plain and ordinary. But her radiance, as usual, shone through. Since she was playing a character not far removed from the image she had projected for so long—vulnerable, poignant—people naturally wondered if Allen had, in creating the character, superimposed the real Mia on the fictional Cecilia. He said he didn't know; on reflection, he acknowledged that might be true but what he saw was merely that she could play the part. He said he wrote the movie because he liked the story, not because it was a vehicle for Mia, but he conceded that Cecilia was a part he'd conceived for her.

As far as Mia was concerned, the character was simple and ingenuous, and she liked her. She said she thought Cecilia was a lot better than she was but admitted she could identify with parts of her and said the character was closer to her than some other characters she'd played.

Mia's fellow actors were impressed with Mia's expertise on the soundstage. Jeff Daniels, who played the matinee idol, defined her style as very simple, very straightforward—she didn't "junk up" a performance—and Daniels emphasized how difficult that kind of simplicity was to achieve.

Whereas many actors—certainly many from the Lee Strasberg–Actors Studio school—require ample time for inner preparation before a scene, as well as time to recover after it, Mia Farrow achieved an equally stunning result simply by stepping into a scene. Jeff Daniels has described how when it was time to shoot, Mia just put down her knitting and came over and did the scene. And did it again and again if necessary.

One scene involved Daniels being beaten up on a church altar and Mia rushing over to him, consoling him and crying. She did at least ten takes, and Woody still wasn't satisfied. During one take the lighting wasn't right; in another he asked her to cry on a different line than the one she'd been crying on. And she did it—according to Daniels, she nailed it every time. Finally, when Woody was satisfied, Mia went back to her knitting.

Farrow's attitude about her work was unusual: She wasn't, like many actors, a constantly anguished and tormented individual. She told critic Roger Ebert she was always surprised by her performances since she always worried that she wouldn't be any good, that she wouldn't be able to do it at all, she'd fail completely and everyone would find her out. If she pulled something off, she was grateful and relieved. She knew she could cry and do all the technical things; she always could, it was no big deal to her and didn't imply good acting. For Mia that had no connection to quality.

For Jeff Daniels *Purple Rose* was a make-or-break film, and he felt himself under a great deal of pressure. He said it was Mia who made him relax. She was intent on getting it right, of course, but the movie wasn't life-or-death to her.

Daniels has recalled how she'd sit on the sidelines and knit and often her kids would visit the set. It was clear that there were things more important to Mia Farrow than whether a film was a good career move. Daniels got the sense that Mia acted because she enjoyed it and because she enjoyed being with Woody.

One of her sons, Fletcher, a preteen, wanted to be an actor and director. Mia joked that perhaps it was because she used to take him backstage in a basket when she was doing shows in London. Fletcher loved being on the set, and according to her, he had a wonderful time with Woody since Allen was doing all the things that Fletcher wanted to do.

One of the twins, Matthew, was inclined in other directions. He'd bought law books a couple of years earlier and, according to his mother, had read them all. He knew exactly what he wanted to do and attended a competitive boys' school.

It's ironic that despite Mia's real-life role as a family-oriented mother in charge of an organized, "conventional" household, the tone of some of the publicity about her still sometimes opted for the sensational. One major women's magazine referred to her as "Woody's Waif-Mistress," proving that the best-laid plans of the most powerful contemporary press agents could go awry.

When *Purple Rose* opened in New York, it received virtually unanimous acclamation (although David Edelstein, of *Rolling Stone,* subsequently wrote that Mia's character was "too much the Chaplinesque innocent"). Some critics felt the ending of the picture a cop-out: Nothing comes true for the heroine, and it seems that everything that has occurred to Cecilia happened only in her imagination. Some found this an affront to audiences, with Allen's moral a turnoff: Reality always lets you down.

In any event the film was an artistic achievement for all concerned, and a prologue to the far greater box office reception that awaited the next Woody-Mia collaboration.

• • •

Since both Mia and Woody are protective of their privacy, give only select interviews, and are reticent about discussing their family life together, fans and detractors alike analyze his scripts for clues to their relationship.

With *Hannah and Her Sisters* people felt they were actually watching the real lives of Mia Farrow and Woody Allen. The story (the title came first, then the script) concerns the complex relationship between three sisters and the men in their lives.

Once again there were definite elements from real life. Hannah (Mia) is the cohesive force keeping a large, disparate family together. Allen's character, as always, is neurotic, a hypochondriac trying to come to grips with life's greater questions. In the story he deals with children who are not biologically his, then ends the film with his character settling into an imperfect but stable relationship and awaiting more children, this time his own biological offspring.

It was one of Allen's most human and incisive tales, but while the script was brilliant, the role of Hannah had presented an obstacle: Allen had had difficulty clearly defining the character. For Mia and Woody it was the hardest role they'd collaborated on to date because Hannah, according to Allen, was the trickiest role in the movie; if it wasn't presented and played just right, the film wouldn't work.

Mia later admitted it *had* been difficult because of the subtlety involved (the characters of Hannah's two sisters, in contrast, were precisely drawn).

It turned out that the solution to discovering the essence of Hannah—a character who's a successful actress juggling a career to raise a family—was to find it as they went along, rather than having it at the start.

The picture featured an exceptional cast: Barbara Hershey and Dianne Wiest as Hannah's two sisters; Michael Caine, Max Von Sydow, Sam Waterston, and Woody as the men in their lives; Carrie Fisher, Julie Kavner, and Lloyd Nolan in featured roles. Perhaps the most interesting casting, from Mia's perspective, was the actress selected for the role of Hannah's mother.

When Maureen O'Sullivan had first been approached to play the part, she turned it down flat. She gave a variety of excuses, the most amusing that she was too old for the role. Mia replied that she *was* her mother! Yes, acknowledged O'Sullivan, but would it photograph properly? She also turned down the part because she feared people might think the script was biographical (which of course they subsequently did).

Perhaps O'Sullivan's early refusal may also have been due to the description of the character in the script: "a boozy old flirt with a filthy mouth." The deciding vote, however, came from Maureen's husband, James Cushing, who said that he thought she was crazy if she turned down the role—it was only a movie! Her agent strongly advised her to take the part and pointed out she'd find it fun to work with Woody Allen. She relented and later said she was glad she had.

Lloyd Nolan played her husband, and Maureen credited Nolan with having more than a little to do with how well she came across. She explained that Woody hadn't told her very much in advance. She came on the set one morning; it was the first time she'd met Lloyd Nolan and she didn't really know what she was going to do. But when she looked at him and caught the expression on his face and in his eyes, she knew that their characters had had many years of love behind them and that while they would say terrible things to each other, there was always that love that united them.

According to Maureen, her scenes with Mia weren't affected by their real-life relationship (although both were nervous at first). She said there was never a problem—Mia immediately became an actress, and Maureen went into her part; it was simply a job they each had to do. However, in their major scene together, Mia had the thrill of appreciating her mother's talent ("My goodness, she's good!") while sharing the experience with her.

Maureen said she enjoyed working with Woody and had no difficulty catching on to his methods. In some respects he reminded her of Mia's godfather, George Cukor, Hollywood's legendary director of women (he'd directed Maureen a half century earlier in *David Copperfield*). Maureen said she preferred Woody to Cukor because Cukor insisted actors follow his preconceived ideas of a role, whereas Woody, if he liked what you were doing, would let you grow and add to the character. But she noted that if he *didn't* like what you were doing, he could be very, very "meticulous."

Maureen understood how exciting it was for an actress like Mia to be working with Woody in what was virtually a cinema repertory company. It was a situation that was particularly right for Mia because Mia thought along the lines of a character actress and didn't care how she looked as long as she got the character right. When, on a later film, a concerned Maureen commented on the unflattering hairdos and accessories Mia planned on wearing, Mia explained that she needed to be very *plain* in the part.

Maureen recognized that Mia was both a character actress *and* a star, and her theory was that while Mia didn't choose to use her star quality a lot of the time, it still made her work much more interesting. And when Mia *wanted* to turn on the glamour—and she didn't do that very often—then, as far as her mother was concerned, she lit up the sky.

Maureen's reaction to Mia in the finished *Hannah and Her Sisters* was fascinating: She said she liked her daughter's performance very much because she'd felt it had been "a complete exposure of herself. She wasn't being anything—she was being Mia."

When others presented Mia with a similar opinion, Mia was emphatic: *Hannah was not her.* And she was equally emphatic that she had no desire or ambition to be perceived or revealed via a character in a film.

Questions concerning similarities between Mia and Hannah were legitimate. Many of the scenes in the movie were actually filmed in Mia's Central Park West apartment, and three of her children appeared in the picture as her children. The Hannah character, like Mia, successfully balances motherhood and a career—and manages the lives of her mother and her siblings as well.

As to speculation on how biographical the film was regarding the relationship between Mia and her real sisters, Mia pointed out that Diane Keaton had sisters too (Keaton had appeared in Woody's *Interiors,* another serious Allen script about relationships between sisters).

Everyone knew Woody's scripts were an amalgam of everyone he knew and everything he'd experienced, plus a very fertile imagination. "When I write for Mia, I write the part with her in mind," he said. "If, for example, the part were going to be played by, say, Diane Keaton, I would write it differently. The idiom, the style of speaking, a number of little things just would be written differently."

The scenes in the film between Woody and Dianne Wiest were at times intensely intimate and tender, and Woody watchers speculated that a new romance might be on the horizon.

Meanwhile in 1985 Mia had adopted another child, Dylan O'Sullivan Farrow. Woody told Mia he had no idea how he'd feel about the baby—maybe he wouldn't feel anything. Fair enough, said Mia, he could simply participate to the extent he wanted to. Subsequently Woody discovered himself *very* much involved with Dylan and even used the baby in his next film. People on the set were amazed at his devotion to her and his ease at dealing with all of Mia's children. Mia observed that Woody was better with the kids than he was with most other people.

Woody and Mia were in production on *Radio Days* when *Hannah* was released early in 1986 and quickly became the hottest Woody Allen picture since *Annie Hall.* It was acclaimed by many critics as a masterpiece and would be nominated for both the Oscar and the New York Film Critics Award.

Despite the acclaim for his films—almost two decades of praise by this point—according to Mia, Woody would never, ever think of himself as a major filmmaker. She noted he could never seem to feel any satisfaction about his work; he derived no pleasure out of success. By his own standards he was still striving to make better and better films—only he was always disappointed.

Mia said that when Woody made a film, it was as though he were nineteen and had never had any success at all and was hoping against hope that the next one would be "it."

Mia's past resurfaced briefly when, in 1985, 20th Century-Fox produced a movie-for-television, *Return to Peyton Place.* It was set in the present, but many of the original series regulars re-created their characters: Dorothy Malone, Barbara Parkins, Ed Nelson, Pat Morrow, Chris Connelly, and Tim O'Connor. But Mia Farrow and Ryan O'Neal were not reunited with the *Peyton Place* cast; they appeared via clips from the original shows. It was fascinating to observe how they'd looked and performed back then. The styles of Farrow and O'Neal didn't seem dated. Their star quality in *Peyton Place* was as apparent and effective today as it had been when the show debuted.

Mia's relationship with Frank Sinatra came back into the spotlight in 1986, when Kitty Kelley's unauthorized biography of the singer was published. Mia did what she had never done before: She made a formal comment on her former marriage for the record; she had her press agents issue a terse statement denying the documented allegations of Frank's mistreatment of her presented in the book.

Mia apparently retained fond and warm memories of Frank Sinatra. She told his daughter, Nancy, who'd written her own book around this time, that Frank was "still a part of me. I think of him often and wish him the very best because he deserves it and of course because I love him."

However, she has also recently said that when she married Sinatra, she didn't know what she was looking for—possibly she'd been searching for a father. And she candidly stated that the Sinatra marriage "wasn't an experience I'd want to re-peat."

• • •

Radio Days was Allen's most costly film to date, an elaborately produced attempt to create a poignant satiric comedy-drama set during the golden days of radio. The script certainly had its moments. The anecdotal story borrowed heavily from Woody's early life, the days when he and his family were radio addicts and juxtaposed their mundane existence against the fantasy lives led by radio stars. The cast, including Dianne Wiest, Julie Kavner, and Michael Tucker, was exceptional. The elements were present for a great film, but they didn't quite gel. The script was too episodic, and a synthetic quality pervaded many of the situations, mostly those involving Mia's character.

In the cartoonlike role of a very ambitious, sexy/shrewd dumb-blond cigarette girl who is prepared to do anything (and she does) to become a radio star, Mia used a Judy Holliday-like high-pitched singsongy voice. Her performance was sometimes strained. She had to sing in the film, a straightforward rendition, with simple piano accompaniment, of "I Don't Want to Walk Without You, Baby." She jokingly apologized to cast and crew after the performance.

According to some reports, Mia and Woody's relationship was somewhat strained as a result of the difficulties trying to make the material work. Woody could be *very* demanding, as Danny Aiello, an actor who's worked with Allen in a number of films, has observed. Woody's screen persona was meek, noted Aiello, but the real Woody was not that way at all.

Mia must have felt a touch of nostalgia when filming the big nightclub scenes for the picture in what had been the famous King Cole Bar of the St. Regis Hotel, where she'd met Salvador Dali so many times over the years. The big, original mural was still in place on the wall, but in other aspects the room had been dramatically renovated.

To set an authentic mood for the film and recall the sound of the radio years, a young Frank Sinatra is heard singing on the soundtrack over one key sequence (not one of Mia's). Old recordings of Bing Crosby and the Andrews Sisters, Carmen Miranda, and other period stars set the mood for other scenes.

Diane Keaton appeared briefly in the picture, as a big-band singer. Mia and Diane had no scenes together. Much has been made of Woody's use of his lovers in his films, with the strong implication that he furthered their careers. He discounts this, stating that people who tell Mia or Diane that they're fortunate to be making films with him don't realize the true situation—*he's* the one who's lucky to be able to work with people who can do things consistently, who are stable, pleasant to work with, who can execute his ideas, who are available to shoot his style and to reshoot.

"I can just call up Mia and say, 'Let's go back and reshoot.' When you've got someone who has six other pictures to do, you can't have that freedom." Woody explained it was this situation that went a long way to perfecting the kind of picture he wanted to make and pointed out that *any* director would know how crucial this was.

In Woody's view he'd lucked out with both Mia and Diane. "I'm lucky that they've made this contribution to me," he said. "My contribution is relatively minimal; I can only provide the script, and then they bail me out, they make me look good."

Diane Keaton has told friends that she thinks Mia Farrow is a terrific gal, and Woody Allen has said he would love to do a film with both Mia and Diane.

While *Hannah and Her Sisters* was a great hit and won many Oscar nominations (despite Woody's publicly expressed disdain for the Oscars and the mentality pervading them, the Academy hasn't ignored his achievements over the years), there'd been no nomination for Mia Farrow's performance, and Allen was again overlooked in the best-director category. Michael Caine won the Oscar for best supporting actor, Dianne Wiest for best supporting actress, and Woody won another Oscar for best screenplay.

There were great expectations for *Radio Days,* but it was a major disappointment at the box office.

Meanwhile Farrow and Allen had begun their next project, *September,* a heavy drama featuring a story line that, denials to the contrary, had obviously been inspired by the notorious 1958 murder case in which Lana Turner's teenaged daughter had killed her mother's gangster boyfriend. In Woody's story, with Mia portraying the now-adult daughter, it is the mother who has committed the murder and forced the daughter to take the blame.

Originally Maureen O'Sullivan was cast as the mother. The film was completed, but Allen was reportedly so dissatisfied that he recast and reshot the movie. In the version that was released Elaine Stritch portrayed Mia's mother.

September featured a marvelous cast. In addition to Mia and Stritch, the film starred Denholm Elliott, Jack Warden, and two members of Woody's unofficial repertory group, Sam Waterston and Dianne Wiest. Around this time there were further rumors (which had initially begun circulating around the time of *Hannah and Her Sisters*) that Woody and Ms. Wiest were an item and that perhaps a turning point had finally been reached in the relationship between Woody Allen and Mia Farrow. But the news of that possibility was almost as quiet as the release of *September.*

The critics didn't rave about this film, released in 1987. All agreed Stritch was the best element in the picture, but it didn't bail out the project commercially, although the advertising campaign was excellent. (All advertising campaigns on Woody's films, over which he exercises strict control, have been unique and brilliant.)

• • •

Several years ago, with "only" seven children, Mia had confided to a friend that she wanted at least nine. She was about to reach her goal, and wasn't adopting this time: In April 1987 she discovered she was pregnant. For the first time Woody Allen, fifty-two, was going to be a father. Those in the inner circle speculated that in her quiet way Mia had won back Woody's wavering attention.

Before the news went public, Woody was already behaving like a father. He and Mia were often spotted strolling through Central Park wheeling their new adopted daughter in her baby-walker. He told friends he was anxiously awaiting his first child and also said he'd developed deep feelings of love for Dylan and believed there'd be no difference between the love he'd feel for the new baby and what he felt for Dylan. Woody had experienced what Mia had predicted: Adoption was not what you could do for the child but what the child could do for you.

Maureen wasn't surprised by Mia's pregnancy and said Mia was very happy about it and so was she. According to Maureen, someone at a film studio had leaked the news (Mia subsequently had to turn down a role) and Maureen didn't think Mia had meant for word to get out so soon. O'Sullivan dismissed the notion that her forty-one-year-old daughter was too old to have a baby, pointing out that she'd been forty when she gave birth to her youngest child, Tisa. Mia's baby would be Maureen's twentieth grandchild!

Maureen also said she didn't care at all if Mia and Woody

did or didn't get married—it was clear they were good for the children (Woody was now the legal father of two of Mia's five adopted children) and good for each other. Who was she to push bondage on them?

Woody detested talking about his personal life but admitted that Mia's pregnancy wasn't anything they'd planned and said they were both surprised by it. However, "Mia would never think of having an abortion. And I don't think that I would either."

• • •

Woody joked that he thought he'd be a profoundly wise, generous, liberal, and understanding dad and said he'd be surprised if he were less than a perfect father. He told CBS correspondent Harry Reasoner on *60 Minutes* that he didn't foresee "the kid" having any problems and thought fatherhood would either deepen him or put him in a crazy house.

Woody and Mia had no plans to alter what Allen described as their extremely comfortable living arrangement: their apartments were only five minutes apart.

On December 9, 1987, Mia gave birth to a son, Satchel, a healthy nine-pound four-ounce baby delivered by cesarean section. Woody said the baby was fine—the only problem was that he looked like Edward G. Robinson.

Shortly after the baby's birth the couple posed with Satchel for an official "portrait," which was released to the press. It was the old Previn-days maneuver to diffuse interest in pursuing unauthorized photographs, and the ploy was again successful.

The following summer Woody and Mia traveled to Europe with the entire brood, including the infants. Traveling with children was, to say the least, atypical for Woody Allen, but according to Mia, Allen was the perfect parent—a friend to the older kids and a father to the youngest three.

The Woody-Mia professional collaboration, however, wasn't proceeding so smoothly. It had run into artistic snags. Their latest films together had flopped. *September* sank almost without a trace, and *Another Woman,* released in 1988 and featuring in addition to Mia such heavyweights as Gene Hackman and Gena Rowlands, was a total box office disaster. It created the least stir of any picture Woody Allen and Mia Farrow had made together in the last seven years.

Things looked brighter with the release of *New York Stories* in 1988. This was a three-part feature, each segment directed by a major *auteur:* Martin Scorsese, Francis Ford Coppola, and Woody Allen. Woody's segment, "Oedipus Wrecks," starred himself, Mia, and Mae Questel, and roamed familiar Woody comedy territory: His character hasn't resolved his relationship with his overbearing mother; there's the ever-present psychiatrist; and Mia portrays the *shiksa* with three children whom he wants to marry (his mother calls her a *corveh,* the Yiddish word for whore).

Surprisingly there's a love scene between an undressed Woody and Mia in bed together, and he abandons her at the end of the story for a nice Jewish girl ("You wake up one day and suddenly you're out of love," his character says).

It was by far the best of the three stories, and the Disney organization, the film's producer, subsequently tried to lure Woody to star in one of their forthcoming pictures, to be directed by someone other than Woody Allen. Woody said he'd consider it.

There was a great deal riding on the next Woody-Mia project. No artist can retain creative control and continue to obtain financing if their product doesn't return big profits. Network television didn't guarantee extra millions of dollars in revenue for Woody's pictures; the networks didn't regard them as hot properties because they didn't attract the audiences network advertisers were interested in. The recent emergence of cable television and networks of independent stations, however, have opened up lucrative markets for Woody's pictures, in addition to income from videocassettes.

The industry questioned whether the prolific Allen had finally dried up creatively—and wondered how that would affect his relationship with Mia.

The next project was tentatively titled *Brothers* (retitled *Crimes and Misdemeanors*) and offered an interesting personal detail regarding Woody's choice for director of photography—Sven Nykvist, the man Mia had been romantically involved with a decade earlier, at the time she made *Hurricane*. In the highly sophisticated and somewhat incestuous world of big-time filmmaking, where people's paths are constantly crossing and backtracking, no one blinked an eye.

Crimes and Misdemeanors was about families, of course, but represented a major departure for Woody in that, for once, brothers, not sisters, were the focal point of the story. It dealt with the universal themes Woody Allen has explored continuously over the years, but with a fresh intensity. The script was provocative from a philosophical point of view, sure to stir controversy and debate. (Critic David Denby subsequently articulated it perfectly: "More pessimistic than ever, Allen gives us a pleasant social world in which crime goes unpunished while misdemeanors are greeted with a scorn close to annihilation.")

There were a dozen key characters in the film, and Allen assembled a virtuoso cast. In addition to Mia, there was Martin Landau, Anjelica Huston, Alan Alda, Jerry Ohrbach, Claire Bloom, Joanna Gleason, Sam Waterston, Caroline Aaron, and Martin Bergmann (a noted psychiatrist portraying a noted psychiatrist who commits suicide). Woody would play a key role, that of an unhappily married documentary film producer of decidedly noncommercial documentaries who falls in love with Farrow, a woman ambitious to be a TV producer. She in turn is ardently pursued by an obnoxious, unscrupulous TV mogul (Alan Alda).

An interesting aspect of *Crimes and Misdemeanors* concerned the relationship between Woody's character and that of his preteenage niece in the film. It shows Woody as a mentor, friend, and father figure to a precocious child—not unlike his relationship with Fletcher Previn.

As usual Allen didn't reveal much about the picture while it was in production, and as the release date approached, expectations were guarded. Many were waiting for a bomb to drop.

This time Woody delivered a critical winner. Vincent Canby of *The New York Times* described this film as Allen's "most securely serious and funny film to date." Canby saw the picture as a "kind of companion piece to *Hannah and Her Sisters,*" and he stated outright, "He [Allen] hits the bull's-eye again." Mia was "a standout," and Canby pointed out that virtually all the actors in the film were standouts (Martin Landau would win an Oscar as best supporting actor).

Canby made a highly pertinent observation: that it was Woody Allen's presence "that fuses the various elements. . . . The writer and director continues to be his own most vital on-screen force."

Siskel and Ebert gave the film a unanimous "thumbs-up." "It's a movie about the values of the 80s," said Roger Ebert, calling it "one of the very best [films] Woody Allen has ever made." "Shockingly good," said Gene Siskel. At a later date Siskel said he'd decided the film was literally Woody's direct tackling of the question "Is there a God?" and Allen's answer, in Siskel's view, was a resounding no.

It's fascinating how Allen sees both sides of the spiritual coin yet keeps flipping it, endlessly, in film after film, expecting, waiting for—what? And while he struggles with the great philosophical questions on-screen, personifying, in effect, the quintessential "loser," off-screen he's wealthy (indeed a connoisseur of the finest in food, art, and sophisticated living), a fighter, and a survivor. He's managed to summon the energy and creative ideas to continuously stir the brew of his discontent for over two decades; few (if any) artists of his caliber have been so prolific and endured the kind of backbreaking movie-making schedule Woody Allen has adhered to, with no end in sight. Certainly Mia and the children have been essential elements in Allen maintaining his creative intensity.

An atypical dilemma faced Woody on the very day, in the fall of 1989, that *Crimes and Misdemeanors* opened in New York City. Woody found himself in the thick of a controversy involving fellow comedian Jackie Mason and New York mayoral candidate David Dinkins, whom Allen supported. Dinkins, the press, and Woody were present at a Dinkins fund-raiser at the luxurious Manhattan town house of Orion Pictures chairman Arthur B. Krim (whose wife, Dr. Mathilde Krim, is the world's foremost medical authority on AIDS) when Woody was queried about allegedly racist remarks Jackie Mason had made about Dinkins. Woody, to Dinkins's (and many other people's) astonishment, expressed the opinion that Mason was no racist, was not a malicious man, and that his remarks should never have been taken seriously. Woody blamed the press (shades of Frank Sinatra!), calling them pious and foolish, and said Mason had gotten a raw deal.

While Mia was nowhere in sight on this occasion, one must assume that she was there in spirit. The girl who was never afraid to voice her opinions, to speak out on any and all subjects, had indeed found a soul mate.

• • •

It was an evening in February 1990, and tongues wagged and heads turned when Woody showed up at Elaine's with Diane Keaton. "Where was Mia Farrow? No one was talking," went one report. Only a week later Woody was back at the restaurant for dinner with Mia *and* Diane. Columnist Suzy described it as "the friendliest table at Elaine's," and commented, "Don't you love it, all that chum-chum-chummy stuff?"

Was a film project in the works featuring the famous trio? Not yet, although on the career front Keaton was certainly cooking. She was reprising her role as Michael Corleone's (Al Pacino's) wife in Francis Ford Coppola's *The Godfather III* and was being paid a reported $2 million.

To the surprise of many, Allen had finally consented to make a picture for Disney's Touchstone Pictures that he would *not* direct. *Scenes From a Mall,* teaming Allen and the outrageous "Divine Miss M," Bette Midler, was described as a comedy about marriage and infidelity, and the writer-director was Paul Mazursky (*Bob and Carol and Ted and Alice, Down and Out in Beverly Hills*).

Mazursky had been instrumental in reestablishing Midler as an enormous box-office draw (she's known in the industry as Disney's "$300 million-dollar woman"), and if the picture with Woody was a big hit, it would introduce him to a segment of the moviegoing public who didn't even know who he was.

Woody was reportedly unhappy, however, during rehearsals and production, not accustomed to functioning without total control and having to contend with a leading lady who wielded as much clout as he did. One can assume Bette Midler was not as malleable or accommodating an artist, vis-à-vis Woody Allen, as Mia Farrow.

Not that Mia is always an angel. According to one of her neighbors in her New York apartment building, who chooses to remain anonymous, Mia can be imperious and unfriendly with an attitude of being better than everybody else (at least as far as this particular neighbor is concerned). There's often a chauffeured limousine at her beck and call, which Mia some-times utilizes to do the grocery shopping (*unlike* neighbor Carly Simon, who, according to this source, is always pleasant, walks to the supermarket, and does her *own* shopping).

As this book goes to press, Mia is forty-six years old. She's not starred in any "outside" (that is, non–Woody Allen) pic-tures in many years but has completed a starring role in Al-len's newest film, *Alice,* in which she portrays a wealthy wife, a good Catholic who has lost her way and goes through a re-markable series of experiences at a crucial point in her life. Alec Baldwin, Blythe Danner, William Hurt, Cybill Shepherd, and Gwen Verdon rounded out the all-star cast.

Released during the 1990 Christmas movie rush, the film was heralded by an ad campaign that undoubtedly made Mia the envy of every other actress in the business—a full-page head shot of Farrow with absolutely no copy, no other photos of her high-powered costars, not even the usual line of credits at the bottom of the ad to detract from the likeness of Mia.

Alice received dramatically mixed reviews. Had the critics all seen the same picture? "A splendid and sometimes uproari-ously funny film," raved Vincent Canby in *The New York Times,* naming *Alice* one of the ten best of the year. "Playing what is, in effect, the Woody Allen role, that of someone who is both fearful and determined, both romantic and pragmatic, Ms. Far-row gives the kind of performance that, if there is any justice, will win her an Oscar nomination this year, maybe even the award."

Canby noted that the film was Allen's "apotheosis of Miss Farrow, who has never looked more beautiful (she has bones to rival Katharine Hepburn's) and has never been more surprisingly funny and affecting. In this, their eleventh collaboration, Miss Farrow gives a performance that sums up and then tops all of the performances that have preceded it."

USA Today, however, panned the movie, terming it "a Catholic-guilt comedy . . . but hold on. Woody isn't the Catholic—in fact, he's not even in the picture. And is he missed."

David Denby described *Alice* as "a beautifully designed vessel with nowhere to go," and found the title role to be "one of Woody Allen's meek and fluttering women . . . she's meant to be lost and rather dim but also adorable and even noble. This woman doesn't know what to do with herself, yet somehow she's better than everybody else."

Denby wryly commented that "Woody Allen appears to be nestling contentedly inside Alice's mink," and observed "there's a softening in Allen that's dismaying. Why make movies about people who don't know what they want to do, people who are lost?"

He further noted, "There's something creepy about Allen's love for dithering women. Diane Keaton had to get away from him and work for other directors before some iron came into her voice."

What's next for Mia Farrow? As her mother has often said, Mia is a person who can do *anything* she sets her mind to. She's finally come to realize she's a *serious* actress, that's how she makes her living, and she's delighted she's good at it because she's a woman with a lot of responsibilities.

Her life to date has certainly been more exciting, colorful, meaningful—and rewarding—than any fictional character she's portrayed. In the case of Mia Farrow, the best is possibly yet to come.

She's a star, but an atypical one. She's recognized in the streets of course, but there's sometimes a twist. On occasion she's told of being mistaken for Sissy Spacek. Or Twiggy. But on these occasions, which would have rattled or insulted most other so-called stars, Mia's response was uniquely Mia and very revealing of her character. She was polite on Sissy's behalf —someone was happy to see Sissy, realized Mia, so why spoil it?

Therein, too, lies the secret of both Mia's success *and* her survival. *She* knows who she is—it doesn't matter to her if other people do or not.

Maureen O'Sullivan, speaking today in a voice that sounds about thirty years old, has something emphatic to say about her daughter. She doesn't hesitate to get right to the heart of the matter: "Look, Mia is a *wonderful* girl. She always was and she always will be, until the day she dies."

Index

Index

Index

Index